STUDIES IN THE REFORMATION:
LUTHER TO HOOKER

This volume is published with the help of a
grant from the late Miss Isobel Thornley's
Bequest to the University of London

W. D. J. CARGILL THOMPSON

Studies in the Reformation: Luther to Hooker

Edited by
C. W. DUGMORE
Emeritus Professor of Ecclesiastical History
University of London

With a Foreword by
A. G. DICKENS
F.B.A.

THE ATHLONE PRESS
London

First published 1980 *by*
THE ATHLONE PRESS
at 90–91 *Great Russell Street, London* WC1
The Athlone Press is an imprint of Bemrose UK Ltd

Distributor in USA and Canada
Humanities Press Inc
New Jersey

British Library Cataloguing in Publication Data
Cargill, Thompson, W. D. J.
   Studies in the Reformation.
   1. Reformation
   I. Title   II. Dugmore, Clifford William
   270.6   BR305.2
   ISBN 0 485 11187 X

Printed in Great Britain by
WESTERN PRINTING SERVICES LTD
Bristol

To
Alexander and Edmund
in Memory of
their father

Foreword

A mere glance at the titles of these essays by James Cargill Thompson might well give an impression of Olympian specialisation. This would be mistaken, for the publication of the volume is no mere act of piety toward a friend but rather an educative event of a high order. They are by no means run-of-the-mill articles, and the more I re-read them, the more I am convinced that no library of standing can afford to overlook this unique collection. Nobody has done this sort of job better! Each essay begins by defining a knotty problem: it usually broadens into far wider perspectives, and it always ends by making an incisive contribution to Reformation studies. By all rights, this clarity and liveliness should attract not a few educated general readers, quite apart from those many students, researchers and teachers whom it provides with such impressive methodological examples. Over and above a mastery of his materials, Cargill Thompson had a remarkable ability to communicate not only with specialist colleagues but also with people whose primary allegiance was not to Reformation studies. Notice for example how, in the first four pages of 'Luther and the Right of Resistance', he outlines the whole context, and even the sort of solution he will propound: from that point we march on confidently to the detail. He chose some of the very hardest problems, thought his way through them and then presented his answers in civilised English that would have been intelligible to William Robertson or Samuel Johnson. More than might appear at first sight, the clear and spirited presentation came from something within the man himself which transcended academic training and logic. Despite his cool, no-nonsense writing, James was a genial character, hearty but gentle, a swift, forthcoming talker, yet disarming toward the inexperienced and never allowing his own formidable learning to become an obstacle. Coming from a family life of singular happiness, he liked people, enjoyed both teaching and learning and, whether he spoke or wrote, never forgot about the recipient. All this I know very well, because for several years he taught along with me in our weekly Reformation seminar at the Institute of Historical Research. Left together, we talked little else but shop, yet I never felt more inspired by, or more in harmony with, a colleague.

What our mutual friend Clifford Dugmore has here so admirably chosen and presented is by no means the whole of James's work, for he wrote a considerable number of other pieces worthy of very close attention. Indeed, I do not think he published anything which lacked the alpha-quality. And while he gave exact and sufficient references, he never produced a page in which a thick layer of footnotes cloaked a paucity of ideas, or in which the antiquarian gargoyles blurred the outline of the building. Certainly he never thought of ecclesiastical history as a more or less self-explanatory and insulated field, and with great ease he moved to and fro across the old, outdated frontiers. He was among those few historians armed with a theological knowledge to match his grasp of the mundane sources and the politico-social background. At the same time he never wore the chains of any rigid ecclesiastical system and never forgot that theology operates within an all-too-human world.

The present volume does not instruct from a narrow front: despite its basic unity, it shows a remarkable range. The essays on Luther-themes confidently explore huge fields demanding an expertise very different from those of the English essays which follow. Well abreast of international research, they rebuke by implication that insularity which has marred so many of our contributions, even those dedicated to our own national history. Despite its unique qualities the English Reformation remained deeply indebted to foreign minds and movements, while almost until the end of the century, *ecclesia anglicana* was still an international mass of aspirations rather than a territorial legatee of Rome, armed with a *magisterium* over and above the Bible.

Even among themselves, Cargill Thompson's English studies also display a wide variety of themes and approaches. Though not primarily a researcher into 'new' manuscript sources, he could exert a precise control over massive and varied groups of materials, mostly in print yet still imperfectly understood. The essays on *The Supper of the Lord* and on Sir Francis Knollys exemplify that waiting multitude of close investigations which we need to undertake before we can progress much further with Tudor religion and philosophy. The 61-page analysis of Richard Hooker's political thought is broader both in scale and in subject-matter. Judicious yet original, it forms rather more than the skeleton of a major work, and it needs at least this space in order to sort out the elements of a confused and changing scene of controversy. While the Hooker study operates on a rather elevated plane, the succeeding essay on Strype remains by contrast functional and gritty: the material for a couple of teaching-seminars somehow made readable as well as useful. Which of us in early life would not have been grateful for such guidance when confronted by Strype, by that huge and leathery expanse of bindings, 'full of pitfalls for the unwary'. Neither unrelated nor overlapping, the English essays illuminate not merely each other but their creator and his *modus operandi*. For him one subject did not smoothly and gradually emerge from another under some lifelong programme. Though far from aware of his own shortage of time, James enjoyed leaping around from one fascination to another: this suited the perfectionist and kept him ever lively and refreshed. Had he lived longer he might well have tied up many of these themes into some notable syntheses, yet of their kind such big books could hardly have been so perfect as the items of this present collection, which after all grew out of a synthesis already well-developed within his mind. He had all the gifts of enthusiasm, all the intellectual equipment: we can only be grateful that he taught us so much while he could.

A. G. DICKENS

Contents

Acknowledgements

The thanks of the editor and publishers are due to the following for permission to reprint material that first appeared as specified below:

The Ecclesiastical History Society: 'Luther and the Right of Resistance to the Emperor' from *Church, Society and Politics* (Studies in Church History, 12, ed. Derek Baker, Oxford 1975), 159–202; 'The Problem of Luther's "Tower Experience" and its Place in his Intellectual Development' from *Religious Motivation: Biographical and Sociological Problems for the Church Historian* (Studies in Church History, 15, ed. Derek Baker, Oxford 1978), 187–211; 'John Strype as a Source for the Study of Sixteenth-Century English Church History' from *The Materials, Sources and Methods of Ecclesiastical History* (Studies in Church History, 11, ed. Derek Baker, Oxford 1975), 237–47.

The Editors of the *Journal of Theological Studies*: 'The "Two Kingdoms" and the "Two Regiments"': some Problems of Luther's *Zwei-Reiche-Lehre*' from *JTS*, N.S. xx (1969), 164–85.

The Editors of the *Harvard Theological Review*: 'Who Wrote "The Supper of the Lord"?' from *HTR*, liii (1960), 77–91.

The Ohio University Press: 'Sir Francis Knollys's Campaign against the *Jure Divino* Theory of Episcopacy' from *The Dissenting Tradition*, ed. C. Robert Cole and Michael Moodie [Festschrift for Leland Carlson], (1976), 39–77.

'The Philosopher of the "Politic Society"': Richard Hooker as a Political Thinker' appeared in *Studies in Richard Hooker: Essays preliminary to an edition of his works*, ed. W. Speed Hill, Case Western Reserve University Press 1972.

Introduction

BY THE EDITOR

Some of the friends and colleagues of the late Professor James Cargill Thompson suggested that it would be a fitting tribute to his memory to issue in book form a collection of his published writings, and I was invited to act as editor of such a volume. I gladly accepted this task out of affection for him and his widow and out of admiration for his scholarship. The result is this book, which contains seven of his published articles, some long, some comparatively short, which I have divided into two parts representing his two main interests, viz. Luther and the English Reformation mainly in the reign of Elizabeth.

William David James Cargill Thompson came from a thoroughly Scottish background. In the seventeenth and eighteenth centuries the family was of basically farming and seafaring stock from the Angus and Perthshire areas of the East Coast. In the nineteenth century pressures on agriculture turned them into mercantile entrepreneurs. The Cargills and Thompsons became linked in 1855 when William Mills Thompson, a coffee planter in Ceylon, married his planter neighbour's sister Helen Cargill. Thus, William David Cargill Thompson, the father of James, after serving in World War I, became an East India merchant, joining the firm of Finlay, Fleming & Co. in Rangoon, who at that time managed the Burmah Oil Co. Ltd. which had been founded by a brother of Helen Cargill. James's father, as managing director, wound up the Rangoon side of the firm in March 1939. He had married an Anglo-Scot, Helen Mary Sutherland Reed, in 1929. So James was born to them in Rangoon on 17 December 1930. In due course he was entitled to bear the family coat of arms which is registered with the Lyon Court in Edinburgh. He was also a member of the Merchants House in Glasgow, where his grandfather had been a leading solicitor while keeping his connexion with the East.

Meanwhile, James was shipped home to school at Lathallan

School, Colinsburgh, Fife, in his ancestral Scotland, at the tender age of five and brought up in the homes of his grandparents. As was said by the Dean of Salisbury (Very Revd. Sydney H. Evans, C.B.E., D.D.) in his memorable address given at the Thanksgiving Memorial Service for James in the Chapel of King's College London on 21 March 1978: 'the loss of fun and companionship: the loss of that special confidence given to sons who have the good fortune to have a friend in their father . . . perhaps it was his own deprivation of that invaluable relationship that caused James the more to value his children and attend to them with a particular care and affection'.

From the Preparatory School in Fife he won a scholarship to Harrow, where he was in Ronnie Watkins's house and, although James was clearly destined to be a historian, he remained, perhaps wisely, on the classical side of the school and won a classical scholarship to King's College, Cambridge, in 1948. After doing National Service in the Royal Army Educational Corps as a Sergeant Instructor from 1949 to 1951 he went up to King's as an undergraduate, 1951–4, and a research student, 1954–6. While leading a very full social life, he obtained first class honours in the Historical Tripos Part I (1953) and Part II (1954). He was awarded the Members' English Essay Prize in 1952 for an essay on 'The English Political Novel', and won the Lightfoot scholarship in 1955—surely a portent of what was to come! He was a Fellow of King's College, Cambridge from 1956 to 1965 and Lay Dean from 1959 to 1964, working in close harmony with the Revd. Dr. Alec Vidler, Dean of King's College. During this period he held a Commonwealth Fund Fellowship to Harvard and the Huntingdon Library (1957–8) and spent a few months in 1962 as a Visiting Lecturer at the University College of Rhodesia and Nyasaland. His increasing interest in the history of the Continental Reformation led to an Alexander von Humboldt Fellowship for the year 1964–5 at the University of Göttingen, where, as the writer of 'The Annual Report of the Council [of King's College, Cambridge] under Statute D, III, 10', for November 1978 says, 'he perfected his German and steeped himself in Lutheran studies—with the long-term objective of a *magnum opus* on Luther's political ideas'. Alas! he did not live to complete this work, on which he had been engaged for some years in between teaching and administrative duties, but the reader will find printed below three learned studies of Luther's thought which will provide some idea of the contribution to scholarship that that *magnum opus* would have provided.

After this brilliant promise of his Cambridge days, during which he published two bibliographical articles in the *Transactions of the Cambridge Bibliographical Society*, namely 'Notes on King's College Library, 1500–1570, in particular for the period of the Reformation', (1954), and 'The Two Editions of Thomas Bilson's *True Difference between Christian Subjection and Unchristian Rebellion*' (1955), and a remarkably perceptive article in the *Harvard Theological Review*, on 'Who Wrote the "Supper of the Lord"?' (1960),* in which he argued most cogently that the treatise should be attributed to George Joye and not to William Tyndale as most previous writers, except Bale, had believed, James was appointed a Lecturer in History in the University of Sussex in 1965. In the following year he married Jennifer Warren, daughter of the bishop of Christchurch, New Zealand, whom he met in Athens where she was studying coins in the British School of Archaeology.

During his time at the University of Sussex, James published the first of several articles on the debate about 'the divine right of bishops', the conflict over episcopacy and presbyterianism which lay at the heart of the Elizabethan Puritan Movement. This was an essay included in a memorial volume to Norman Sykes (*Essays in Modern English Church History*, ed. G. V. Bennett and J. D. Walsh, London 1966, 44–75) entitled 'Anthony Marten and the Elizabethan debate on Episcopacy'. This was followed in 1969 by 'A reconsideration of Richard Bancroft's Paul's Cross Sermon' (*Journal of Ecclesiastical History*, xx, 253–66). Other related papers came later.

But James always seems to have kept several pots boiling at the same time. He had already laid the foundations of his lasting interest in Martin Luther some years earlier, during his stay at Göttingen, and the April 1969 issue of the *Journal of Theological Studies* carried a most important contribution to Luther studies. This was his 'The "Two Kingdoms" and the "Two Regi-

* An asterisk indicates inclusion in the present volume. Full details of original publication will be found in the list of Acknowledgements.

ments"'*, in which he dealt in masterly fashion with Luther's theology of the two orders of government which God has established for mankind—the spiritual order through which God carries out the work of Redemption, and the temporal order through which he provides for the needs of Man's earthly existence. Working carefully through the apparent confusions in Luther's use of language (*die Welt* and *weltlich, geistlich*: *Reich* and *Regimente*), he insisted that for Luther, while the two orders are distinct, they are also complementary since both were instituted by God. But Luther also held an eschatological doctrine of the two kingdoms, derived from Augustine, in which 'they represent the weapons which he employs in his struggle against the *regnum diaboli*'. Salvation is preached to all men, and though the members of Satan's kingdom reject it, the Christian on earth is a citizen of both kingdoms.

In October 1969 James took up his appointment as Lecturer in Ecclesiastical History at King's College London, where he proved to be not only an industrious researcher but an excellent and conscientious teacher, loved and respected by students and colleagues alike. He was promoted to be Reader in 1975 and when I retired under the age limit in September 1976 he was appointed Professor. He had already been elected Dean of the Faculty of Theology in the College, so he shouldered a considerable burden in October 1976, at a time when King's College was petitioning the Crown for a new Charter and endless meetings were taking place to thrash out new Statutes and Regulations, amid a certain amount of controversy. In all this he kept his head and proved to be an extremely able administrator and Dean of the Faculty. Nor did he let it interfere with his teaching or research, though it clearly took its toll. After a very distinguished tenure of the Chair for just over one year and a quarter, without warning, he dropped dead in a street near the College on 21 February 1978 at the early age of 47. This was, as I said in my Obituary Notice in *The Times*, not only a terrible loss to scholarship, but a severe loss to King's College and to the whole University of London, where he had established himself as a valuable member of the Board of Studies in History, and its Standing Committee, as well as the Board of Studies in Theology. He was also a Governor of Harrow School from 1962 and of Bishop

Otter College (1967–9) and acted as Assistant Editor of the *Journal of Ecclesiastical History* from 1975 and a member of the Board of Advisers for the Folger Library Edition of the works of Richard Hooker from 1973.

Despite his academic and other activities James Cargill Thompson's literary output continued unabated almost to the end. He kept the various pots boiling. Thus, he followed up his article on Luther in *JTS* with two learned papers read to the Ecclesiastical History Society and subsequently published, on 'Luther and the Right of Resistance to the Emperor'* and 'The Problem of Luther's "Tower Experience" and its place in his intellectual development'*. Both show the very wide extent of his reading and his ability to put across to the reader in clear, lucid prose the most subtle and complex ideas. A more popular version of his *JTS* article was published as a chapter entitled 'Martin Luther and the "Two Kingdoms"' in *Political Ideas*, ed. David Thomson, Pelican Books A 1054, London 1966, 34–52. This has not been included in this volume since the *JTS* article is a later, fuller and more detailed discussion of the same subject. Nor has his article on 'Thomas Erastus' in the *Encyclopaedia Britannica* (1963); nor his chapter on 'The English Reformation' in *Civilization, II: Journey to the Modern World*, Del Mar, California: CRM Books 1973.

His studies on Luther were not the only contributions to scholarship which James made after his appointment to the Chair at King's College. He pursued his earlier interest in the English Reformation in the reign of Elizabeth with a Bibliographical Note in *JEH* (1976) on 'Thomas Brett's Puritan Papers: a lost Collection of Elizabethan Manuscripts' and 'Sir Francis Knollys's Campaign against the *Jure Divino* theory of Episcopacy' in *The Dissenting Tradition*, ed. C. Robert Cole and Michael Moodie, the second of which is reproduced here.

Richard Hooker was another great source of interest to James. It has already been mentioned that he was on the Board of Advisers for the Folger Library Edition of Hooker's works. To the second of two volumes of Preliminary Essays to this great new critical edition of Hooker's Works in six volumes, he contributed a remarkably fine essay on 'The Philosopher of the "Politic Society": Richard Hooker as a Political Thinker',* published in the U.S.A. (1972), under the editorship of William Speed Hill, for whom James had a great regard. It was one of his longer pieces, running to over 70 pages in the original edition. The subject of political theory was one of his main concerns and he possessed in his fine, specialised library a very good collection of books on the subject, some quite rare. A short bibliographical note (*JEH*, xxv (1974), 75–81) on 'The Sources of Hooker's knowledge of Marsilius of Padua' is not included here but as a tail piece to the volume I have added another paper that he read to the Ecclesiastical History Society, this time on 'John Strype as a source for the study of sixteenth-century English church history', in which he noted the valuable contribution of Strype as an antiquarian collector of original documents, while pointing out how unreliable he is as an editor and transcriber of those documents.

He has left us much to be grateful for. It was the irony of fate that he did not live to complete his book on Luther's political ideas. When he died he was in the process of preparing an Inaugural Lecture. He left behind a first draft in the form of rough notes, written in his own appalling hand-writing, such that his widow wrote of them to me 'I am afraid I find them relatively illegible... I think it should be stressed that they may well be far from what he intended as the final version: you know what a perfectionist he was'. It is clear from his introductory jottings that he had intended to deliver a historiographical lecture on the study of Church History. 'Ecclesiastical History has in one sense an unchanging theme—the history of the Church. It is how we approach it and what we understand by the Church that has changed, and at no time more startlingly than over the past 100–150 years'. It would be unfair to him to try to guess from these rough notes how he would have developed his theme in the final version and they are best left in his family archives.

For James Cargill Thompson was, indeed, a perfectionist. As a scholar he was exact and thorough. His mind was clear and his prose style superb, so that he was able to conduct his reader through the intricacies of Luther's thinking or the sometimes tedious arguments of the Elizabethans with absolute lucidity and to build up a case, always strictly tied to the evidence, with forceful and persuasive clarity. He was never pompous or pedantic.

As a man he was, to quote the Dean of Salisbury's Memorial

Address again: 'Shy, sensitive to pain in others but loving the company of others, clear thinking, discreet, courteous, practical in giving help, this fundamentally humble man illumined for us all the sentiments expressed by Francis Bacon: "Certainly it is heaven upon earth to have a man's mind move in charity, rest in providence and turn upon the poles of truth" '.

Abbreviations

ARG	*Archiv für Reformationsgeschichte*, Berlin/Leipzig/ Gütersloh 1903–
CR	*Corpus Reformatorum*, ed. C. G. Bretschneider and others, Halle 1834–
DNB	*Dictionary of National Biography*, London 1885–
EHR	*English Historical Review*, London 1886–
H.M.C	Historical Manuscripts Commission
HTR	*Harvard Theological Review*, New York 1908–9; Cambridge, Mass. 1910–
HZ	*Historische Zeitschrift*, Munich 1859–
JEH	*Journal of Ecclesiastical History*, London 1950–65; Cambridge 1966–
JTS	*Journal of Theological Studies*, London 1899–1904; Oxford 1905–49; N.S., Oxford 1950–
PhK	Philosophisch-historische Klasse
P.R.O.	Public Record Office
SVRG	*Schriften des Vereins für Reformationsgeschichte*, Halle/Leipzig/Gütersloh 1883–
TLZ	*Theologische Literaturzeitung*, Leipzig 1876–
WA	*D. Martin Luthers Werke*, ed. J. C. F. Knaake and others, Weimar 1883– [Weimarer Ausgabe]
WA Br.	*Briefwechsel*
WA TR	*Tischreden*
ZKG	*Zeitschrift für Kirchengeschichte*, Gotha 1877–1930; Stuttgart 1931–
ZRG	*Zeitschrift der Savigny-Stiftung für Rechtsgeschichte* (Weimar)
ZRG KA	*Kanonistische Abteilung*, 1911–67

PART ONE
LUTHER STUDIES

I

Luther and the Right of Resistance to the Emperor

Like most problems connected with Luther, the question of his attitude to the right of resistance to the emperor is one that has attracted a great deal of attention from German scholars. Sixty years ago, at the height of the First World War, Karl Müller published his pioneering essay, *Luthers Äusserungen über das Recht des bewaffneten Widerstands gegen den Kaiser*, in which he provided the first detailed analysis of the development of Luther's views:[1] since then the problem has been extensively debated by a succession of German historians and theologians.[2] Yet it is perhaps typical of the insularity of so much English historical writing on the continental reformation that these debates have largely been ignored on this side of the Channel. Even today there is no adequate study of the problem in English. It is, of course, common knowledge that Luther changed his views on the question of resistance to the emperor after the Diet of Augsburg under pressure from the protestant princes; but one will search most English biographies of Luther in vain for more than a passing mention of this episode[3] or for a clear analysis of what the change involved, while the subsequent evolution of Luther's ideas in the later 1530s has escaped notice almost entirely. If, therefore, I am only too conscious that in choosing to discuss this subject I am venturing into territory that has already been intensively explored, I may perhaps be allowed to justify my choice on three grounds: first, that it is particularly germane to the theme of this volume; secondly, that it is a topic which has hitherto received too little attention from English historians; and thirdly, that even today there is considerable disagreement among German scholars over the way in which Luther's development should be interpreted, so that it is perhaps worth making a fresh attempt to draw the strands of the story together.

A study of the development of Luther's views on the question of resistance to the emperor enables us to explore the theme of 'the Church and Politics' from a number of different angles. In the first place, it provides an opportunity to see how Luther, who has so often been accused—quite wrongly—of being indifferent to politics, attempted to deal with a concrete political issue. Secondly, it brings out very clearly the tensions which existed within the reformation almost from the beginning between the conflicting demands of religious principle and political necessity. No issue of practical politics presented the first generation of German reformers with such acute moral problems and it was one with which Luther was continually concerned throughout the last twenty-five years of his life. During these twenty-five years his ideas changed slowly but radically, largely in response to the pressure of political events. A study of the problem, therefore, reveals not only the strains to which Luther's teaching was exposed, but also the extent to which his thinking was influenced, both consciously and unconsciously, by external factors. In addition, it has important implications for the general history of political thought in the sixteenth century: for the debate over the right of resistance to the emperor in Germany gave rise to the later protestant doctrine of the right of inferior magistrates to resist their superiors.

From the publication of the Edict of Worms in 1521 until the outbreak of the Schmalkaldic War in 1546 the German protestants had to face the continual possibility that Charles v would at some time or another take active measures to suppress the reformation. It was a threat which varied in intensity at different times. Throughout the greater part of the 1520s the prospect of imperial intervention remained fairly remote. But the question was always there in the background—even if it did not become acute until after 1529—what action, if any, should the protestants take if the emperor were to try to enforce the Edict of Worms against them? In practice, the issue with which the protestants were concerned was whether it was lawful for the estates of the empire (*die Reichsstände*)—the princes and the imperial cities—to resist the emperor in defence of the gospel. At this period it was taken for granted that the common people did not possess the right to resist their superiors: the only question that was seriously considered was whether the princes and the cities had the right to defend themselves if attacked by the emperor in the cause of religion.

It was a question that involved a number of different issues— political, legal, moral and theological—all of which tended to cut across one another, but which need to be distinguished. On the political plane, there was the practical question of whether the princes and cities were prepared to take up arms against the emperor and under what circumstances. On this issue there were marked differences between the attitudes of the leading protestant estates, especially in the 1520s.[4] Philip of Hesse, for example, never appears to have had any scruples about the concept of resistance; Saxony, on the other hand, while supporting the idea of a defensive league against the catholic princes, vacillated for a considerable time before accepting the principle that the emperor might be resisted; while a few states, of which Nuremberg is the outstanding example, ended by repudiating the principle of resistance to the emperor altogether, partly on theological grounds but also for reasons of state. Closely bound up with the political question was the legal question, whether the estates of the empire possessed a constitutional right to resist the emperor under certain circumstances? Here, however, once the political will to resist existed, the jurists attached to the Saxon and Hessian courts found little difficulty in producing an array of arguments from roman and canon law, and from the laws and customs of the empire, to justify the right of resistance, arguments which eventually exercised a considerable influence on the views of the theologians.

Finally, there was the moral and theological question, was resistance compatible with the teaching of the gospel? Luther had always taught that resistance to properly constituted authority was forbidden by divine law. 'The powers that be are ordained of God. Whosoever therefore resisteth the power, resisteth the ordinance of God: and they that resist shall receive to themselves damnation' (Rom. xiii 1–2). It was the Christian's duty to endure oppression, however tyrannical his rulers might be. If his ruler commanded him to do something that was contrary to divine or natural law, then he must refuse obedience and be prepared to suffer the consequences.[5] *Leyden, leyden, Creutz, creutz ist der Christen recht, des und keyn anders,* as he admonished the peasants in 1525.[6] The question was whether this principle extended to the estates of the empire in their relations with the emperor. Initially Luther held that it did, and he repeatedly advised the elector Frederick the Wise and his successor, the elector John, against engaging in any form of opposition to the emperor. But after the Diet of Speyer of 1529 he came under increasing political pressure to modify his position, and eventually at the end of 1530 he did so, at first reluctantly and equivocally, but later at the end of his life with increasing enthusiasm.

Thus there are, in fact, three stages in Luther's development with which we shall be concerned in this paper. First, the period down to 1530, when he opposed resistance to the emperor under all circumstances; secondly, the period after the Declaration of Torgau in October 1530, when he conceded with extreme reluctance that there might possibly be a valid legal right of resistance, although as a theologian he refused to pronounce on the question which he insisted was a matter for the lawyers. Finally, there is a period at the end of his life, in the late 1530s, when he reversed many of his earlier views and emerged as an outspoken champion of resistance to the emperor on theological as well as on legal grounds.

The possibility of a confrontation between the princes and the emperor—and with it the problem of how the princes should act in such a situation—was first raised by the publication of the Edict of Worms in 1521, although initially only in a limited form. In the long term the edict was to provide the main legal justification for Charles v's later moves against the protestant estates and the question of its enforcement was to become one of the most divisive issues of German politics of the next twenty-five years. But in 1521 this still lay in the future. At the time the edict was promulgated there were no protestant estates. Consequently, the question of whether the estates had the right to resist the emperor for the sake of religion did not arise directly. Nevertheless, the edict raised one immediate issue which was a potential source of conflict. This concerned the fate of Luther himself. The edict was addressed to the electors, princes and other ruling authorities of the empire. Under clause 27 it was laid down that after the expiry of Luther's safe-conduct no one was to harbour him, 'but in whatever place you'—that is, the recipients of the edict—'shall find him, if you have sufficient power, you shall take and bind him and bring him or cause him to be brought to us in close custody, or at the least you shall instantly notify us where he may be taken, and in the meanwhile you shall guard him carefully in prison until you receive our instructions as to how he shall be dealt with further'.[7] This clause posed a potentially acute problem for the elector of Saxony. Up until the Diet of Worms Frederick the Wise had been able to justify his refusal to surrender Luther with strong legal arguments[8] and Charles v had tacitly acknowledged the strength of Frederick's position when he agreed to summon Luther to Worms. The publication of the Edict of Worms altered the situation radically. Luther had now been formally placed under the ban of the empire—even though he had challenged the validity of his excommunication by appealing to a general council—and Frederick would have been put in a difficult legal position if Charles had proceeded to call upon him to surrender Luther. In fact, Charles appears to have been as anxious as Frederick to avoid an open confrontation and he secretly took steps to ensure that a copy of the edict was never officially sent to the elector.[9] But it was largely in order to find a way around this dilemma that Frederick arranged for Luther to be kidnapped on his way back from Worms and concealed in the Wartburg, and it is clear that Luther was only persuaded to acquiesce in this arrangement in order to rescue the elector from an embarrassing situation, and not from any fears for his own safety.[10]

Luther outlined his own views on the question, some months later, in the famous letter which he wrote to Frederick the Wise on 5 March 1522,[11] in which he announced his decision to leave the Wartburg and return to Wittenberg without the elector's permission in order to deal with the religious disturbances that had arisen there during his absence. This letter is best known for the forthright manner in which Luther justified his decision to disobey the elector's commands on the grounds that his duty to God must override his obligations to his temporal sovereign. But in the concluding paragraphs he went on to advise Frederick on how he should proceed in the difficult situation that Luther's return would create for him. In fact, his advice was that the elector should do nothing, since he had already done too much, and he should on no account take any steps to protect Luther from the imperial authorities. 'Because I will not obey your Grace, your Grace is excused before God if I am captured or put to death. Before men your Grace should conduct himself thus: namely, as an elector you should be obedient to the magistrate and allow his Imperial Majesty to exercise authority over life and property in your Grace's towns and lands, as he is entitled to do according to the constitution of the empire, and you should not defend nor resist nor require anyone to resist or hinder the [imperial] power, if it wishes to arrest or kill me. For no one should destroy or resist the power except only he that has ordained it, otherwise it is rebellion and against God'. On the other hand, Luther insists, there is no obligation on the elector to become his executioner. It is enough if he permits the envoys of the imperial government to enter his lands and arrest Luther, in which case Luther will allow himself to be taken without causing any trouble or danger to the elector—'For Christ has not taught me to be a Christian at another's expense'. But should the imperial authorities be so unreasonable as to require the elector himself to lay hands on Luther, then Luther will give the elector further advice at the appropriate time on what he should do; but he undertakes that, whatever happens, the elector will come to no harm in body, estate or soul for his sake.[12]

Here in a nutshell is a classic statement of the basic principles of Luther's original position on the question of resistance to the emperor. As far as he personally is concerned, he is ready to suffer arrest and the elector must not intervene to protect him. The princes of the empire have no right to resist the emperor, however just the cause. For within the empire the emperor represents the powers that be that are ordained of God. In relation to the emperor the princes are merely subjects: for them to oppose his commands is to be guilty of rebellion, which is itself a sin against God. On the other hand, the princes are not obliged to assist the emperor in the performance of ungodly acts. Provided that the elector does not prevent the emperor's representatives from entering his territories, he is under no moral obligation to take active steps himself against Luther. Luther leaves open the further question of what is to be done if the imperial authorities should order the elector to arrest him—probably deliberately, because he did not want to trouble Frederick's conscience any further, but also perhaps because he was confident that the issue would not arise.

The letter also contains certain other ideas which are fundamental to the understanding of Luther's attitude to the question of resistance to the emperor in the 1520s. First, there is his strong moral conviction that the gospel ought not to be defended by force, an ideal which he was to develop more fully in his treatise *Of Temporal Authority* of 1523; closely associated with this there is, secondly, his confident belief that God will protect and promote the gospel without any human assistance.[13] Both these ideas were among Luther's most deeply-held convictions during the first decade of the reformation and together they do much to explain the emotional fervour with which he initially opposed the idea of resistance to the emperor. It was a basic axiom of Luther's thought in the 1520s that the battles of the spirit could only be fought with spiritual weapons, with prayer and preaching, and this led him to condemn the use of force in support of the gospel under any circumstances.[14] Equally he believed passionately that God would never allow his cause to fail, but would always intervene to defend the gospel in ways which man could not foresee; consequently, he tended later in the decade to interpret any moves on the part of the protestant princes to form a defensive alliance on behalf of the gospel as evidence of lack of faith, since it indicated that they were not willing to put their trust in God alone.[15] Significantly, it was when Luther's faith in these two concepts began to weaken, as it did in the 1530s, that his attitude to the question of resistance to the emperor also underwent a change.

As it turned out, Frederick the Wise was never called upon to face the decision whether or not to surrender Luther. Following Charles v's return to Spain in the summer of 1521, the imperial governing council (*das Reichsregiment*), which was responsible for the administration of the empire in Charles's absence, showed extreme reluctance to enforce the Edict of Worms and for the next eighteen months it successfully side-stepped the issue. However, the question of the enforcement of the edict could only be postponed; it could not be avoided altogether, and it re-emerged as a critical issue at the second Diet of Nuremberg which sat from November 1522 to February 1523.[16] At the diet the papal legate presented the estates with a formal request from the new pope,

Adrian VI, calling on them to implement the papal bull and the Edict of Worms against Luther and his followers. At the same time, a group of catholic princes, led by Frederick's dynastic rivals, the elector Joachim I of Brandenburg and duke George of Albertine Saxony, began to press for active measures to be taken against electoral Saxony. In the end the crisis blew over. The estates finally resolved not to enforce the edict until the abuses in the Church had been dealt with and they called instead for a new general council to be summoned within a year—although as a sop to the papal legate it was agreed that Frederick should be required to prevent Luther and his followers from writing or publishing any new works—a demand with which Luther not surprisingly refused to comply.[17] However, in the weeks before the diet reached its decision, the outlook for Saxony appeared so threatening that Frederick took the step of consulting the Wittenberg theologians on whether he might lawfully engage in a defensive war if he were to be attacked for Luther's sake. It is to this crisis that we owe the first formal *Gutachten* that we have on the subject of resistance. These consist of four short statements by Luther, Melanchthon, Bugenhagen and Amsdorf, which were drawn up at the beginning of February 1523 at the request of the elector's secretary, Georg Spalatin.[18]

Because of their early date these *Gutachten* are of particular interest, but they also present problems of interpretation. The difficulty arises from the fact that Spalatin's original letter to the Wittenberg divines does not survive and we do not know the precise form of the questions that he put to them.[19] As a result, most historians have tended, in practice, to treat these statements as if they represented opinions on the question of whether it was lawful to resist the emperor.[20] But it is clear from the answers of Luther's colleagues—though not from that of Luther himself— that Spalatin's questions were couched in more general terms and that the problem with which the elector was immediately concerned was not whether he might resist the emperor, but whether he might offer any resistance in the event of his being attacked on Luther's account by an alliance of catholic princes. This problem was particularly pressing at this juncture for two reasons: first, because of Luther's previously-declared opposition to the use of force in defence of the gospel; and secondly, because of the real, if short-lived, threat that the elector of Brandenburg and duke George might attempt to invade Saxony under the pretext of enforcing the Edict of Worms.

Luther's answer is terse to the point of ambiguity and it presents the most problems of interpretation. He begins by insisting that so long as the elector maintains his present position of neutrality in regard to Luther's cause[21] he should not go to war on account of it, but 'ought to yield to the imperial power' and permit it to 'arrest and proceed against those whom it wishes in his territories, since the emperor is his lord by the consent of God and of men, even though they be ungodly'. However, he then goes on to concede that 'if the elector wishes to undertake war for the sake of this cause' (*si autem vellet bellum suscipere pro tuenda ista causa*) he may do so under strictly defined conditions. In the first place, he must publicly acknowledge that Luther's cause is just and abandon his previous attitude of neutrality. Secondly, he may not go to war for the reason that these people are his subjects, 'but he may as a foreigner coming from a foreign land go to the assistance of foreigners' (*sed tanquam alienus alienis ex aliena terra veniens succurrat*).[22] Thirdly, he may act if he has a special divine calling (*vocante singulari spiritu et fide*). Otherwise he must yield to the superior sword and die with those whom he acknowledges to be Christians. Fourthly, provided that the dispute is between him and his equals—if, for example, duke George or the elector of Brandenburg or some one else should attack him 'not with the emperor nor at the emperor's command, but out of their own arrogance'—then he may act in the same way as in wars involving secular causes; in other words, he should first offer justice and peace; then, if that is refused, he may 'resist force by force on behalf of his subjects'.[23]

This document has usually been interpreted as meaning that Luther was prepared to concede the possibility that the emperor might be resisted under certain hypothetical conditions, but these conditions were so stringent that, as Karl Müller put it, it was unthinkable that they could be fulfilled.[24] Consequently, Luther may effectively be said to have ruled out the idea of resistance to the emperor in practice, while admitting it in theory. Certainly, Luther's answer can be read in this sense, if one starts with the preconception that the only question he was discussing throughout

the paper was that of resistance to the emperor. But this interpretation is impossible to reconcile with Luther's other statements at this stage of his career. On no other occasion in the
period down to 1530 did he concede that it could be lawful to
resist the emperor under any circumstances and it is difficult to
believe that he was prepared to do so, even momentarily, in 1523.
If, however, one sees the paper as being concerned not with the
specific question of resistance to the emperor, but with the more
general question of whether it was lawful for the elector to go to
war if he were to be attacked on Luther's account, then Luther's
answer emerges in a different light. For it becomes clear that the
conditions that Luther laid down in the second part of the paper
do not relate to the question of resistance to the emperor but
rather to the circumstances in which the elector might take up
arms for the protestant cause[25]—a very different matter.

   That Luther's paper was not primarily concerned with the
question of resistance to the emperor is also suggested by the
answers of his colleagues. All three answers are concerned simply
with the general question of whether the elector might defend his
people, if attacked for Luther's sake, and none of them makes any
mention of the emperor. Melanchthon went a step further than
Luther in insisting that it was wrong for the elector to undertake
war 'in any cause', unless he was convinced that the cause was
just and that it was pleasing to God that it should be defended by
war. Apparently in answer to points raised by Spalatin, he also
put forward two other arguments against armed intervention by
the elector. First, he insisted that if it was wrong for a prince to go
to war 'without the consent of his people, from whom he receives
his authority' (*nisi consenciente populo, a quo accipit Imperium*),[26]
then it must follow that the elector ought not to go to war in this
case. For it was evident that the people of Saxony would not wish
to go to war for the sake of the gospel, since they did not believe
—a clear-sighted, if perhaps unexpected comment on the small
progress the reformation had made in Saxony at that date.
Secondly, he dismissed as irrelevant the precedent of the Old
Testament kings of Judah: for whereas the people of Judah were
expressly commanded by God to wage war in defence of the faith,
'our people have no command to defend themselves, but those
who are Christians ought to give up their lives for the Gospel, not

wish to be defended by others'.[27] Bugenhagen's answer reveals most clearly the moral dilemma which the issue posed for the Wittenberg reformers: for after tying himself up in knots in an agonised attempt to reconcile the Christian's duty to suffer with the magistrate's duty to defend his subjects, he finally gave up the struggle and referred the issue to God, with the prayer that he would guide their consciences to act aright when the time came.[28] By contrast, Amsdorf argued unequivocally that although in his private capacity as a Christian the prince ought not to wage war on account of the gospel, he is also a 'public person' and bears the sword. Consequently, it is his duty to defend his subjects against attack. Amsdorf, therefore, had no hesitation in saying that the elector might lawfully resist, if attacked, even without the consent of his people—for, as he pointed out with a side-glance at Melanchthon's reply,[29] the prince does not bear the sword by the will of the people. All that is necessary is that he should act with a secure conscience, strengthened and confirmed by the pure word of God.[30] Taken together—despite their differences—these three answers demonstrate that resistance to the emperor was not the question on which the Wittenberg theologians were asked to give their advice in February 1523. That Luther alone should have felt it necessary to touch on the matter in his reply is perhaps not surprising in view of his earlier advice to Frederick on the subject; but there can be little doubt that Luther, like his colleagues, was primarily concerned on this occasion with whether the elector might resist an attack by his enemies and it is almost certainly wrong to interpret his paper as conceding a hypothetical right of resistance to the emperor.

For an unambiguous statement of Luther's views at this period it is only necessary to turn to his treatise *Of Temporal Authority*, which was published in March 1523 barely a month after he wrote his memorandum for the elector. There he states categorically, in language which echoes some of the phrases of his memorandum,[31] that for princes to resist their superiors is always wrong: 'I say that to act here in a Christian manner no prince should wage war against his overlord, be he king, emperor or other liege lord, but should let him who takes take. For no one should resist the magistrate with force, but only with confession of the truth. If he is converted thereby, it is good; but if not, you are excused and suffer wrong for God's sake. But if your opponent is your equal or inferior to you or a foreign ruler, you should first offer him justice and peace, as Moses taught the children of Israel. But if he will not accept it, then do your best and defend yourself with force against force; as Moses has so well written, Deut. 20'.[32]

In practice, because of the reluctance of the diet and the imperial governing council to take any steps to enforce the Edict of Worms, the threat of direct intervention by the imperial authorities gradually receded and it remained a relatively remote contingency until after the Diet of Speyer of 1529. On the other hand, the protestants had to face the continued possibility of an attack by the catholic princes and this danger became increasingly acute after 1525 as a small but growing number of princes and cities began to adopt the reformation officially—some, though by no means all, of whom were eager to take active counter-measures against the catholics. In consequence, during the second half of the 1520s the question of the right of resistance to the emperor, although it could not be ignored completely, tended to be subordinated to the more immediate issue which confronted and divided the protestant estates—the question of whether, and under what conditions, it was lawful for them to engage in a defensive alliance against the catholic princes.

In so far as Luther discussed the question of resistance to the emperor between 1525 and 1529 it was largely in the context of the debate over the formation of a protestant league. Thus in an opinion which he wrote for count Albrecht of Mansfeld, probably early in 1525 at the time when the possibility of an alliance between Saxony and other princely states was first being mooted, he insisted categorically that no league could be lawful which was directed against the emperor. 'Your Grace knows well', he wrote, 'that against the magistrate [the emperor] no alliance is valid. For God requires that the overlords be honoured, be they evil or good, Rom. xiii and 1 Pet. iii'. On the other hand, he was prepared to allow that a general defensive league might be permissible, provided that no attempt was made to specify its objectives and it was directed solely against some 'unnamed mischance', in which case it might usefully serve as a deterrent to the catholic princes.[33]

Luther reaffirmed his fundamental opposition to resistance to

the emperor in his tract, *Whether soldiers too can be saved?* of
1526, in which he argued at length that it was always wrong for
inferiors to wage war against their superiors, however tyrannical
they might be. This maxim, he insisted, applied equally to
'peasants, townsmen, noblemen, counts and princes. For all these
also have overlords and are underpersons in relation to some one
else. Therefore, just as one cuts off the head of a rebellious
peasant, so one should cut off the head of a rebellious nobleman,
count or prince, the one like the other, and no wrong is done to
anyone'.[34] Some of the arguments that Luther used in this tract
are of particular interest in view of the subsequent development
of the controversy. For example, he refused to accept the validity
of any historical precedents for rebellion, whether taken from
classical antiquity, or from the Old Testament, or from more
recent historical events, such as the revolt of the Swiss against the
Habsburgs or the Danes against king Christian II, arguing that
what matters is not what has been done in the past, 'but what one
should and can do with a good conscience', and that even if rebellion seems to prosper to begin with God will always punish it in
the end.[35] He also specifically rejected the argument that where
a king or lord has bound himself by a formal oath to his subjects
to observe certain articles of government, he may legitimately be
resisted if he breaks his oath; for God alone has the right to punish
tyrants.[36] On the other hand, he did not dispute that war might
be justified between equals, but only under certain conditions.
Above all, he insisted that a prince must not go to war unless he is
attacked first, in which case 'war may be called not only war, but
a necessary protection and self-defence';[37] and secondly, that a
prince must always fight in the fear of the Lord and not put his
trust in his own might, however just his cause; for it is God who
decides the outcome of wars and he will punish those who, in their
arrogance, believe that they can win by the strength of their own
resources without his aid.[38]

From 1528 relations between the catholic and protestant estates
became increasingly strained, at first largely because of the aggres-
sive policies of Philip of Hesse, later because of the renewed
threat of imperial intervention after the Diet of Speyer of 1529.
In consequence, a new impetus was given to the negotiations over
the formation of a protestant league, although in practice the

protestant estates proved to be so deeply divided over the issue that it was not until nearly three years later, when the political situation had become much more threatening after the Diet of Augsburg, that the League of Schmalkalden was finally concluded.[39] During these three years Luther and his colleagues were frequently consulted by the elector John on the moral implications of taking part in such a league and some of Luther's most important *Gutachten* both on the question of a protestant league and the related question of resistance to the emperor date from this period. In general down to the closing months of 1530 there is little discernible alteration in Luther's position except on one issue. By 1529 he appears to have quietly abandoned his earlier insistence that the reformation should not be defended by force. In other respects his views remained unchanged. While he accepted that a defensive alliance was not in itself unlawful, he continued to insist that it must not be directed against the emperor and that it must be purely defensive. Throughout this period he repeatedly emphasised that the protestant estates must on no account embark on a preventive war: they must wait to be attacked before attempting to defend themselves; otherwise they would be breaking God's law and God would surely punish them. At the same time he remained firmly convinced that the truly Christian course of action which the protestants ought to follow was not to take defensive measures of any kind, but to put their trust in God who had protected them in the past and who would continue to do so provided that they did not let their faith fail. Thus, although Luther's attitude tended to fluctuate with the political situation, on balance he viewed the idea of a protestant league with considerable reservations and this is clearly reflected in his letters of advice to the elector.

In March 1528 Luther was called upon to advise the elector at the time of the so-called 'Pack affair', when it was widely believed by the protestants on the strength of a forged document passed on to Philip of Hesse by Otto von Pack, a former councillor of duke George of Albertine Saxony, that the leading catholic princes had made a secret treaty the previous year to launch an attack on the protestants.[40] Luther, like the Saxon government, was at first convinced that the secret treaty was genuine and in a memorandum, which he drew up for the elector's chancellor, Gregor Brück, on

28 March 1528, he had no hesitation in recommending that the elector might defend himself with a good conscience if he were attacked by the catholic princes, since 'as an elector of the Empire he has no overlord who has the right and power to punish or judge his Grace except only his Imperial Majesty himself'. The elector, he advised, could safely disregard any claims by the catholic princes to be acting in the emperor's name, since it was evident that this was only a pretext and that they were acting 'without his Imperial Majesty's knowledge, will and command'. On the other hand, as he was to do again and again over the next three years, he warned the elector in the strongest terms that he must on no account take part in a preventive war against the catholics. If the protestants were to attack first, they would immediately put themselves in the wrong, while the catholic princes would be able to claim that they were acting in self-defence. 'No greater dishonour could befall the Gospel; for the outcome would be not a peasants' uprising, but a princes' uprising (*nicht ein Bauraufruhr, sondern ein Fürstenaufruhr*), which would destroy Germany utterly, something which also Satan would gladly see'. He therefore urged that if Philip of Hesse refused to follow this course of action and persisted with his plans for attacking the catholics, the elector should stand aside; for he was not bound to hold to the alliance, if it would involve him in breaking God's laws.[41] A few days before this memorandum was written Luther had expressed himself even more forcibly on this point at a private interview with the elector, at which he had warned John that if he and Philip were to proceed with the idea of launching a preventive attack against the catholics, then Luther and his colleagues would feel obliged to leave Saxony in order to protect the good name of the gospel from the scandal which would inevitably ensue.[42] In the end, after considerable hesitation, the elector was persuaded to withdraw his support from Philip; and Philip, whose troops had already begun to invade the territories of the archbishop of Würzburg, was forced to call off his planned campaign against the prince bishoprics of the Main. Shortly afterwards, the crisis was defused when Pack's revelations were exposed as fraudulent. But the whole incident left Luther with a lasting suspicion of Philip's intentions and it served to reinforce his reservations about the idea of a protestant league.

Luther's distrust of Philip and his reluctance to support Philip's schemes for a protestant league is reflected in the series of letters which he wrote to the elector in the months that followed the second Diet of Speyer of 1529. The decision of the catholic majority at the diet to annul the recess of the 1526 Diet of Speyer, coupled with the announcement that Charles v was planning to return to Germany before the next diet, provoked a new crisis for the protestants and it once again made the question of a protestant league a matter of urgency. The first steps were taken at Speyer itself. Before they left the diet, five of the leading states which had signed the protestation against the recess—Saxony, Hesse, Nuremberg, Ulm and Strassburg—agreed in principle to the formation of a new protestant league, although the details were left to be settled later. Luther's reaction was immediate and hostile. As soon as news of the Speyer agreement reached him in Wittenberg, he wrote to the elector to express his vehement disapproval of the proposed league. 'Such an alliance', he protested, 'is not of God, nor is it based on trust in God, but on human wisdom and the desire to seek and trust in human help alone'; as such, it 'has no good foundation and therefore may bring forth no good fruit'. He warned the elector against becoming involved in any new alliance with Philip after his experiences of the previous year; for the landgrave is 'a restless young prince' (*ein unrugig junger Fürst*), who could not be relied upon to keep the peace but would endeavour to find some excuse to attack their enemies.[43]

In fact, the unity which the protestant states displayed at Speyer turned out to be short-lived. Almost as soon as the diet was over, splits began to appear in their ranks and although the negotiations for a league continued until the beginning of the following year it proved impossible for them to reach any definite agreement on the form the alliance should take.[44] The two major issues which divided the protestant estates were, first, the question of who should be admitted to membership of the league, and, secondly, the question of whether it should be directed against the emperor as well as against the catholic princes. The initial agreement at Speyer in April 1529 had been signed by the representatives of two cities with Zwinglian leanings, Ulm and Strassburg. It soon became clear that Philip of Hesse's aim was to construct a comprehensive anti-catholic and anti-Habsburg alliance that would include not only the Zwinglian cities of southern Germany, but also some of the Swiss cities as well. By contrast, Saxony for both political and theological reasons favoured a more cautious policy and, as the summer wore on, it began to insist that membership of the league should be restricted to those states that accepted the Lutheran doctrine of the eucharist. This policy was strongly supported by the Wittenberg theologians. Both Luther and Melanchthon had been deeply disturbed by Philip of Hesse's plans to include the Zwinglians in the league and in his letter of 22 May 1529 Luther had advanced as one of his principal objections to the Speyer agreement the fact that it would have involved the Lutherans in allying themselves with those who 'strive against God and the Sacrament'.[45] He repeated these views in a formal opinion which he wrote at the end of July or the beginning of August on behalf of his Wittenberg colleagues, in which he insisted that any alliance must be based on unity of faith. In this paper he specifically condemned the inclusion of the Zwinglians in the league on the ground that this would mean lending support to their heresies, while he once again warned the elector against the dangers of taking part in an alliance with Philip of Hesse.[46] During the coming months Saxony's intransigent demand that the members of the league should subscribe to a common statement of faith was to become one of the principal factors which prevented the negotiations from making any progress.

The other major issue on which the negotiations eventually stalled was the question of resistance to the emperor, although this did not become a serious point of controversy until the autumn. At an early stage in the negotiations a proposal had been put forward by Lazarus Spengler, the city secretary of Nuremberg, that the treaty should include a clause specifically excluding resistance to the emperor from the terms of the league. But this proposal was initially rejected not only by Philip of Hesse but also by the elector of Saxony and the margrave of Brandenburg–Ansbach without serious opposition from the other states.[47] At this stage there appears to have been little public discussion of the issue. Perhaps deliberately the elector did not consult Luther, although he did consult Bugenhagen in September 1529 at a time when Luther and the other leading Wittenberg theologians were absent at the Colloquy of Marburg. Bugenhagen replied in a letter, dated 29 September, in which he tentatively agreed that the elector might lawfully defend his people if they were unjustly attacked by the emperor, although he insisted that this was only his personal opinion and he begged the elector to keep his advice secret until his colleagues had had the opportunity to consider the matter.[48] In this situation the question might have been allowed to go by default, especially since the legal councillors of Saxony and Hesse were agreed that resistance to the emperor could be justified on grounds of natural and positive law.[49] That this did not happen was largely due to Lazarus Spengler.[50] At the beginning of November Spengler produced a long and carefully reasoned memorandum for the city council of Nuremberg, in which he argued that resistance to the emperor was absolutely forbidden by divine law.[51] Spengler succeeded in winning over both the council of Nuremberg and the margrave of Ansbach to his views and this had the effect of reopening the debate among the protestant estates. While Nuremberg and Ansbach now came out against any alliance that was directed against the emperor, Philip of Hesse, not surprisingly, championed the opposite point of view and insisted that the princes of the empire possessed both a moral and a constitutional right to defend themselves if the emperor were to attack them without just cause.[52] The issue came to a head at a meeting of the Lutheran estates held at Nuremberg in January 1530 to discuss the future of the league, following the withdrawal of the south German cities from the negotiations because of their refusal to accept an alliance based on the Schwabach Articles. At this meeting the question of resistance to the emperor emerged as the dominant issue. While the chancellor of Saxony expressed himself in favour of resistance, the representatives of Nuremberg and Ansbach refused to take part in any alliance against the emperor, with the result that the meeting ended without any agreement.[53]

Following the Nuremberg meeting the elector of Saxony decided to refer the matter to the Wittenberg theologians. Up to this point he appears to have been unwilling to seek Luther's advice on the question, preferring instead to rely on Bugenhagen's opinion of September 1529,[54] partly, no doubt, because he was afraid of what Luther's answer might be. Thus it is almost certainly no accident that neither of the two *Gutachten* which Luther wrote for the elector on 18 November and 24 December 1529 is concerned directly with the moral question of resistance to the emperor, although on both occasions he advised the elector very strongly against taking part in an alliance with Philip and in the second letter he advanced a number of practical reasons why the elector should not accede to Philip's latest suggestion that the protestants should mobilise their forces in readiness to meet an attack by the emperor.[55] It is clear from the content of Luther's answers that he was not asked to discuss the *principle* of resistance to the emperor and there can be little doubt that at this stage the elector did not wish to have the matter raised. The reports of the debates at Nuremberg, however, unsettled the elector and on 27 January 1530 he wrote to Luther to ask him to consult with Justus Jonas, Bugenhagen and Melanchthon and to present their considered opinion on whether the emperor might lawfully be resisted if he were to attack the protestants while their formal appeal to a general council was still pending, especially since such an attack might be regarded as a breach of his election capitulation by which the emperor had bound himself to observe the due process of law in all his dealings with the estates.[56] The form of the question is particularly interesting, since it encapsulates two of the main arguments which the protestant lawyers were beginning to develop as the basis of their case for resistance—first, the claim that it was unlawful for the emperor to proceed against the protestants until their appeal to a general council had been heard, and, second, the claim that the estates were entitled to resist the emperor if he failed to observe the promises he had made in his election capitulation.[57]

Luther replied on behalf of his colleagues on 6 March 1530 in a long and carefully composed letter which later came to be regarded as one of his most important pronouncements on the question of resistance to the emperor.[58] In this letter he reviewed the principal arguments that had been put forward in support of resistance and rejected them in turn, taking his stand, as he had always done, on the principle that resistance to superiors was absolutely forbidden by divine law. He began by examining the claim that the emperor might be resisted if he broke the terms of his election oath. While he was prepared to accept that a case could be made out for this on the basis of imperial and temporal laws, he insisted that it was entirely contrary to the plain teaching of Scripture. 'According to the Scripture it is in no way meet that anyone who would be a Christian should resist his ruler, irrespective of whether he acts justly or unjustly, but a Christian should suffer force and injustice, especially from his ruler'. However unjustly the emperor acts, he still remains emperor and 'neither his imperial authority nor his subjects' duty of obedience is abrogated so long as the empire and the electors still acknowledge him as emperor and do not depose him'. This is so, even if he transgresses God's laws: otherwise there would be chaos, since subjects would always be able to justify any act of resistance by claiming that their ruler had broken God's laws. But if the emperor may not be resisted, 'even if he breaks all of God's commandments simultaneously, yea, even if he were a heathen', then it must follow that 'until he is removed or is no longer emperor' he may not be resisted if he breaks his oath to his subjects; for the duty he owes to God is of a far higher order than the duty he owes to men. At this point in his argument, however, Luther introduced an important distinction: for he suggested that although sin did not abrogate the emperor's authority, punishment did—in other words, he could be deprived of his authority, if he were unanimously deposed by the empire and the electors. In that case he might lawfully be resisted since he would no longer be emperor. 'Otherwise, so long as he is unpunished and remains emperor, no one may withdraw his obedience from him or resist him. For that is to initiate mob-violence and rebellion and discord'.[59]

Having disposed of the argument of the emperor's election oath, Luther then proceeded to deal more briefly with two other arguments that had been put forward to justify resistance. The first was an argument which was strongly favoured by Philip of Hesse's lawyers, that resistance to the emperor could be justified on the basis of the natural law right of self-defence. Luther rejected this out of hand. He pointed out that the natural law maxim *vim vi repellere licet* which the lawyers cited, only applied, if at all, to cases in which one was attacked by one's equals: it did not give inferiors the right to defend themselves against their superiors. To drive the point home with a local example, he insisted that, since all the princes' subjects were also the emperor's subjects the princes had no more right to defend them against the emperor than the burgomaster of Torgau had to defend his towns-men against the princes of Saxony. He gave even shorter shrift to the argument that resistance was justifiable on the grounds that the emperor intended to ignore the protestants' appeal to a general council. With cold common sense Luther pointed out that it made no difference whether the emperor allowed the protestants' appeal to be heard or not, since both he and the protestants knew perfectly well that, even if the appeal were heard, the protestants would certainly be condemned, so that in ignoring the appeal the emperor would merely be treating them as if they had already been condemned.[60]

As in 1522, Luther advised that the proper course of action for the princes to follow was to 'let their land and people stand open to the emperor, since they are his, and entrust the matter to God'. No one, he maintained, should expect the prince to do otherwise: for each person ought to stand up for his own faith and be pre-pared, if necessary, to lay down his life for it without bringing his prince into danger by seeking his protection. On the other hand, if the emperor were to go further and require the princes to attack and persecute their subjects for the sake of the gospel, they should refuse to obey: for it is enough if they leave their lands and people undefended and they should on no account cooperate with the emperor in doing evil. In the meanwhile, Luther urged, as he had done in all his letters in 1529, that the protestants ought to put their trust in God and not seek to anticipate events, for God would find ways to help them and to protect his Word as he had done ever since the foundation of the Church. To do otherwise was to show a lack of faith in God.[61]

Luther's arguments and even some of his phrases are strikingly reminiscent of his letter to Frederick the Wise of March 1522. The one novel element in this letter—which does seem to mark the beginnings of a shift in his position—is that he was now apparently prepared to recognise the possibility that the emperor might be deposed by the unanimous judgment of the electors and the estates.[62] But the shift—if it can be counted as such—was essentially academic; for it did not affect the existing situation. As Luther was at pains to point out, Charles v was still recog-nised as the lawful emperor by the empire and so long as this remained the case the protestants had no right to resist him, however unjustly he might behave towards them. Moreover, given the existing divisions within Germany, it was inconceivable that Charles could ever be removed by a unanimous decision of the electors and estates, so that the situation could never arise in which it would be lawful for the protestants to resist him.

In March 1530, in other words, Luther's position and that of his colleagues was still in essentials what it had always been: they remained convinced that resistance to the lawful emperor was absolutely prohibited by Scripture and they refused to allow that there could be any exceptions to this rule. Yet only seven months later they were to abandon their uncompromising stance and were to concede—admittedly with the greatest reluctance—that a legal right of resistance might exist. How did this change come about and what did it involve?

The answer to the first part of the question lies in the outcome of the Diet of Augsburg of 1530. The diet altered—or, perhaps it would be more accurate to say, appeared to alter—the political situation in Germany dramatically. The return of Charles v to Germany, his rejection of the Augsburg Confession and the subsequent recess of the diet, which called for the strict enforcement of the Edict of Worms, faced the protestants once more with the threat of direct intervention by the emperor. In practice, the recess was to prove no more enforceable than that of 1529, but its effect was to reunite the protestants and steps were immediately taken to resume the negotiations for a protestant league which had been suspended since the failure of the Nuremberg talks in January.[63] The seriousness of the threat of imperial intervention removed any lingering doubts that the elector of Saxony still had on the question of resistance to the emperor and from this time on the policies of the Saxon and Hessian governments were in close accord on this issue.[64] The one major difficulty remained the attitude of the Wittenberg theologians, who now came under increasing pressure both from the electoral government and from Philip of Hesse to accept the legality of resistance to the emperor.

So seriously did the elector regard the situation that in October 1530, shortly after his return from the diet, he summoned Luther, together with Melanchthon and Justus Jonas, to a meeting at Torgau to discuss the matter with his legal councillors. At this

meeting they were presented with a paper drawn up by Gregor
Brück, the elector's principal councillor and former chancellor,
and several of the jurists attached to the Saxon court, in which a
case was made out for resistance on the basis of arguments drawn
from Roman and, rather surprisingly, canon law.[65] At about the
same time—apparently while he was actually at Torgau[66]—
Luther received a letter from Philip of Hesse in which he advanced a number of reasons why resistance might be considered
lawful. In particular, Philip argued that the constitutional position of the German princes was quite different from that of the
magistrates of the Roman Empire in the time of the apostles,
since they were not appointed officials of the emperor but
hereditary rulers who possessed rights which the emperor—who
was himself not hereditary, but elected—was bound to observe:
in consequence, if the emperor exceeded his jurisdiction, or failed
to keep his oath to the princes, they were fully entitled to resist
him, since he automatically forfeited his authority and made himself 'a common person', who could 'no longer be regarded as a
true emperor, but as a peace-breaker'.[67] However, it is noteworthy
that, although the argument that the princes possessed constitutional rights against the emperor later came to play an important part in protestant political theory, it was not used by the
Saxon jurists in their memorandum[68] and there is no evidence
that it was accepted by Luther at this stage. Instead the Saxon
councillors relied on the much narrower legal argument, which
Luther had previously rejected in his letter of 6 March 1530, that
if the emperor were to attack the protestants for the sake of
religion, while their appeal to a general council was still pending,
he would be guilty of *notoria iniuria*, since he would be acting in
a matter in which he had no powers of jurisdiction, and that,
therefore, according to the views of both Roman lawyers and
canonists, he might lawfully be resisted.[69]

We do not have a full report of the Torgau meeting, but the
discussions continued over three or four days[70] and we know from
subsequent letters by both Luther and Melanchthon that the
matter was hotly debated.[71] From these letters two points are
clear: first, that the talks were not confined to the issues raised in
the jurists' memorandum, and, secondly, that initially the Wittenberg theologians refused to make any concessions. In particular,

Luther resolutely refused to go back on the opinion, which he had expressed in his letter of 6 March, that resistance to the emperor could not be justified on the basis of the natural law right of self-defence (*vim vi repellere licet*).[72] In the end, however, without formally retracting their belief in the principle that resistance to superiors was forbidden by Scripture, they were persuaded to withdraw their opposition to the arguments used in the jurists' paper and they agreed to the famous statement known to historians as the Torgau Declaration. This statement was presented in the names of Luther, Jonas, Melanchthon, Spalatin 'and certain other theologians', whose names are not recorded, although it is usually assumed that the text was drawn up by Luther.[73] Although its grammar is rather tortuous and it shows signs of having been written in haste, the declaration was worded with considerable care and it is, therefore, necessary to quote the greater part of it verbatim: 'A paper has been presented to us, from which we observe what the doctors of law conclude in regard to the question, in what cases it is lawful to resist the magistrate. If now this has therefore been established by the said doctors or experts in the law, then seeing that we are certainly placed in such a situation in which (as they show) the magistrate may be resisted, and [secondly] that we have at all times taught that one should accept and uphold the validity of temporal laws in what concerns them so long as (*weil*)[74] the Gospel does not teach anything contrary to the temporal law, we cannot oppose it with the Scripture if in this case it is necessary to defend oneself, whether it be against the emperor in his own person or anyone acting in his name . . . With regard to the fact that we have hitherto taught that the magistrate should on no account be resisted, this is because we did not know that the magistrate's law itself permitted this—which law we have always diligently taught should be obeyed'.[75]

Hedged about with reservations as this statement is, the theologians then proceeded to qualify their remarks still further by submitting a supplementary memorandum to the elector in which they presented their advice as to how the protestant estates should act in the present crisis. Far from lending their support to the idea of resistance, they recommended that the protestants should continue to seek peace from the emperor and that they should send him an embassy to explain why they could not in conscience accept the recess. If, however, he persisted in his determination to enforce the recess, they should inform him that in order to avoid causing bloodshed they would not offer any resistance to the restoration of catholicism, but that they would not cooperate in any way. If this course of action were followed, the divines concluded hopefully, the reintroduction of catholicism would take place without the use of military force or bloodshed and it would probably collapse of its own accord within one or two years.[76]

The Torgau Declaration is rightly regarded as a crucial turning-point in the development of Lutheran political theory,[77] since from this time on the Wittenberg theologians abandoned their outright opposition to resistance to the emperor. But it is important not to exaggerate the nature of the change in their views at this period. While the practical implications of the declaration were far-reaching, the shift in the intellectual position of Luther and his colleagues was at first relatively small. As the wording of the declaration makes clear, they did not positively assert the existence of a right of resistance nor did they abandon their basic belief that resistance to superiors was forbidden by Scripture. The most they were prepared to concede was the possibility that positive law might permit resistance in certain circumstances, in which case they declared that they would not oppose it on scriptural grounds. But even this concession was strictly qualified. In the first place, they refused to commit themselves as to whether such a right of resistance did exist, insisting that it was a matter for the lawyers to decide. Secondly, they did not state, as some historians have suggested through a misunderstanding of Luther's use of the word *weil*, that Scripture did not contradict temporal laws: they merely said that temporal laws were to be regarded as valid in their own sphere *so long as* they did not conflict with the teaching of the gospel.[78] Thus it was in accordance with this principle that in the course of the debate they rejected the argument that resistance to the emperor could be justified on the basis of the natural law right of self-defence as being contrary to Christ's teaching.[79] In practice, it is clear that the only legal argument that they were prepared to consider at this stage was the one put forward by the Saxon jurists in their memorandum, that grounds for

resistance might exist if the emperor exceeded his powers of jurisdiction by attacking the protestants for the sake of religion while
their appeal to a general council was still pending. Significantly,
it was not until several years later that they came to accept Philip
of Hesse's argument that the princes of the empire were not mere
'private persons', but possessed constitutional rights in virtue of
the nature of their office which entitled them to resist the emperor
if he acted tyrannically.[80] Equally, it is clear from their second
paper, which needs to be read in conjunction with the first, that
in October 1530 Luther and his colleagues were still opposed to
resistance in any form and that they would have preferred to see
the protestants submit to the emperor if he attempted to enforce
the Edict of Worms against them. Thus the Torgau Declaration
is an equivocal document. It represents not so much a change of
front on the part of the Wittenberg theologians as an abdication
of responsibility. They withdrew their formal opposition to the
lawyers' arguments; but instead of coming out openly in support
of resistance themselves, they took up a position of guarded
neutrality, declaring that it was not for them as theologians, but
for the lawyers to determine what the law allowed. As Luther
wrote in a letter to Wenceslas Link in Nuremberg in January
1531, 'I may not advise nor judge concerning that law itself, but
remain in my theology'.[81]

How little Luther was prepared to admit that his views had
changed is shown by this letter and two others which he wrote to
Link's associate Lazarus Spengler, the city secretary of Nuremberg, in the early months of 1531.[82] As in the previous year, the
two Franconian States, Nuremberg and Ansbach, had continued
their policy of total opposition to the principle of resistance to the
emperor, even after the Diet of Augsburg. While the motives of
the Nuremberg city council were as much political and com-
mercial as religious,[83] this stance was strongly supported on theological grounds by Wenceslas Link and Lazarus Spengler.[84] When,
therefore, rumours began to circulate after the meeting of the
protestant estates at Schmalkalden in December 1530 that Luther
had changed his mind on the issue of resistance, both Link and
Spengler wrote to him to express their concern. Luther's replies
throw a revealing light on his attitude. In these letters he indig-
nantly repudiated the charge that he had altered his views and

insisted that neither he nor his colleagues had advocated resistance —indeed, they had continued to argue against it. What had happened at Torgau, he wrote, was that after a sharp debate, in which they had reaffirmed their opposition to resistance, they had been presented with the argument that the 'imperial law' (*das Kaiserliche Recht*—that is roman law) permitted the emperor to be resisted in cases of notorious injustice (*in notorie iniustis*). In this situation they had concluded that they could not oppose resistance, if it was permitted by the law, since they had always taught that the laws should be obeyed.[85] Thus, as he put it in his first letter to Spengler the issue could be reduced to a syllogism: ' "Whatever the emperor or the emperor's law has laid down is to be obeyed; but the law has laid down that he is to be resisted in such a case; therefore he must be resisted, etc." Now we have hitherto taught the major: that the sword is to be obeyed in political matters. But we neither assert nor know the truth of the minor. Wherefore I may not draw any conclusions, but we have referred this wholly to the jurists, that they may judge. We wish neither to lay down nor advise nor assert nor urge anything except this major: the emperor is to be obeyed. But if they prove the minor, which does not pertain to us, we cannot deny the conclusion, since we teach the major'.[86] In his letter to Link Luther displayed an even more casuistical attitude. 'I console myself', he wrote in conclusion after admitting that his advice was likely to go unheeded, 'that if they altogether decline to accept our advice, they sin less or act more safely, if they have acted in accordance with the civil law than if they have acted directly against conscience and in clear and voluntary opposition to the scriptures. In the meantime they themselves believe that they are not acting against the scriptures, since they are not acting against the civil law. So I let them act. I am free'.[87] Disingenuous and even complacent as these arguments are, they indicate that even after the Torgau Declaration Luther remained anxious to dissociate himself from the idea of resistance and he declined to take any responsibility for what the lawyers and politicians might decide.

Nevertheless, as Mme de Deffand remarked in another context, '*il n'y a que le premier pas qui coûte*'. Having once taken the step of admitting the possibility that a right of resistance might exist, the Wittenberg reformers found it difficult to resist the temptation to go further and in the course of the next few years they quietly abandoned the cautious position they had adopted at Torgau and began to emerge as active exponents of the necessity of resistance. Precisely when this conversion took place is uncertain. Most probably it was a gradual process which occurred almost unconsciously as the reformers became increasingly acclimatised to the idea of resistance. Such evidence as there is suggests that throughout 1531 Luther continued to maintain his position of ambivalent neutrality, neither supporting nor condemning resistance to the emperor, but insisting that it was a matter for the lawyers;[88] while after the Nuremberg standstill of the following year the issue became for a time less urgent, as the threat of imperial intervention was once again postponed. However, from the mid-1530s there is a marked change in the attitude of the Wittenberg theologians which is apparent both in the formal *Gutachten* which they prepared for the electoral government at times of renewed political crisis and in some of Luther's later writings.

The first clear signs of this change are to be found in an official opinion, dated 6 December 1536, which was signed by all the leading Wittenberg theologians—Luther, Jonas, Bugenhagen, Amsdorf, Caspar Cruciger and Melanchthon.[89] This opinion represents a radical break not only with their earlier views but also with the position they had taken up at Torgau. It was written at the request of the elector John Frederick at a time when the protestants were facing a new crisis as the result of pope Paul III's decision to summon a general council to meet at Mantua the following year and it was widely feared that the council would proceed to pass judgment against the protestants' appeal, thus providing the emperor with a fresh excuse for attacking them.[90] The opinion is concerned with two issues: first, what attitude the protestants should adopt towards the forthcoming council, and second, the question of resistance. On the first question the Wittenberg divines urged a policy of caution and they strongly attacked the proposal, which had been put forward by the elector, that the protestants should summon a rival council of their own on the grounds that this would lay them open to the charge of schism which it would be difficult for them to rebut.[91] By contrast, on the second question they now abandoned their earlier neutrality and came out openly in favour of resistance to the emperor.

This section of the paper is remarkable for the number of points on which the Wittenberg divines reversed opinions that they had held earlier. They began with what might appear at first sight to be a conventional restatement of the principles of the Torgau Declaration, insisting that the gospel is a purely spiritual doctrine which 'does not concern external, temporal government, but rather confirms it and values it highly'. But they immediately proceeded to give this principle a new and much more far-reaching significance by adding 'therefore it follows that the Gospel permits all natural and equitable protection and defence that is authorised by natural laws or else by temporal government'—a phrase which can only be interpreted as meaning that they were now prepared to accept the validity of the natural law argument for resistance (*vim vi repellere licet*) which they had so strenuously opposed in 1530.[92] Even more striking is the change in their conception of the duties of temporal rulers. Whereas in the 1520s Luther had repeatedly affirmed that the magistrate, in his capacity as magistrate, was not concerned with matters of faith and that the gospel must not be defended or promoted by force, they now stated categorically that it was the duty of each prince 'to protect and maintain Christians and the external worship of God against all unjust force'. This duty, they insisted, was enjoined on princes by Scripture, both by the example of the godly kings of the Old Testament and by the teaching of the second commandment, 'wherein the rulers are commanded that they should preserve God's name from being dishonoured . . . Therefore the princes are bound to plant and uphold true doctrine in their territories, and as God threatens those who dishonour his name so also will he help those who abolish idolatry and protect pious Christians'. On the strength of this argument they had no difficulty in concluding that it was the duty of every prince to defend his Christian subjects and true religion not only against attacks by princes of equal rank or by private persons but also against the emperor. How far the ideas of Luther and his colleagues had changed since 1530 is shown by the fact that they now unhesitatingly accepted the legal argument, which the Saxon jurists had put forward at Torgau, but which at that time they had regarded as unproven, that if the emperor were to attack the protestants, while their appeal was still pending, he would be guilty of *notoria iniuria* and, therefore, might lawfully be resisted.[93]

The pope's decision to summon a general council raised the further question of how the protestants should act if the council were to pronounce judgment against their appeal, thereby enabling the emperor to proceed against them with the semblance of law. Here too the Wittenberg divines had no hesitation in declaring that resistance would be permissible: for, even if the council were to condemn the protestants in accordance with the procedures of canon law, the decision would have been reached unjustly and the whole process could therefore be regarded as void, since it was 'contrary to natural equity'. Similarly they argued that, if the pope by his sentence were to confirm public idolatry, the princes would be entitled to oppose him and to protect their subjects; just as they would have the right—and, indeed, the duty under the second commandment—to oppose the Turks, if they attempted to establish the religion of Mahomet in their territories, in the same way that Judas Maccabaeus opposed Antiochus.[94]

Unlike the opinions of the 1520s this paper was not drawn up by Luther, but by Melanchthon,[95] and it is arguable that some of its ideas are more typical of Melanchthon's thinking than of Luther's. In particular, the emphasis which is placed on the prince's duty to protect and uphold true religion and the appeal to the second commandment and the precedents of the Old Testament kings are characteristic of Melanchthon's doctrine of the *ius reformandi* of the magistrate which he was beginning to develop at this period in order to justify the princes' role in the Church[96] and which went considerably further than Luther's limited concept of the prince as *Notbischof*. Nevertheless, if the ideas are Melanchthon's and it cannot necessarily be assumed that Luther accepted them in their entirety, there can be no doubt that the main conclusions of the paper had his support. At the beginning of the section on resistance it is expressly stated that the theologians 'have today concluded unanimously' on what follows, while Luther not only signed the document, but he added the flamboyant endorsement—*Ich Martinus Luther will auch dazu thun mit Beten, auch (wo es seyn soll) mit der Faust.*[97] Over the next few years the Wittenberg divines were to reaffirm their support for resistance in a number of other opinions.[98]

As far as Luther himself is concerned, the main evidence for his later views comes from a series of pronouncements which he made in the early part of 1539. During the winter of 1538/39 the relations between the catholic and protestant estates in Germany had once more reached a point of crisis and for several months it looked as if the war, which had been so long delayed, was finally about to break out. In the end—as so often in the past—the crisis subsided and a new religious truce known as the Frankfurt standstill was arranged in April 1539.[99] But in the period before the truce was signed, when the danger was at its height, Luther succumbed to the general war hysteria which infected the protestants and he began to assert the necessity of resistance to the emperor and the pope more vehemently than he had ever done in the past.

The two most important statements of Luther's position at this period are his letter to Johann Ludicke of 8 February 1539 and the theses which he drew up for the *Zirkulardisputation* of April/May 1539. Luther's letter to Ludicke may be classed as a semi-official *Gutachten*. Its recipient was a Lutheran preacher in Brandenburg, who had apparently been asked—or was expecting to be asked—to advise the elector of Brandenburg, Joachim II, on the question of resistance, and Luther's letter was written to give him guidance on the form his reply should take.[100] In it Luther began by stating that it was too late to discuss the question of whether it was lawful for 'our princes' to resist the emperor, since they had already made up their minds to resist, and that it was lawful for them to do so, and they were unlikely to be influenced by anything further that he might say. Nevertheless, while protesting that he still hoped that Christ would render his advice unnecessary by intervening to prevent the emperor from embarking on 'such a mad war', he now declared that he had 'the gravest reasons' (*gravissimas causas*) for not opposing the plans of the princes.[101] The remainder of the letter is devoted to outlining some of these reasons.

As his principal argument Luther now took over the claim, which had been developed by the propagandists of the Schmalkaldic League[102] but which had not figured at all in the Wittenberg theologians' opinion of December 1536, that if the emperor were to attack the protestants, he would not be acting on his own account, but simply as the agent of the pope, and therefore might lawfully be resisted. For it was the pope and the bishops who were the real instigators of the war against the protestants and who wished to use the emperor 'as their soldier' (*velut milite*) for defending 'their horrible tyrannies and diabolical crimes' against the truth. Now the pope may undoubtedly be resisted: for 'if it is lawful to wage war or defend oneself against the Turk, how much more so is it to do so against the pope who is worse'. In consequence, if the emperor who has no grounds of his own for attacking the princes chooses to involve himself in the pope's war, he must expect the same fate. 'For these reasons', Luther informed Ludicke, 'our princes judge that in this case the emperor is not emperor, but the soldier and robber of the pope' (*militem et latronem papae*)—for it is the pope who is the true emperor in this war. However, Luther was clearly conscious that in adopting this argument he was laying himself open to the charge of contradicting his earlier views, for he hastily added by way of extenuation that, while this was the opinion of the princes, he himself had not previously given any advice on the position of the emperor as 'the soldier of the pope'. In an attempt to underline the consistency of his attitude, he went on to suggest that it was only because the pope and his followers were guilty of blasphemy in claiming to be acting in the name of Christ that it was lawful to resist them: if they were to lay aside the name of Christ and confess themselves to be the servants of Satan, he would continue to urge the necessity of submitting to 'heathen tyrants' (*gentilibus tyrannis*), as he had done in the past.[103]

In addition to the concept of the emperor as *miles papae*, Luther cited two other arguments in this letter which he did not develop in such detail. First, he appealed briefly, as he and his colleagues had done in 1536, to the example of Judas Maccabaeus and various Old Testament precedents. Secondly, he now adopted the constitutional argument that Philip of Hesse had put forward in 1529 and 1530, but which at that time he had declined to accept, that the empire was not an absolute monarchy and that the princes of Germany possessed the right to resist the emperor if he failed to observe the laws and customs of the empire: for they 'govern the Empire in association (*communi consilio*) with the emperor: the emperor is not an absolute king (*monarcha*), neither can he alter the form of the Empire against the will of the electors, nor should it be endured, if he were to try'. If this principle applies in civil matters, it must apply equally, Luther insisted, in cases where the emperor seeks to subvert the constitution of the empire in the cause of the pope and the devil.[104]

The concept of the emperor as *miles papae* also plays an important part in Luther's theses for the *Zirkulardisputation* on *Matt.* xix. 21,[105] where it took on a new significance by being coupled with Luther's eschatological conception of the pope as the beast of the book of Daniel. These theses were drawn up early in April 1539 for a regular academic disputation at the university of Wittenberg, at a time when the prospect of war between the catholics and protestants seemed inescapable. In the event the Frankfurt standstill was signed before the disputation was held and Luther subsequently added a further twenty-one theses attacking the validity of ecclesiastical laws made by the pope.[106] The original seventy theses—with which we are concerned—fall into two sections: theses 1–50, dealing with the Christian's position in the world; and theses 51–70 on the pope. In theses 1–50 Luther put forward what was, in essentials, his conventional teaching on the place of the Christian in the world, his duties under the first and second tables of the law and his obligations to secular rulers. He insists that the Christian has a dual role as a Christian and as 'a citizen of this world' (*civis huius mundi*). As the latter, he is bound to do and suffer everything that is required of him according to the second table of the law (Th. 30). Thus as a pious citizen of the world, you may lawfully resist a robber who attacks you, even if he seeks to kill you on account of Christ: for the magistrate has commanded that robbers are to be resisted and this is therefore in accordance with the second table of the Law (Th. 31–5). On the other hand, if the magistrate persecutes you for Christ's sake—whether he be a heathen magistrate or a bad Christian—it is your duty to suffer and offer no resistance. For the magistrate is not a robber, but is instituted by God to preserve law and order. Therefore, even if the magistrate breaks the first table of the law, he is not to be resisted; for we are forbidden to destroy the magistrates and governments which God has ordained on account of human wickedness (Th. 36–50).[107]

Such statements are entirely in accord with the views that Luther had expressed in the 1520s and, taken on their own, they might suggest that he had reverted to his earlier standpoint. But in theses 51–70 Luther turned to deal with the position of the pope and in the process of attacking the papacy he reaffirmed, but in more passionate language, the arguments of the letter to Ludicke. He began by insisting that the pope is not a magistrate of any kind, either ecclesiastical or civil, since he does not belong in any of the three divine hierarchies which God has ordained against the devil—the family, civil government or the Church[108] (Th. 51– 55). Rather he is the monster foretold in the book of Daniel. He is what 'we Germans call a *Beerwolf*, what the Greeks, if perchance it had been known to them, would have called *arktolukos*'—a wolf which is possessed by a demon and which destroys everything in its path (Th. 56–9). Such a monster can only be destroyed if all the people from the surrounding countryside and towns gather together to hunt him down. Nor is it necessary to wait for orders from the magistrate before attacking him, for present necessity is enough (Th. 60–1). So, likewise, if the pope provokes war, he must be resisted 'like a furious and possessed monster or a true *arktolukos*: for he is not a bishop nor a heretic nor a prince nor a tyrant, but the beast who lays everything waste, as Daniel declares' (Th. 66–7). But equally—and here Luther returned once again to the theme of the emperor as *miles papae*—whoever fights for the pope must be resisted, regardless of whether they be princes, kings, or even emperors: for whoever 'fights under a robber (whoever he may be)' has to face the risks both of war and of eternal damnation. 'Nor will it save kings, princes, or even emperors that they claim to be acting as defenders of the Church, since it is their duty to know what the Church is' (Th. 68–70).[109] By identifying the pope with the beast of the book of Daniel and by insisting that any ruler who went to war on his behalf must be resisted, Luther had effectively undermined the conclusions of the first fifty theses.

By the time the disputation was held on 9 May 1539 the immediate threat of war had been removed. But it is clear from the three anonymous reports of the disputation which survive[110] that the news of the Frankfurt standstill had in no way diminished Luther's obsessive horror of the papacy and, despite the wide-ranging character of the original theses, the greater part of the debate seems to have been taken up with the discussion of the twin questions of whether it was lawful to resist the pope and the emperor. In the course of the disputation Luther repeatedly reaffirmed his apocalyptic view of the papacy in language which appears from the reports to have been even more extreme than that of the theses. In passage after passage, he reiterated his belief that the pope was not 'a legitimate magistrate',[111] nor even a tyrant in the conventional sense of the term,[112] but 'a monster',[113] an 'arktolukos',[114] 'a minister of the devil who is possessed by the devil',[115] a creature who is worse even than the Turk since he destroys men's souls.[116] Consequently, he is to be resisted at all costs.[117] So equally are those who seek to defend him, including the emperor.[118] But Luther did not stop there. To the question whether it was lawful to resist the emperor *propter doctrinam Dei*, if he were to act as an ordinary tyrant by persecuting Christians on his own initiative, and not at the behest of the pope, Luther replied just as emphatically, 'This evil is to be resisted. For we ought to leave our descendants this doctrine and the Church well established'.[119] In answer to another question he also repeated the argument, to which he had alluded briefly in his letter to Ludicke, that the constitution of the empire gave the princes the right to resist the emperor. The prince electors, he now maintained, in striking contrast with the view he had so often expressed in the 1520s, were not private persons. Rather, the seven electors were the equals of the emperor, since they were a constituent part of the empire, of which the emperor was the head.[120] Moreover, since the magistrates were now Christians, not heathens (*gentiles*), they all had an equal duty along with the emperor to prevent blasphemy and they therefore might resist him in defence of the first table of the law.[121]

Fate was kind to Luther, for he died before the Schmalkaldic War broke out and he was spared the disaster of Mühlberg and the dismemberment of Ernestine Saxony. As a result, we cannot know for certain how he would have reacted to these events. But in view of his attitude in the late 1530s there can be little doubt that, had he lived a few months longer, he would have joined Melanchthon and the other Wittenberg theologians in their support for the war. Certainly, Melanchthon was to make extensive use of Luther's writings to justify the position which the Witten-berg divines adopted in 1546 and the theses for the *Zirkulardispu-tation*, in particular, were reprinted several times in both Latin and German in the early months of the war.[122] It is interesting to speculate how Luther would have reacted to the defeat of Mühlberg. Twenty years earlier he would have treated such a defeat as divine retribution on the protestants for the sin of rebel-lion. One can only conjecture that, had he been alive in 1547, he would have rationalised it as the triumph of anti-Christ.

In Luther's later pronouncements and the opinion of 1536 one finds three main lines of argument which represent a radical departure from the views he had held in the 1520s. First, there is the idea, which is developed more fully in the 1536 opinion than in Luther's own writings, that the Christian magistrate has a duty to uphold true religion and suppress idolatry, and that it is there-fore incumbent upon the German princes to defend the gospel and their Christian subjects against all attacks, whether from other princes or from the emperor—an idea which is utterly at variance with the principle which figures so prominently in Luther's writings of the early 1520s that the gospel is a purely spiritual doctrine which must not be defended by force. Secondly, there is the constitutional argument, which Philip of Hesse had first put forward in 1529 and 1530, that the princes of the empire are not mere 'private persons' in relation to the emperor, as Luther had maintained throughout the 1520s, but are associated with him in the government of the empire and are therefore legally empowered to resist him if he acts tyrannically—an argument which Luther had initially opposed, but which by 1539 he had quietly come to accept. Thirdly, there is the claim that the emperor may be resisted if he attacks the protestants for the sake of religion, since he is not acting as emperor, but merely as the agent of the pope, as *miles papae*. This argument too did not originate with Luther, but with the theorists of the Schmalkaldic League. But, in taking over the idea, Luther radically transformed it: for, by combining it with his doctrine of the pope as the beast of the book of Daniel, the *Beerwolf* who must be resisted at all costs, he turned what had originally been a purely legalistic argument into an apocalyptic call to arms. The fanaticism of Luther's language in the *Zirkular-disputation* is not in itself surprising: for it is in keeping with his increasingly obsessive hatred of the papacy which is to be seen in so many of his writings of the period.[123] But it is, perhaps, indicative of the idiosyncratic character of Luther's later views that he should have chosen in both the *Zirkulardisputation* and the letter to Ludicke to place his main emphasis not on the constitutional claims of the princes, but on the concept of the emperor as *miles papae*.[124]

Historically, however, it was the first two arguments which were to prove to be the most influential for the subsequent development of protestant political thought. For it was out of a fusion of these two sets of ideas that there evolved the standard protestant theory of resistance of the mid-sixteenth century—the doctrine that the inferior magistrates (though not the common people) had not only the right but the duty to resist the supreme magistrate in defence of true religion. This doctrine is popularly associated with Calvinism rather than with Lutheranism. But it is important to note that it originated in Germany in the confessional conflicts of the 1530s and 1540s and that Calvin, Beza[125] and the English Marian exiles who amplified the doctrine in the 1550s were not propounding a new political theory, but were building on foundations that had already been laid by the German Lutherans. As will be clear from what has been said, Luther's personal contribution to the development of this theory was relatively small. He did not originate either the idea that the German princes had the legal right to resist the emperor or the more general claim that the Christian magistrate had an ex-officio duty, which was laid down in Scripture, to defend the faith by force against all attacks, although he later endorsed both these arguments and by so doing helped to popularise them. So far as I have been able to discover, the main credit for introducing into protestant political thinking the principle that it was lawful for inferior magistrates to resist their superiors in defence of religion must go to Philip of Hesse and his advisers; for it was they who first developed the main outlines of the theory in relation to the German princes, although it was not perhaps until the appearance of the Magdeburg *Bekenntnis* in 1550 that the doctrine was fully worked out in its classic mid-sixteenth century form.[126]

At the same time, it is equally clear that the conventional picture of Luther as acquiescing in the idea of resistance only with the greatest reluctance under pressure from the princes needs considerable modification. While this is true of his position in 1530 at the time of the Torgau Declaration, by the end of the 1530s a profound change had taken place in his attitude and he had emerged as a passionate advocate of the need to resist both the pope and the emperor. Contrary to the popular image of the two reformers, the later Luther was far more outspoken than Calvin ever was in his support for resistance. Indeed, it could be argued that in the *Zirkulardisputation* he came close to anticipating the views of John Knox. For, although it is probable that Luther did not fully understand where his remarks were leading, the logical conclusion to be drawn from the *Beerwolf* analogy is that it is not only the princes but the common people who have the right to resist the pope, and therefore by implication any secular ruler who fights on his behalf—a claim which most mid-sixteenth century supporters of the rights of inferior magistrates would have repudiated with horror.

In general, the tendency among historians has been to stress the contradictions between Luther's earlier and his later views. It should be said, however, in conclusion that in recent studies of the problem there has been something of a reaction against this approach. Both Johannes Heckel and, in a different fashion, Hermann Dörries have attempted to qualify the charges of inconsistency which have usually been levelled against Luther: Heckel, by claiming that most earlier writers had failed to take sufficient account of the theological and juristic assumptions underlying Luther's thought and that, if this is done, there is a greater degree of unity to his pronouncements than might appear at first sight;[127] Dörries, more convincingly, by pointing out that even at the end of his life Luther did not so much abandon his earlier principles as allow them to be overshadowed by new ideas, and that even in his 1539 writings there are elements in his thinking that go back to the early 1520s.[128]

Nevertheless, while there is some substance in these arguments and it is clear that there is more continuity in Luther's thought than has sometimes been allowed, the fact remains that in the 1530s he did alter his position radically and for reasons that had more to do with politics than with religion. The years after 1529 were a period of intense and continuing crisis for the German protestants and, even though war did not finally break out until 1546, the psychological pressures on Luther and his colleagues to abandon their earlier opposition to resistance to the emperor were very strong. It is, therefore, hardly surprising that, having once taken the initial step at Torgau of conceding that resistance might be permitted on legal grounds, they should gradually have given up their attempt to maintain a position of neutrality and identified themselves completely with the policies of the Schmalkaldic League. In this sense the evolution of their views is exactly paralleled by that of the more radical English exiles in the 1550s and the French Huguenots in the 1570s. But it means that, if one wishes to understand the transformation which took place in the attitude of the Wittenberg divines in the 1530s, it is more important to look at the political and psychological factors which influenced them than at the intellectual arguments which they used to justify the change. There is undoubtedly a logic to the development of Luther's views on the question of resistance to the emperor, but it is a logic deriving from events rather than from the underlying principles of his theology.

II

The 'Two Kingdoms' and the 'Two Regiments': Some Problems of Luther's *Zwei-Reiche-Lehre*

Among the most significant developments in modern German and Scandinavian Luther-scholarship has been the growth of interest in Luther's *Zwei-Reiche-* or *Zwei-Regimente-Lehre*—his doctrine of the 'Two Kingdoms' or orders of government through which God exercises his lordship over mankind. Since 1930, and more particularly since the war, there has appeared a succession of studies by such scholars as Franz Lau, Gustav Törnvall, the brothers Harald and Hermann Diem, Paul Althaus, Johannes Heckel, and others, whose researches have focused attention on the fundamental importance of the study of the *Zwei-Reiche-Lehre* not only for the interpretation of Luther's social and ethical teaching but also for the understanding of his theology as a whole.[1] Nevertheless, in spite of the emphasis which has been placed on the role of the *Zwei-Reiche-Lehre* in recent discussions of Luther's thought, the precise interpretation of the doctrine still remains a matter of controversy, as the continuing spate of books and articles on the subject suggests. While this can partly be explained by the inherent complexity of the doctrine and the fact that it is closely interwoven with so many other aspects of Luther's theology, the study of the *Zwei-Reiche-Lehre* is also complicated by the fact that Luther's treatment of the doctrine is ambiguous and appears to involve a number of inconsistencies, with the result that scholars have been sharply divided over the correct interpretation of his teaching. The aim of this paper is, therefore, to try to clarify the discussion of the *Zwei-Reiche-Lehre* by examining some of the problems which Luther's treatment of the doctrine presents.

The first major source of difficulty lies in Luther's terminology; for much of the confusion which surrounds the interpretation of the *Zwei-Reiche-Lehre* has its origins in the ambiguities of his vocabulary. Although Luther was by no means such an unsystematic or contradictory thinker as some modern critics have maintained, on one point at least he cannot escape the charge of inconsistency and that is in his use of words. Luther's language is often extremely imprecise: he had little regard for verbal exactness, while he frequently employs even technical theological terms in a variety of ways. Usually it is clear from the context in what sense he is using a particular term in a given instance; however, the fact that the same word or phrase can have several connotations makes the task of trying to expound his thought an extremely difficult undertaking for modern scholars, since it is often hard to define precisely what he means by a specific phrase or concept. This looseness of language is particularly marked in the case of the *Zwei-Reiche-Lehre*; for many of the terms which Luther uses, such as *Reich, Regiment, Welt,* and *weltlich* are highly elastic in meaning, while it is significant of the extent to which his vocabulary can be a source of confusion that even the phrase *die zwei Reiche* itself is ambiguous since it can be applied to two quite separate concepts in his theology. In order to avoid misunderstanding, it is therefore essential to begin by examining the meaning of some of the principal terms which Luther uses in connexion with the doctrine of the *zwei Reiche*.

In the first place, it is important to observe that the word *Reich*, like its Latin equivalent *regnum*, has two quite distinct meanings in Luther's thought.[2] Just as in medieval Latin usage the word *regnum* can mean either 'kingdom', in the modern sense of the realm over which a king rules, or the office or authority belonging to a king, as in the phrase *regnum et sacerdotium*, so in Luther's vocabulary the word *Reich* can also be used in two ways to signify either the realm or people over whom a monarch rules or the dominion which he exercises over them. Thus Luther employs the words *Reich* and *regnum* in the first sense in such phrases as *Reich Gottes, regnum dei, Reich Christi,* and their antonyms, *Reich der Welt, regnum mundi, regnum Satanae, Teufels Reich,* which he uses to describe the kingdom of God in the sense of the true Church or *communio sanctorum*, over which Christ rules, and its adversary, the kingdom of the World or the Devil, which consists of all those who do not believe in Christ and are therefore under the dominion of Satan.[3] On the other hand, it is important to note that when Luther employs the terms *das geistliche Reich* and *das weltliche Reich*, the word *Reich* is normally to be understood in its second sense of government or rule. Broadly speaking —although it is dangerous to try to define his terms too precisely— Luther uses the phrases *das geistliche Reich* and *das weltliche Reich* not to refer to two kingdoms but rather to denote the two ways in which God governs mankind or the two orders of government which he has instituted for the world, namely the spiritual order of the Word and the temporal order of the sword.[4] Thus the word *Reich* in this usage is closely related to the word *Regiment*, meaning government, and it is significant that Luther frequently treats the two words as if they were interchangeable.[5] However, even in this context Luther's use of the word *Reich* is by no means wholly consistent; for, while the primary connotation of the terms *geistliches Reich* and *weltliches Reich* is that of the two orders of government through which God rules the world, Luther also uses the terms equally freely to describe the two spheres of human existence, the spiritual sphere and the temporal sphere, which correspond to the two divine orders of government.[6]

Similarly the word *Regiment*, as Luther uses it, can also have several shades of meaning. Basically *Regiment* signifies 'rule' or 'government': thus it is the equivalent of the Latin *gubernatio* or of *Reich* in its second sense of the authority exercised by a king, while it also corresponds very closely to the original meaning of the English word 'regiment', which in the sixteenth century was invariably used as a synonym for government and by which it can perhaps be conveniently translated.[7] Hence, the primary idea which characterises Luther's doctrine of the 'two Regiments' (*das geistliche Regiment und das weltliche Regiment*) is again that of the two ways in which God governs the world;[8] however, by a natural extension of language Luther can also use the terms *geistliches Regiment* and *weltliches Regiment* to refer either to the actual instruments through which God exercises his two-fold government on earth—namely, the Word and the sword or the office of the temporal magistrate—or to the spiritual and temporal order in general,[9] with the result that in practice there is a very close similarity between the way in which Luther uses the terms *geistliches und weltliches Regiment* and *geistliches und weltliches*

Reich and it is often difficult to draw any clear distinction between them.

Another equally important source of confusion is to be found in Luther's use of the terms *die Welt* and *weltlich*, and *Reich der Welt* and *weltliches Reich*.[10] In Luther's vocabulary *die Welt* and *weltlich* can possess two quite distinct and even contradictory meanings. While Luther normally employs the adjective *weltlich* in a neutral sense to mean 'temporal' or 'natural'—something belonging to this world as opposed to *geistlich* or 'spiritual'[11]— when he speaks of *die Welt* it is very often in the pejorative sense of the fallen world which is the embodiment of sin and corruption.[12] For Luther the 'World' in this sense is to be identified with the kingdom of Satan: for, as a result of the Fall the world is utterly turned away from God and given over to the power of the Devil.[13] Thus he uses the term *das Reich der Welt* (*regnum mundi*, 'the kingdom of the World') as a synonym for the kingdom of the Devil (*regnum diaboli, regnum Satanae, Teufels Reich*) in the same way that St. Augustine equates the term *civitas terrena* with *civitas diaboli*.[14] On the other hand, when Luther uses the term *das weltliche Reich* it is almost always in a quite different sense of both *weltlich* and *Reich*, in order to denote the temporal order of government which God has instituted in the world or, more broadly, the natural order in general which he also regards as divine since it is both created and maintained by God.[15]

This distinction is of fundamental importance to the understanding of the *Zwei-Reiche-Lehre*, since it explains the fact that the term *Zwei-Reiche-Lehre* can be applied to two quite separate, though related, concepts in Luther's thought which need to be carefully distinguished. In general the term is primarily used by modern scholars to describe Luther's doctrine of the two orders of government through which God rules the world (*das geistliche Reich und das weltliche Reich*), in which sense it is closely allied to the term *Zwei-Regimente-Lehre*.[16] However, it is characteristic of the confusion which surrounds the study of the *Zwei-Reiche-Lehre* that the term can also be applied with equal validity to Luther's doctrine of the conflict between the kingdom of God and the kingdom of the Devil (*Reich Gottes* and *Reich der Welt* or *Teufels Reich*) and a number of scholars prefer to use it in this sense.[17] In practice, both of these concepts need to be taken into account in any discussion of the *Zwei-Reiche-Lehre*, for although they are essentially distinct, there is a close connexion between them in Luther's theology and neither of them can be properly understood except in relation to the other.

The essence of the first doctrine, or *Zwei-Regimente-Lehre*, consists in the idea that God has appointed two orders in the world through which he governs mankind—the spiritual order (*das geistliche Reich* or *Regiment*) in which he governs men through the Word and the temporal order (*das weltliche Reich* or *Regiment*) in which he governs them through the sword.[18] These two orders are quite distinct both in character and function. The spiritual *Reich* or *Regiment* is 'God's kingdom' or 'government of the right hand' (*Reich Gottes zur Rechten* or *mit der rechten Hand*)[19] the spiritual order of salvation in which he carries out his *opus proprium*, the work of redemption. It is essentially an inward and invisible government, a government of the soul; for it is not concerned with men's external lives but only with their eternal salvation.[20] In it God rules through the Word and the Holy Spirit, by means of which he operates secretly in men's hearts to draw them away from sin and make them righteous.[21] The *geistliches Reich* or *Regiment* is, therefore, in Luther's phrase *ein Hörreich*, a 'kingdom' or 'government of hearing';[22] for it is only through the instrument of the Word and not by force that men can enter the kingdom of heaven.[23] The temporal *Reich* or *Regiment*, on the other hand, is 'God's kingdom of the left hand' (*Reich Gottes zur Linken* or *mit der linken Hand*),[24] his government of the temporal order which he has instituted for the punishment of sin and the maintenance of external peace in the world, and through which he provides for the needs of man's earthly existence.[25] Here God governs men by means of temporal laws and the power of the sword which he has entrusted to secular rulers and magistrates to exercise on his behalf.[26] The temporal *Regiment* is, therefore, a purely external government, a rule of force; for its primary function is the enforcement of law and order in the world, without which human life would be impossible, and it is only concerned with the regulation of men's external behaviour and not with the inward condition of their souls.[27] Nevertheless, the *weltliches Reich* or *Regiment* cannot be regarded simply as the antithesis of the *geistliches*: for, although as Luther repeatedly insists, the two orders are as distinct 'as heaven and earth' and must on no account be confused,[28] they are also complementary in that they are both instituted by God and each is essential for the fulfilment of his divine purpose.[29]

By contrast, when the term *Zwei-Reiche-Lehre* is used in its second sense it refers to the eschatological doctrine, which Luther derived from St. Augustine, of the conflict between the kingdom of God and the kingdom of the Devil. In this context Luther employs the terms *Reich Gottes* or *Reich Christi* (*regnum dei, regnum Christi*) and *Reich der Welt* or *Teufels Reich* (*regnum mundi, regnum diaboli, regnum Satanae*) to signify the two opposing communities into which, like St. Augustine, he sees mankind as being divided. The *Reich Gottes*, in this sense, is God's everlasting kingdom, the true Church or *communio sanctorum*, which consists of all those, both in heaven and on earth, who truly believe in Christ and accept his lordship, and who together constitute the members of Christ's 'spiritual body' (*corpus Christi*); the *Reich der Welt*, on the other hand, is the kingdom of the Devil or *corpus diaboli*, which includes all the rest of mankind who do not accept Christ and are, therefore, in bondage to Satan.[30] These two kingdoms, like St. Augustine's two cities, are invisible societies or *corpora mystica*, which transcend the boundaries of the natural world, for they embrace both the living and the dead, while on earth their members are inextricably mixed together like the wheat and the tares of the parable since only God knows who truly believes and who belongs to the kingdom of the Devil.[31] Between these two kingdoms there is total opposition: not only are they completely different in character, since the *Reich der Welt* is in every respect the spiritual antithesis of the *Reich Gottes*, but they are locked in a perpetual state of war, for Satan is always striving to overthrow God's kingdom and bring all men into subjection to himself.[32] This conflict is for Luther, as for St. Augustine, the dominant factor in human history, for it governs every aspect of man's existence on earth and it will only come to an end at the Last Judgement, when Satan is finally vanquished and Christ's kingdom is established in glory on earth.[33]

Although these two doctrines are quite distinct and it is important not to confuse them, they are, none the less, closely related;

for Luther's concept of the two divine orders or regiments is profoundly influenced by his doctrine of the eschatological conflict between the kingdom of God and the kingdom of the Devil.[34] In the first place, it is because of the existence of this conflict that God has instituted the *zwei Regimente* on earth in their present form. The two regiments, therefore, possess a dual significance in Luther's theology. They not only constitute the instruments through which God governs mankind, they also represent the weapons which he employs in his struggle against the *regnum diaboli*. Through the Word, God seeks to combat Satan's power by spiritual means and to draw men away from sin and into obedience to himself, while through the temporal government of the sword he endeavours by force to curb the activities of the members of Satan's kingdom on earth and to prevent them from utterly destroying the world by sin.[35] At the same time Luther holds that the two divine regiments are directly involved in the conflict in another sense; for they are under constant attack from Satan who is continually seeking to undermine them and to gain control of them for himself.[36] This he does in two main ways: first, by endeavouring to stir up heresy and rebellion among the common people, so that they reject the authority of those whom God has appointed to govern them; and, second, by attempting to persuade the clergy and the civil magistrates, to whom God has entrusted the administration of his two regiments on earth, to forsake their divine calling and turn themselves into tyrants, thereby perverting the authority which God has given them to the service of the *regnum diaboli*.[37] Thus the two regiments may be said to stand at the very centre of the conflict between the *regnum dei* and the *regnum diaboli*: for just as, on the one hand, God has instituted them in order to protect mankind against the onslaughts of the *regnum diaboli*, so, on the other, Satan is continually engaged in trying to overturn them and bring them under his own domination.

The existence of this basic ambiguity in Luther's terminology is responsible for much of the controversy which has arisen over the interpretation of the *Zwei-Reiche-Lehre* in recent years, since it has led to a heated debate over the question of the relative importance in Luther's theology of the two concepts of the *zwei Reiche* and the precise nature of the relationship which exists between the two divine *Regimente*, on the one hand, and the two kingdoms of God and the Devil, on the other. In general the prevailing tendency among modern German and Scandinavian theologians over the past thirty years has been to emphasise the importance of the doctrine of the *zwei Regimente* or *zwei Reiche* in the first sense by focusing on this as the key to the understanding of Luther's moral theology and his doctrines of God and man, although in practice most of the leading exponents of this usage have also been fully alive to the significance of Luther's doctrine of the conflict between the two kingdoms of God and the Devil.[38] However, this approach to the study of the *Zwei-Reiche-Lehre* has come under heavy criticism during the past fifteen years as the result of the work of the distinguished German legal scholar, the late Johannes Heckel, who challenged the conventional interpretation of Luther's teaching in a series of attacks, published during the 1950s, on the ground that it was based upon a fundamental misconception about the nature of Luther's primary assumptions.[39]

In Heckel's view the proper starting-point for the interpretation of Luther's *Zwei-Reiche-Lehre* is not the concept of the two regiments through which God governs the world, but rather the eschatological doctrine of the conflict between the two kingdoms of God and the Devil.[40] Heckel holds that the basic element in Luther's teaching, which underlies his theory of the two divine *Regimente*, is his concept of the *Reich Gottes* in the sense of the 'kingdom of Grace' (*Reich der Gnade*) over which Christ rules and its antithesis, the *Reich der Welt* or *regnum diaboli*.[41] In this context the terms *Reich Gottes* and *Reich der Welt* are employed by Luther in a personal connotation, for they signify the two opposing communities or *corpora mystica* over which Christ and the Devil respectively preside.[42] Thus the essence of the *Reich Gottes* is that it is the 'people of God' or 'mystical body of Christ', who are bound together in faith under the spiritual headship of Christ, just as the *Reich der Welt* is the 'people of the Devil' or *corpus diaboli*.[43] This concept Heckel calls *die Reichslehre im Grundsinn*,[44] as distinct from the *Regimentenlehre* which he regards as essentially secondary; for he holds that Luther's doctrine of the *zwei Regimente* is ultimately derived from the doctrine of the *zwei Reiche* in the primary sense of the two *corpora mystica* and that the key to the understanding of the *Regimenten-lehre* lies in the fact that the two regiments represent the two different ways in which God exercises his lordship over the members of the two opposing *regna*.[45]

To some extent the dispute is an artificial one, since it is factitious to try to decide which of these two concepts is the more fundamental to Luther's thought. The fact is that Luther's two doctrines of the *zwei Reiche* are closely bound up together and they both play a basic part in his theology. It is, therefore, dangerous to attempt to separate them or to place too much emphasis on one at the expense of the other. Nevertheless, the controversy cannot be dismissed as entirely meaningless, since it raises certain fundamental questions about the interpretation of Luther's teaching on the role of the two regiments in God's government of the world and the position of the Christian in relation to the two divine orders of government, and it is therefore necessary to examine the arguments put forward by Heckel and his opponents in greater detail.

According to the orthodox theory—whether it is expressed in terms of the *zwei Reiche*, as by Paul Althaus and Franz Lau, or in terms of the *zwei Regimente*, as by Gustav Törnvall—the importance of Luther's doctrine lies in the fact that God has appointed the two *Reiche* or *Regimente* for all men universally.[46] They represent not only the two ways in which God governs mankind but also the two divinely appointed orders of human existence; for they correspond to the fact that man has two natures—that he has, in Luther's phrase, 'two persons', a 'spiritual person' as Christian (*Christ-person*) and a 'temporal person' as a member of the natural order (*Weltperson*).[47] As a 'spiritual person' the Christian belongs in *das geistliche Reich* or under *das geistliche Regiment*; as a 'temporal person' he is a member of *das weltliche Reich* in the sense of the natural order or subject to the authority of God's *weltliches Regiment* in the sense of the temporal government of the sword. According to this view, therefore, it is possible to describe the Christian on earth as 'a citizen of two worlds' or 'of both kingdoms' (*ein Bürger zweier Welten* or *der beiden Reichen*), or as subject to the authority of both regiments;[48] for in this world he is not only under the rule of Christ in the spiritual order, he is also involved in the temporal order of the natural world, where he is subject to the rule of the temporal authorities, although here too he is, in reality, as much under God's government as he is in the spiritual order, since both regiments are divine and God has instituted them both for the government of mankind.[49]

Heckel's interpretation of the role of the *zwei Regimente* is quite different. In his view Luther's doctrine of the *zwei Regimente* can only be properly understood if it is seen in the perspective of the conflict between the kingdom of God and the kingdom of the Devil, for the two regiments are in a sense the product of this conflict and their character is largely determined by it.[50] While he does not deny that both regiments are divine, he insists that God has instituted them for separate *Reiche* and it is a mistake to assume that they apply to all men universally.[51] The spiritual regiment of the Word exists for the members of God's spiritual kingdom, the *Reich Gottes*; the temporal regiment of the sword for the members of the *Reich der Welt* or *Teufels Reich*, who refuse to obey the Word and can only be restrained from sin by force.[52] From this it follows that, strictly speaking, only the members of the *Reich Gottes*, the true Christians, can be said to be under the *geistliches Regiment*, while only the wicked who belong to the Devil's kingdom are subject to the *weltliches Regiment*.[53] If, therefore, God expects the members of his own kingdom to submit to the authority of the *weltliches Regiment* while they are on earth, it is not because they are subject to it in the same sense that the members of the *regnum diaboli* are, who need to be governed by the sword, but rather because they ought to devote themselves in this way to the service of their fellow men in the spirit of Christian love.[54] Similarly Heckel rejects the view that the Christian can be said to be a citizen of the *weltliches Reich* as well as of the *geistliches Reich* in any real sense.[55] According to the strict interpretation of Luther's teaching, he argues, the Christian belongs to one kingdom only, the *Reich Gottes* in the sense of the people of God who are under the spiritual rule of Christ, and it is a logical error to equate the Christian's position in the world with his membership of Christ's spiritual kingdom.[56] For although the Christian has to live out his natural life on earth, his position in the world is always that of a 'stranger' (*advena, hospes*); he is in the world, but not of it, just as he is not really subject to the authority of the temporal regiment, even though he must be prepared to submit himself voluntarily to its commands.[57]

The crux of the dispute can, therefore, be summarised quite briefly. Are the two regiments instituted for two separate kingdoms or do they apply to all men universally? Or, to put it in another way, does the Christian belong only to the *geistliches Reich* or can he be said to be 'a citizen of two kingdoms'—the temporal order as well as the spiritual order? It is obvious that he cannot be a member of both the *Reichs Gottes* and the *Reich der Welt* in the sense of the *regnum diaboli*, for by definition the two *corpora mystica* are mutually exclusive, since it is impossible for anyone to belong to both God's kingdom and the Devil's; but is it compatible with this to maintain that a Christian, while he is on earth, belongs equally to both the *geistliches Reich* and the *weltliches Reich* in the sense of the two divine orders which God has instituted for the government of the world?

The issue is by no means clear-cut, since there is considerable evidence in Luther's writings to support both points of view. At first sight the arguments in favour of Heckel's interpretation would appear to be extremely strong. It is possible to find a great many passages in Luther's writings in which he asserts quite explicitly that God has instituted the two regiments for two different classes of men, and that the temporal regiment exists only for the members of the *regnum diaboli*, who refuse to hear the Word and have to be governed by force, while the spiritual regiment exists for the members of the *Reich Gottes* who have no need of the sword since they are ruled by God's Word. Thus in his treatise *Of Temporal Authority* (1523) he writes 'Therefore God has ordained the two regiments, the spiritual, which creates Christians and godly people through the Holy Spirit under Christ, and the temporal, which restrains those who are not Christian and the wicked, so that they must maintain external peace and live in tranquillity against their will'.[58] Similarly in his *Exposition of the Epistle of St. Peter*, also published in 1523, he declares 'Therefore there are now two kinds of government in the world, just as there are two kinds of people, namely believers and unbelievers. The Christians allow themselves to be ruled by the Word of God, therefore they do not need the temporal regiment for themselves. But those who are not Christian must have another regiment, namely the temporal sword, since they will not live in accordance with God's Word'.[59] Nor can it be argued that such remarks are confined to a particular period in Luther's life, for, as Heckel has shown, it is possible to find very similar statements in Luther's writings of the late 1520s and 1530s.[60]

Against Heckel's interpretation, however, one has to set the evidence of numerous other passages in which Luther states that the Christian is subject to both the temporal and the spiritual regiment or in which he propounds the idea that the Christian is not merely a 'spiritual person' but a 'temporal person' as well, and that as such he is necessarily involved in the temporal *Reich* or *Regiment* as well as in the spiritual. This theme is developed particularly in the *Exposition of the Fifth, Sixth and Seventh Chapters of St. Matthew*, where Luther uses the concept of the Christian's 'two persons' or 'callings' as the basis of his explanation of the ethical teaching of the Sermon on the Mount. For example, in a typical passage dealing with the problem of the Christian in society, Luther writes: 'Therefore there is a second question, whether a Christian may also be a temporal man and exercise the office and work of government or the law, so that the two persons or two kinds of office are united in one man and he is at the same time a Christian and a prince, judge, lord, man-servant or maid-servant, which are called purely temporal persons since they belong to the temporal regiment. To this we say yes: for God himself has ordained and instituted this temporal regiment and distinction of persons, and moreover he has confirmed and praised it through his Word. For without it this life could not exist, and we are all included in it together—yea, we are born into it before we become Christians. Therefore we must remain in it so long as we exist on earth, although only in respect of our external bodily life and nature'.[61]

The question, therefore, arises as to how far it is possible to reconcile these two sets of ideas. Are they, in fact, compatible or do they represent a fundamental contradiction in Luther's thought? However, before one rushes in to condemn Luther for being inconsistent, it is important to examine the context in which his remarks occur, for many of the difficulties can be resolved by the fact that Luther is constantly arguing on two different levels of thought.

In part the apparent contradiction can be explained by the ambiguity of Luther's use of the term *das weltliche Regiment*. As we have seen, Luther tends to employ the term in two distinct, though overlapping, senses—in a limited sense to mean 'temporal government' as represented by the power of the sword and the office of the civil magistrate, and in a wider sense to denote the whole temporal order of nature or human society. When he uses it in the first sense to refer to the power of the sword, it is almost always in the context of the fallen world. Like Augustine, Luther holds that temporal government, as it exists in the world today, is a product of the Fall. God has instituted it as a consequence of man's sin in order to control the members of the *regnum diaboli* and prevent them from destroying the world altogether.[62] Thus Heckel is right when he insists that Luther's concept of temporal government is closely bound up with the idea of the *Reich der Welt*; for, strictly speaking, the *weltliches Regiment* in the sense of the power of the sword only exists for the members of the *Reich der Welt*, since God has provided a separate form of government through the Word for the members of his own kingdom.[63] However, Luther also uses the term *weltliches Regiment* in other contexts to refer to the temporal order in general. In this sense the term embraces the whole external order of society and all the institutions and callings of man's natural life—the family, property, trade, agriculture, and other temporal occupations as well as the office of government.[64] From this point of view the *weltliches Regiment* or *weltliches Reich* cannot be regarded simply as a product of the Fall. It is part of God's original creation, and although its character has been profoundly modified as a result of the Fall—as, for example, by the institution of temporal government and the transformation of marriage into a remedy for concupiscence[65]—it has an importance which is independent of the Fall, since it derives its existence from God's original act of creation. In consequence the terms *weltliches Reich* and *weltliches Regiment* cannot be associated exclusively with the *Reich der Welt*, for the natural order embraces all men in so far as they are temporal persons, and not merely the members of the *regnum diaboli*.[66]

Similarly, it is extremely important to distinguish clearly between those passages in which Luther is writing about the

Christian in the abstract and those in which he is dealing with the position of the Christian in the world. Heckel is undoubtedly correct when he maintains that the Christian *qua* Christian cannot be subject to the *weltliches Regiment* in the sense of the sword, since this is instituted only for the members of the *Reich der Welt*, whereas the true Christians are governed by the spiritual regiment of the Word. Where this interpretation falls short, however, is that it does not take sufficient account of the fact that for Luther no one on earth can be regarded simply and without qualification as a 'mere Christian' and nothing else. In the first place, it is a fundamental premise of Luther's teaching that the Christian on earth has two natures, since he is at one and the same time 'flesh' and 'spirit', 'old man' and 'new man', and these two natures are constantly at war with one another within him.[67] It is, therefore, impossible for anyone to become a perfect Christian in this life. In Luther's theology the Christian on earth is always *simul justus et peccator*: although God accounts him righteous for Christ's sake, he remains a creature of sin and he can never entirely escape from the consequences of his sinful nature. It is only in the next world that the process of sanctification will be completed and the remnants of his old sinful nature will be finally extinguished.[68] Secondly, Luther holds that the Christian on earth has always to be seen not merely as a 'spiritual person', who exists only in relation to Christ, but also as a 'temporal person' who lives in the world and is a creature of flesh and blood with the same bodily needs and the same social responsibilities as other men. 'Therefore [he writes in the *Exposition of the Fifth, Sixth and Seventh Chapters of St. Matthew*] only learn the difference between the two persons which a Christian must bear at the same time on earth, because he lives among other men and must use the world's goods and the emperor's just as the heathen do. For he has exactly the same blood and flesh, which he must provide for not through the spiritual regiment but from the fields and the land, which are the emperor's, until such time as he is removed bodily out of this life into the next'.[69] Whereas as a 'spiritual person' the Christian belongs under Christ alone, as a 'temporal person' he exists in the world and has responsibilities towards other people. He is, in Luther's phrase, a person *in relatione*, for he is bound to other people in a complex of relationships as a father, son, husband, master, servant, etc.[70] In the same sense Luther argues that the Christian on earth has two 'callings': in addition to his spiritual calling to salvation God has endowed him with a temporal 'office' (*Amt*) or 'calling' (*Beruf, vocatio*) in the world in which he has a duty to devote himself to the service of his neighbour and in which he is subject to the same laws and obligations as other men.[71] As a 'temporal person', therefore, the Christian may be said to belong under the temporal regiment, although only in respect of his external life or calling: in his inner life as a 'spiritual person', on the other hand, he belongs by faith to Christ's kingdom and here he is under the rule of Christ alone.[72]

Thus, the key to the problem lies in the fact that Luther's argument is conducted on two levels. When he is speaking from a strictly theoretical standpoint he maintains that the Christian is only subject to the spiritual regiment, since the true Christian is a member of the *Reich Gottes* and, therefore, by definition has no need of the temporal regiment of the sword which God has instituted for those who belong to the *regnum diaboli*. When, however, he turns to deal with the position of the Christian in practice this argument no longer applies, since no one on earth can be described simply as a Christian and nothing else. It is an essential condition of the Christian's existence in the world that he is both a temporal person and a spiritual person and that, as a temporal person, he is involved in the external order of society with its complex of earthly callings and duties. Similarly it follows that, although in one sense the two regiments only apply to the members of separate kingdoms, in another sense they apply to all men universally irrespective of whether they belong to the *regnum Dei* or the *regnum mundi*. While it is true that, strictly speaking, only the members of God's kingdom can be said to be under the rule of the spiritual regiment, since they alone hear the Word and obey it, God has not instituted the Word for them alone. On the contrary, the Word exists for all men and must be preached to the world at large, even if the majority of men reject it and close their ears to the promises of the Gospel.[73] Equally there is a sense in which the temporal regiment of the sword may be said to exist for the Christian as well as for the members of the Devil's kingdom. Although the perfect Christian by definition has no need of temporal government, the Christian on earth is not perfect. He is still a creature of sin, even though God no longer holds his sins against him, and in so far as he is a sinner he is under the Law and, therefore, under the rule of the temporal magistrate.[74] In consequence, Althaus and the other exponents of the orthodox interpretation would appear to be justified when they claim that the *zwei Regimente* are instituted for all men or that the Christian on earth can be regarded as 'a citizen of both kingdoms'—of the *weltliches Reich* as well as of the *geistliches Reich.*

This interpretation is confirmed if one examines the character of the *weltliches Regiment* more closely in its relation to God's purpose. If Heckel is correct, Luther's conception of the *weltliches Regiment* is essentially negative, since it is dominated by the notion of the *regnum diaboli.* While he does not deny that Luther sometimes uses the term *weltlich* in the sense of 'corporal' or 'natural', Heckel insists that Luther's use of the antithesis *geistlich/weltlich* to describe the two regiments is not arbitrary, since it reflects the fact that the two forms of government are concerned with different groups of men and that the character of the *weltliches Regiment* can only be properly understood when it is seen in relation to the *Reich der Welt* as a 'kingdom of wrath' (*Reich des Zornes*) whose primary function is the punishment of the wicked.[75] But this interpretation is only partly valid, for it is strictly applicable only to the *weltliches Regiment* in the sense of the power of the sword which can be said to owe its existence to the presence of Satan's kingdom on earth. Even here, however, Luther's position is not entirely negative: while it is true that he constantly emphasises the punitive function of temporal government, he also sees it as one of the highest manifestations of God's goodness and mercy towards men, since it is through the sword that God provides men with the blessing of temporal peace without which human life could not be carried on.[76]

When, however, Luther uses the term *weltliches Reich* or *weltliches Regiment* in the wider sense of the natural order of society, a much more positive conception emerges. The temporal order figures in Luther's thought not merely as *a remedium peccati*—although it has become that in part as a consequence of the Fall—but as the vehicle of God's creative activity, through which he showers men with blessings and provides him with all that is necessary for his earthly existence.[77] Although, like St.

Augustine, Luther ascribes the introduction of government to the Fall, he traces the origins of human society itself back to the Creation; for he holds that the basic institutions of human life— above all marriage and the family—were established by God in Paradise before ever sin entered into the world.[78] Consequently the *weltliches Reich* or *Regiment* in the wider sense of the temporal order can be said to be derived from God's original act of creation in contrast to the temporal government of the sword which only came into existence after the Fall. This is not to deny that the character of the temporal order has been profoundly affected by the Fall. In Luther's view man's sin has affected the whole universe, with the result that not only man himself and the institutions of human life but the entire order of nature have lost something of their pristine purity and innocence.[79] Nevertheless, in spite of man's sin God has not abandoned his creation; on the contrary, he continues to maintain it and govern it and it is his hand alone which preserves it in being—'otherwise it could neither stand nor remain'.[80]

Luther never tires of emphasising the fact that in spite of the Fall the natural order is God's creation. Its institutions are divine *Ordnungen* or *Stände* which God has established for the support of man's earthly existence and however much they may be abused they do not on that account cease to be divine.[81] Through them God pours out his blessings on mankind: he preserves and maintains human society, he provides men with food to eat and clothes to wear, he causes the rain to fall and the corn to grow, for he never ceases to care for his creatures and it is to his continuing munificence that man owes everything that he enjoys on earth including life itself. 'He has created all communities and continues to create them, he still brings them together, nourishes them, increases them, blesses them and maintains them: he gives them fields, meadows, cattle, water, air, sun and moon and everything that they have, even body and life, as the first chapter of Genesis declares'.[82]

At the centre of Luther's concept of the natural order is the idea that God is continuously active in his creation.[83] For Luther God's work as Creator does not cease with the initial act of creation; it is a continuing process which is still going on. In contrast to the eighteenth-century conception of a remote divine clockmaker who sets the world in motion and then leaves it to operate according to its own immutable laws, Luther sees God as actively involved in the world the whole time, upholding it, directing it, replenishing it with new creatures.[84] Viewed from this standpoint all creatures, including man himself, are merely the instruments through which God carries out his purpose in the world. They are, in Luther's phrase, God's 'masks' (*larvae*) behind which he works in secret.[85] For it is of the essence of God's activity in the natural order that he does not reveal himself openly but prefers to remain 'concealed' (*verborgen, absconditus*) and to operate through natural means.[86] In the words of the *Larger Catechism* 'creatures are only the hands, tubes and instruments through which God gives all things'.[87]

This concept of the *weltliches Reich* or *Regiment* as the instrument of God's continuing activity as Creator is essential to the understanding of the *Zwei-Reiche-Lehre*. In Luther's theology the two divine *Reiche* or *Regimente* not only represent the two orders of government which God has established for mankind, they also embody the fact that God is continually active in the world in two ways. Through the spiritual order he carries out his *opus proprium*, the work of Redemption; through the temporal order he executes his 'other work', the work of Creation, by which he provides for the needs of man's earthly existence. In this sense, therefore, the two regiments may be said to pertain to all men, and not merely to the members of separate kingdoms. For just as salvation is preached to all men, even though the members of Satan's kingdom reject it, so too God has established the temporal order for Christians and non-Christians alike. From this it follows that the Christian on earth may legitimately be described as *ein Bürger der beiden Reichen*: for although Heckel is right that as a 'spiritual person' the Christian belongs only in the *Reich Gottes*, in this world the Christian is not just a 'spiritual person', he is a 'temporal person' as well and as such he belongs like other men in the temporal *Reich*.

III

The Problems of Luther's 'Tower Experience' and its Place in his Intellectual Development

The problem of the date and significance of Luther's so-called 'tower-experience' (*Turmerlebnis*)—the moment of illumination at which he came to his new understanding of Romans i. 17—is one of the longstanding cruces of modern Luther-scholarship. Since the problem was first raised in its modern form by German scholars at the beginning of the present century probably no aspect of Luther's biography has attracted so much attention or has been the subject of so much controversy: and even today, although the nature of the debate has changed considerably in recent years as new arguments and new solutions have been put forward, it still remains one of the central issues in all discussions of Luther's early intellectual development, not only because it presents the irresistible fascination of an unresolved conundrum but also because in traditional historiography it has always been closely identified with the complex question of when and how Luther arrived at his reformation theology.[1]

Considering the amount of heat that the controversy has generated, the 'tower-experience' is surprisingly well-documented. Luther himself referred to his discovery of the meaning of Romans i. 17 on numerous occasions in his *Table Talk* and in his writings, although it should be said that most of his explicit references to it date from the 1530s or early 1540s, that is between fifteen and twenty or twenty-five years after the event. Thus in one version of a well-attested conversation which took place in 1532 Luther is reported as saying: 'For these words "righteous" (*Iustus*) and "righteousness of God" (*Iustitia Dei*) were to me as a thunderbolt in my conscience. When I heard them I was filled with terror: for if God is righteous, then he will punish. But by the grace of God, when once in this tower and heated room (*in hac turri et hypocausto*) I was meditating on these words "The just shall live by faith" and "the righteousness of God", presently I came to perceive that if we as righteous men ought to live by faith and if the righteousness of God ought to be for the salvation of all who believe, then it is not our merit but the mercy of God [by which we are saved]. Thereby my spirit was cheered. For the righteousness of God is that by which we are justified and saved through Christ. And these words became more joyful to me. The Holy Spirit revealed the scripture to me in this tower (*in diesem thurn*)'.[2]

A very similar account is dated 12 September 1538: 'That phrase "the righteousness of God" was like a thunderbolt in my heart. For when under the papacy I read "Deliver me in thy righteousness" [Ps. xxxi. 1] and "In thy truth", I at once thought that that righteousness was an avenging anger, namely, of the wrath of God. I hated Paul from my heart when I read "The righteousness of God is revealed in the Gospel" [Rom. i. 16–17]. But afterwards when I saw the words that follow, namely, "as it is written, The just shall live by faith" and when, in addition, I consulted Augustine, than was I joyful. When I understood that the righteousness of God is his mercy by which he reputes us to be righteous, then this provided a remedy for me in my affliction'.[3]

A rather different version appears in the *Table Talk* for the winter of 1542/3: 'For a long time I was in error and was not aware that I was. Certainly I knew something, but nonetheless I did not know what it was until I came to the passage in Romans i: "The just shall live by faith". That helped me. Then I saw what righteousness Paul is speaking of when earlier in the text the word "righteousness" appears. Then I brought the abstract and the concrete into agreement with one another[4] and became certain of my cause; I learned to distinguish between the righteousness of the law and that of the gospel. Before that I lacked nothing except that I made no distinction between the law and the gospel; I regarded them both as the same and held that Christ did not differ from Moses except in the time at which he lived and in perfection. But when I discovered that distinction, namely, that the law is one thing, the gospel another, then I broke through'.[5]

These quotations could be paralleled by numerous other passages.[6] What is clear from the surviving evidence is where the experience is supposed to have taken place. It occurred in the tower of the Augustinian house at Wittenberg—hence the term 'Luther's tower-experience'[7]—probably in the heated room (*hypocaustum*) where Luther had his study, although the alternative reading *cloaca* (lavatory), favoured by Grisar and by psychoanalysts and psychoanalytical historians like P. J. Reiter, Erik Erikson and Norman Brown, still has its supporters.[8] It is also fairly clear from Luther's accounts—although its precise theological significance is still a matter of controversy—what his discovery consisted of. It involved a new insight into the meaning of Romans i. 17, 'For therein is the righteousness of God revealed from faith to faith: as it is written, The just shall live by faith', and, in particular, into the meaning of the term 'the righteousness of God' (*iustitia Dei*). In most of his accounts Luther describes how in wrestling with this passage he came to see, as it were in a flash of illumination, that the term 'the righteousness of God' in this passage was to be understood not, as he had hitherto understood it, in the sense of the righteousness by which God judges sinners—a concept which had caused him so much spiritual anguish[9]—but rather as the righteousness by which God in his mercy justifies those who have faith. In the third of the passages from the *Table Talk*, quoted above, Luther relates his new understanding of Romans i. 17 somewhat differently from his discovery of the distinction between law and gospel; but in most of his descriptions he does not make this connexion and it raises complications both about the exact nature and the date of his discovery which will have to be considered later.

What is unclear from most of Luther's descriptions of his 'tower-experience' is the date at which it is supposed to have taken place. The one exception is provided by the very long and circumstantial account of his discovery of the meaning of Romans i. 17 which he gave in the autobiographical preface which he wrote at the end of his life for the first volume of his collected Latin writings in the Wittenberg edition of his works (1545). In that account he not only presents a very full description of the nature of the discovery and its impact on him, but he also appears (if one takes his words literally) to suggest a precise date for it—namely, that it took place as he was about to embark on his second course of lectures on the Psalms, that is in 1519. However, that account raises a number of problems which have been at the centre of the debate and I will therefore return to it at a later stage in the discussion.[10]

The orthodox view, which held the field until comparatively recently, was that Luther's discovery took place at some point between his return to Wittenberg in the second half of 1511 and the summer of 1515 when he started to deliver his famous course of lectures on Romans. This view became established in the early years of the present century, following the discovery and publication of the MSS. of Luther's early lectures, notably the first series on the Psalms (*Dictata super Psalterium*, 1513–15) and the lectures on Romans (1515–16), which made it possible for the first time to explore the development of his theology in detail.[11] Ironically, the person who was chiefly responsible for initiating the debate over the date of Luther's breakthrough, was not a Lutheran scholar but the catholic historian and polemicist, Heinrich Denifle. In the first volume of his *Luther und Luthertum*, published in 1904, Denifle argued on the basis of the newly discovered and still unpublished lectures on Romans that the crucial turning-point in Luther's development, when he broke away from the traditional teaching of the catholic Church and arrived at his new understanding of justification, took place in 1515 in the early stages of the lectures on Romans and he poured heavy scorn on protestant scholars whom he accused of failing to look critically at the problem of at what period in his career Luther's new theology originated.[12] However, Denifle's challenge was soon taken up and over the next forty years a succession of (mainly protestant) scholars devoted a great deal of effort to trying to establish the precise point at which Luther arrived at his new understanding of Romans i. 17. As a result, a large number of different solutions was put forward. These included: 1508–9, during his first period of residence at Wittenberg (R. Seeberg, O. Ritschl), a view soon discarded by most scholars;[13] c. 1512 or possibly 1511, shortly after his return to Wittenberg but before— and probably some considerable time before—the commencement of the first lectures on the Psalms (Holl);[14] between October 1512 when he took his doctorate and the summer of 1513 when he began the lectures on the Psalms (Scheel, Strohl, Mackinnon);[15] in April or May 1513 when he was composing the *argumenta* for the printed Latin text of the Psalms which he was preparing for use in his forthcoming lectures (Boehmer);[16] early in the first course of lectures on the Psalms, at Psalm xxxi (Hirsch);[17] halfway through the lectures on the Psalms, at or before Psalm lxxi, in other words probably in the autumn of 1514 (Vogelsang);[18] late in the lectures on the Psalms or after their conclusion, but before the commencement of the lectures on Romans (Bornkamm);[19] around the end of 1514, while he was preparing the lectures on Romans (A. V. Müller);[20] before Easter 1515 (Stracke).[21] Of these the solution which has probably attracted most support from subsequent scholars is that of Erich Vogelsang, whose argument, based on a close analysis of the language of the *Dictata*, that Luther's discovery must have taken place in 1514, at or shortly before his comments on Psalm lxxi, was widely accepted as the authoritative answer to the problem in the 1930s, 1940s and early 1950s.[22]

Despite their differences, all these interpretations may be said to start from certain common assumptions which were shared by most early twentieth-century Luther scholars. In the first place, it was accepted more or less without question that the 'tower-experience' represented the moment at which Luther arrived at his reformation theology of justification and it was therefore frequently referred to as his 'reformation discovery' or 'reformation breakthrough' (*reformatorische Entdeckung, Erkenntnis* or *Durchbruch*). Secondly, it was generally believed that Luther's theology was in essentials complete in the lectures on Romans and this in turn led logically to the assumption that his 'reformation breakthrough' must have occurred before or, at the latest, about the time that he embarked on the lectures on Romans. In addition, running through the attempts of scholars like Hirsch and Vogelsang to establish a precise date for the 'tower-experience' was an implicit, and perhaps unconscious, assumption that his new understanding of Romans i. 17 must have been immediately reflected in his academic teaching, so that it should be possible by a close examination of the text of the early lectures to determine the exact point at which it occurred.

One of the very few early twentieth-century scholars to dissent from the prevailing view that Luther's 'tower-experience' must have occurred by 1515 at the latest was the catholic historian,

Hartmann Grisar, who argued for a late date in 1518 or at the beginning of 1519, at the time of the second lectures on the Psalms, as suggested by the 1545 preface.[23] But Grisar's views were universally rejected by his protestant critics and it was not until the 1950s that the traditional interpretation began to be seriously questioned. In the past twenty-five years, however, the pendulum has swung the other way and a growing number of scholars have begun to argue that Luther did not arrive at his mature theology until around 1518/19 and that his 'tower-experience', far from occurring in his early years at Wittenberg, did not happen until about the same date, that is, probably in 1518 or early in 1519.

The first modern scholar to put forward this thesis was a Finnish–American theologian, U. Saarnivaara, in a book which originally appeared in Finnish in 1947 and was subsequently published in English in America in 1951 under the title *Luther Discovers the Gospel*. In this book Saarnivaara set out the two main lines of argument which have characterised the revisionist theory ever since. In the first place, he maintained that, contrary to the traditional view, Luther did not develop the distinctive features of his reformation theology of justification until around 1518/19. Before that, although his thought was in process of evolution, his basic conception of justification was Augustinian and even in the lectures on Romans, despite evidence of a deepening evangelical insight, it still conformed to an orthodox, pre-reformation type.[24] Secondly, Saarnivaara argued that Luther's account of the 'tower-experience' in the 1545 preface, where it is dated to about 1519, should be taken literally, for the 'tower-experience' was associated not with the beginnings of his spiritual development in his early years at Wittenberg but with the final emergency of his reformation teaching in the winter of 1518/19 and, in particular, with his second lectures on the Psalms.[25]

However, Saarnivaara's book attracted little attention when it first appeared and even in recent years its influence has largely been confined to English and American scholars.[26] Consequently, the debate did not really get under way until the publication in 1958 of Ernst Bizer's important monograph *Fides ex auditu*,[27] which reopened the question of the interpretation of Luther's early development by challenging the accepted views of Vogelsang and his followers. While Bizer does not appear to have been aware of Saarnivaara's work at the time he published the first edition of *Fides ex auditu*[28] and his own investigation into the evolution of Luther's thought between 1513 and 1519 was inspired by different principles and went considerably deeper than Saarnivaara's, their general conclusions were very similar. Like Saarnivaara, Bizer argued—though on different grounds—that Luther's 'reformation breakthrough' did not take place until 1518 or early 1519 and that Luther's account of the 'tower-experience' in the 1545 Preface was substantially correct, for the emergence of his mature doctrine of justification was closely linked with a new understanding of Romans i. 17 which is apparent in his writings from the end of 1518.[29] Where Bizer's theory differed from Saarnivaara's was, first of all, in the emphasis that he placed on *humilitas* as the key-note of Luther's theology of justification down to 1518[30] and, secondly, in the claim that the decisive element in Luther's breakthrough was his discovery of the Word as the means of grace and that it was this, not the concept of passive righteousness, that constituted the essence of his new insight into the meaning of Romans i. 17 in the 'tower-experience' of 1518.[31]

The significance of the revisionist theory for the interpretation of Luther's biography lies in the fact that it entails a crucial reversal of the order of events—and therefore, by implication, of cause and effect—in his early career. The traditional view, by placing Luther's 'reformation discovery' before the ninety-five theses and the indulgences controversy, encouraged historians and biographers to assume—not necessarily justifiably—that the one led logically to the other and that Luther's attack on the Church was a direct, not to say inevitable, outcome of his new theology of justification. By contrast, according to the revisionist theory, Luther did not develop the distinctive features of his reformation theology until after the outbreak of the indulgences controversy, although he had, of course, been attacking scholastic theology before that. This means that the development of his mature theology and his 'tower-experience' have to be seen as taking place within the context of the debate over indulgences; and while not all the protagonists of the revisionist theory would make this connexion explicitly, some, including Bizer himself, would argue that Luther's 'reformation discovery' not only occurred at the time of the indulgences controversy but was inspired, directly or indirectly, by his need to grapple with the issues that it raised,[32] so that, in effect, the traditional view is turned on its head and Luther's reformation teaching emerges not as a cause but rather as a consequence, in part at least, of his attack on indulgences.

Inevitably a theory that involves such a radical reinterpretation of Luther's early development has aroused considerable controversy. The publication of Bizer's book sparked off a heated debate which continued throughout the 1960s.[33] Not surprisingly, many scholars found it difficult at first to accept the implications of a theory which challenged so many preconceptions about the early history of the Reformation[34] and it is only gradually that the revisionist thesis that Luther did not arrive at the distinctive features of his reformation theology until around 1518/19 has begun to gain widespread, though by no means universal, acceptance.[35] Even so the debate is far from over. Not only are there still many supporters of the traditional view who remain unpersuaded by the arguments of the revisionists, but the revisionist theory itself leaves a number of loose ends and, even if one accepts (as I do) the general argument for a late date for the emergence of Luther's reformation theology, it cannot be said that the biographical problem of Luther's 'tower-experience' has yet been satisfactorily resolved.

It is this that I want to look at in the remainder of this paper. Let me say at once that I am not going to pull a new rabbit out of the hat. I cannot claim to have found the solution to the mystery that has defeated everyone else until now. In fact, I suspect that the problem is ultimately insoluble. What I want to do is simply to draw attention to a methodological confusion which, it seems to me, has bedevilled the discussion of the problem ever since it was first raised at the beginning of the century and which needs to be cleared out of the way if one is to approach the problem afresh.

This confusion lies in the fact that in modern research two quite distinct problems have been unconsciously conflated: the problem of the date of the emergence of Luther's reformation theology of justification and the problem of the date and significance of his 'tower-experience'. In discussions of Luther's early intellectual development it has generally been taken for granted that the 'tower-experience' was directly connected with the emergence of his reformation theology, either in the sense that what he discovered in the tower was the doctrine of justification by faith or in the sense that his new understanding of *iustitia Dei* was the essential insight which led him to the discovery of justification by faith. In other words, it has generally been taken for granted that the 'tower-experience' represents what German scholars call his 'reformation discovery' or 'reformation breakthrough'. Consequently, there has been an inbuilt tendency on the part of many scholars to assume that if only one can solve the problem of the date of Luther's 'tower-experience', then one has solved the problem of when he achieved his 'reformation breakthrough', or vice-versa—if one can discover from an analysis of Luther's early writings when his 'reformation breakthrough' occurred, then one has also solved the problem of the date of his 'tower-experience'.

It is easy to understand why this assumption should have been made by the older generation of Luther scholars who first formulated the theory of a date between 1512 and 1515 for the 'tower-experience', since they started from the premiss that Luther's reformation theology was in essentials complete by the time he embarked on his lectures on Romans. Given the assumption that the lectures on Romans were to be seen as a clear statement of Luther's mature teaching on justification, it followed that his 'reformation breakthrough' must have taken place before that and it was only natural that they should have identified it with the moment of illumination that he described in his accounts of the 'tower-experience'. At the same time the tendency to treat the two problems as if they were one and the same was undoubtedly fostered by the methodological assumption made by Emanuel Hirsch and his followers that it must be possible to pin-point the precise moment in Luther's lectures at which he came to his new understanding of Romans i. 17; and one legacy of the obsessive endeavours of successive German scholars to establish such a precise turning-point in his writings has been to encourage the belief that there must be a clear-cut solution to the problem of the 'tower-experience', when probably there is not.

What is more remarkable, however, is that for the most part this basic assumption that the two problems are identical has been carried over into the revisionist theory. In part, one suspects, because it had become such a well-established tradition among Luther scholars to equate Luther's 'tower-experience' with his 'reformation breakthrough', the newer generation of scholars like Saarnivaara and Bizer, who contend that Luther did not arrive at the distinctive features of his mature theology until around 1518/ 1519, have continued to make the assumption that the 'tower-experience' must be linked with the emergence of his mature theology and they have argued—admittedly also partly on the basis of the 1545 preface—that it cannot have taken place until 1518 or early 1519. Similarly, again following in the tradition of earlier German Luther scholarship, they have continued to be greatly concerned with trying to detect the exact point in Luther's writings at which his new understanding of Romans i. 17 begins to emerge.

The question I want to put, therefore, is whether the two problems are necessarily identical or, at least, as closely interrelated as most scholars have tended to assume. As I see it, there are really two distinct problems which need to be kept separate. The first— and from a historical point of view the more important—problem is when did Luther arrive at the distinctive elements of his reformation theology? Was it before 1515 or only after the outbreak of the indulgences controversy, around 1518/19? The second is the much more limited biographical question, when did Luther undergo his 'tower-experience' and what precisely did it involve? Only by looking at these two questions separately can one try to establish what connexion there is, if any, between Luther's 'tower-experience' and the emergence of his reformation theology.

The first is an immensely complex and technical problem which cannot be explored here. To do justice to it properly would require a detailed, step-by-step analysis of the progress of Luther's thought in his early writings of the kind provided by Bizer or by Gordon Rupp in *The Righteousness of God*. It would also involve an examination of the highly controversial question of how one defines the difference between the 'reformation' (*reformatorische*) and the 'pre-reformation' (*vorreformatorische*) elements in Luther's thought.[36] Such an analysis, even if I had the competence to undertake it, is clearly outside the scope of this paper. I will therefore confine myself to a few brief general observations. In the first place, it is now clear that the evolution of Luther's thought in the period 1512 to 1520 was a much more gradual process than used to be assumed. If the controversy has failed to produce any agreement on when Luther's breakthrough occurred, it has served to show that Luther did not formulate his new theology all at once, but rather over a period of several years, and it is significant that even those scholars who would place the decisive turning-point in his development relatively early would admit that on a number of important issues he did not work out his ideas in full until considerably later.[37] Secondly, again partly (although not exclusively) as a result of the controversy, there has been a marked change in the interpretation of the lectures on Romans over the past thirty years.[38] Although passions still run high over whether the lectures should be seen as a statement of his 'reformation' or his 'pre-reformation' thinking,[39] the researches of Saarnivaara, Bizer and others have demonstrated that Luther's theological position in the lectures on Romans is considerably more ambiguous, not to say transitional, than was perceived by most early twentieth-century scholars and, on balance, it seems to me that the weight of the evidence supports the revisionists' contention that at this stage his teaching on justification was still essentially Augustinian in character, and that he had not yet arrived at his distinctive reformation doctrine of justification as an instantaneous process.[40] Thirdly, a number of recent scholars have tended to argue that a general reorientation took place in Luther's thinking around 1518–19, following the outbreak of the indulgences controversy, and it is now fairly clear that certain key concepts of his mature theology, such as his teaching on law and gospel and his new understanding of the Christian as 'flesh' and 'spirit', *simul iustus simul peccator*, only began to crystallise in his thought at this period.[41] While recognising that the matter is still far from settled, I am therefore myself largely convinced by the revisionist argument that Luther did not come to a full understanding of his reformation teaching on justification until around 1518/19, and that before that his thought progressed through an Augustinian phase, represented *par excellence* by the lectures on Romans, during which he was actively engaged in attacking scholastic theology but had not yet achieved his final break-through.

Such a protracted view of Luther's development should not really seem surprising. On the contrary, when one reflects on the problem, it is the older belief that Luther arrived at the main principles of his reformation theology very early which makes the greater demands on our credulity. As he himself remarked, 'I did not learn my theology all at one time; rather I had to dig for it ever deeper and deeper where my trials took me'.[42] It makes much better sense psychologically, as well as of the evidence of his early writings, to see Luther's thought developing gradually over a period of six or seven years, as he worked out his ideas stage by stage—*scribendo et legendo*, as he put it in the 1545 preface.[43] Not only was Luther by temperament a conservative thinker, who always found it difficult (even in later years) to free himself completely from the traditional ideas in which he had been reared; but the task he was engaged on—at first unconsciously—was an immensely difficult one, since in effect it involved break-ing away from one theological system and creating a new synthesis of his own. By its very nature this was bound to be a relatively long drawn out process: although the beginnings of Luther's evolution as a reformer can be traced back to the first lectures on the Psalms, the final clarification of his teaching on justification almost certainly did not occur until around 1518/19, and it is only at this stage that he can properly be said to have arrived at his reformation theology.

The second problem—the problem of the 'tower-experience'—is much narrower in scope in that it concerns a particular moment in Luther's intellectual biography. Essentially it comprises three interrelated questions. First, at what point in Luther's early years at Wittenberg did it take place? Secondly, what exactly did his discovery consist of? Thirdly, what is the significance of the 'tower-experience' in the overall pattern of Luther's intellectual development?

At this point we need to turn to the famous account of his dis-covery which Luther gave in the 1545 preface to the first volume of his collected Latin writings. There, after describing the origins and development of the indulgences controversy and the mission of Miltitz, he writes: 'Meanwhile in that year [1519] I had returned once more to interpreting the Psalms, confident that I was better trained after I had expounded the epistles of Saint Paul to the Romans and the Galatians and the epistle to the Hebrews in the schools. Certainly I had been seized by an extraordinary ardour to understand Paul in the epistle to the Romans, but what had hindered me thus far was not any coldness in my heart's blood but that one phrase in the first chapter, "The righteousness of God is revealed in it." For I had hated that phrase "the righteousness of God" (*iustitia Dei*), which by the use and custom of all the doctors I had been taught to understand philosophically in the sense of the formal or active righteousness (as they termed it) (*iustitia (ut vocant) formali seu activa*), by which God is righteous and punishes sinners and the unrighteous. Although as a monk I lived an irreproachable life, I felt that before God I was a sinner with a most unquiet conscience, nor was I able to believe that he was appeased by my satisfactions. I did not love, nay rather I hated that righteous God who punishes sinners, and if not with silent blasphemy, then certainly with a great murmuring, I was angry with God . . . Thus I raged with a furious and troubled conscience; yet I continued to knock importunately at Paul in this passage, thirsting most ardently to know what Saint Paul meant. Until at last, by the mercy of God, as I meditated day and night, I began to consider the connexion of the words,[44] "The righteousness of God is revealed in it, as it is written: The just shall live by faith". Then I began to understand that the righteousness of God is that righteousness by which the righteous man lives by the gift of God, namely by faith, and that this phrase, "The righteousness of God is revealed through the gospel", is passive, meaning the righteousness by which God in his mercy justifies us through faith, as it is written, "The just shall live by faith". Now I immediately felt that I had been reborn and that I had entered through open gates into paradise itself. Then forthwith the face of the whole of scripture appeared different to me. After that I ran through the scriptures, as memory served, and I found the same analogy in other phrases, such as the work of God (*opus Dei*), that which God works in us; the power of God (*virtus Dei*), by which he makes us powerful; the wisdom of God (*sapientia Dei*), by which he makes us wise; the strength of God (*fortitudo Dei*); the salvation of God (*salus Dei*); the glory of

God (*gloria Dei*). Now, just as before I had so hated that phrase "the righteousness of God", so with equal intensity I began to love and extol it as the sweetest of words, so that that passage in Paul became for me the very gate of paradise. Afterwards I read Augustine, *On the Spirit and the Letter*, where beyond my expectation I found that he too interprets the righteousness of God in the same manner, namely, as that with which God endues us when he justifies us. And although this is expressed somewhat imperfectly and he does not explain everything clearly about imputation, nevertheless it was pleasing to find that he taught that the righteousness of God is that by which we are justified. Made better armed by these thoughts, I began to interpret the Psalms for the second time. . . '.[45]

The fullness of this account is remarkable and it contains many points of detail that are of interest. However, at the risk of over-simplifying a complex problem, it is possible to single out four points that are particularly crucial to the discussion. 1. If one interprets Luther's words literally, his chronology implies quite specifically that his discovery took place in 1519 when he was about to embark on his second series of lectures on the Psalms.[46] 2. He connects his difficulties over the meaning of the term *iustitia Dei* with the personal spiritual crisis which he experienced as a monk. 3. He relates his new understanding of Romans i. 17 to the discovery that *iustitia Dei* can be interpreted not merely in an active sense as the righteousness by which God judges (and con-demns) sinners, but also in a passive sense as the righteousness by which men are made righteous through faith. It is this 'passive' righteousness[47] which God bestows on men as a gift through faith, that is, the righteousness by which men are justified and to which Paul refers in Romans i. 17. This description is more or less identical with that which Luther gave in the first two passages from the *Table Talk*, quoted at the beginning of this paper: in the third, he suggested rather differently that it was connected with his discovery of the distinction between law and gospel.[48] 4. In the 1545 preface Luther states that after he had come to his new understanding of Romans i. 17 he read Augustine's *De spiritu et littera*, where *praeter spem* he found that *iustitia Dei* was interpreted similarly, although somewhat imperfectly.[49]

The crux arises from the fact that not only, so far as is known, were Luther's spiritual struggles as a monk over well before 1519, but that both in the 1545 preface and in most of the other accounts in the *Table Talk* and elsewhere he appears to describe his discovery in terms of a new understanding of *iustitia Dei* which he arrived at not in 1519, or even in 1518, but several years earlier—certainly by 1515 when he began the lectures on Romans and very probably at some point during the first lectures on the Psalms. One has only to turn to the beginning of the lectures on Romans where Luther outlines the theme of the epistle to see that he regarded the central message of Romans as being that man is not saved by his own righteousness, but 'by an external righteousness' (*per extraneam iustitiam*)—'which does not originate from ourselves, but which comes to us from outside, which does not arise on our earth, but which comes from heaven'.[50] Moreover, if one turns specifically to Luther's exposition of Romans i. 17 in the 1515–16 lectures, one finds that he interprets *iustitia Dei* in a manner which clearly resembles the language of his later accounts of his 'tower-experience'. 'But only in the gospel', he writes, 'is the righteousness of God revealed (that is, who is righteous and by what means he becomes righteous before God) through faith alone by which one believes the word of God . . . For the righteousness of God is the cause of salvation. And here again the righteousness of God is not to be understood as that righteousness by which God is righteous in himself, but that by which we are justified by him, which happens through faith in the gospel'.[51] Nor do the parallels with the 1545 preface stop there, for in the very next sentence Luther goes on to cite Augustine's *De spiritu et littera* in support of this interpretation of *iustitia Dei*;[52] and, in fact, throughout the lectures on Romans he refers to Augustine's tract on numerous occasions, so that it is evident that he was thoroughly familiar with it by the time he came to write the Romans lectures.[53]

What is one to make of these discrepancies in Luther's account? To the supporters of the traditional theory the chief source of difficulty lay in Luther's apparent dating of his discovery to 1519 and they attempted to get round this in various ways: for example, by suggesting that his use of the pluperfect tense (*captus fieram*, etc.) at the beginning of the passage indicates that he was going back in time to an earlier period in his career and that the whole passage should be regarded as a digression from the main course of his narrative;[54] that he did not intend to give a precise date for his discovery here;[55] that he simply made a mistake and confused his second course of lectures on the Psalms with the first;[56] or that in 1545, when the preface was written, he was a relatively old man, so that it is hardly surprising that his narrative is somewhat incoherent and rambling.[57]

However, none of these explanations is very convincing, as has frequently been pointed out. Luther's language is too precise to make it easy to accept the view that he intended the passage to be treated as a digression and there is nothing in the rest of the preface to suggest that his memory of events had become confused or that he was becoming in the least senile.[58] The revisionists would therefore argue that Luther's dating must be taken seriously: that the 'tower-experience' did occur around 1518 or early 1519 and that it was related to the emergence of his mature teaching on justification which first becomes apparent in his writings of 1518–19. In support of this Bizer quotes a number of passages from the sermon on two-fold righteousness (1519) and the second lectures on the Psalms (*Operationes in Psalmos*) where Luther's ideas and the language in which he clothes them appear to parallel very closely the ideas and phraseology of the 1545 preface.[59] On the other hand, it has to be said that the revisionist argument fails to deal satisfactorily either with the major problem that in the 1545 preface and most of his other accounts Luther appears to describe his discovery in terms of a new understanding of *iustitia Dei* which he had certainly acquired by 1515, and probably earlier, or with the lesser difficulty that Luther was well acquainted with Augustine's *De spiritu et littera* when he commenced the lectures on Romans. On the first point, Bizer argues that there is a crucial difference between Luther's concept of *iustitia Dei* as it appears in the lectures on Romans and the first lectures on the Psalms and as he restated it in 1518/19, in that in 1518/19 he began for the first time to make justification dependent not only on faith but on the Word as the means of grace. According to Bizer, the essence of Luther's new insight into the meaning of Romans i. 17 lay in the realisation that the words *Iustitia Dei revelatur in illo* meant not merely that the righteousness of God is revealed *in* the gospel, but that it is revealed *through* the gospel. In other words, what

Luther discovered in 1518/19—and this, Bizer claims, is what the 'tower-experience' consisted of—was the idea of the Word as the essential means of grace.[60] The difficulty with this is that it is not what Luther appears to be describing in his account of the 'tower-experience' in the 1545 preface where he quite specifically identifies his new understanding of Romans i. 17 with the realisation that *iustitia Dei* can be interpreted passively.[61] Even less persuasively Bizer and other supporters of the revisionist theory have tried to argue that when Luther referred to Augustine's *De spiritu et littera* in the 1545 preface he did not mean to imply that this was the first time that he had read it, since clearly he had read it before 1518/19, but that he read it again with new eyes shortly after his discovery when he was amazed to find (*praeter spem*) how closely Augustine's views corresponded to his own new conception of *iustitia Dei*.[62] No doubt it is possible to interpret Luther's words in this way, but again it is hardly the obvious impression that they convey.

My own view is that the problem of reconciling these conflicting strands of evidence is insoluble and it is unlikely that we shall ever arrive at a satisfactory explanation that tidies up all the loose ends in Luther's account. This does not necessarily mean that no explanation of the 'tower-experience' is possible: simply that we cannot reconcile the contradictions in Luther's accounts and we ought to recognise this. In examining the problem of the 'tower-experience' we therefore need to go back to what we can be certain of.

What is beyond dispute—or almost beyond dispute[63]—is that Luther did at some period in his early years at Wittenberg experience a moment of illumination which he himself always remembered as a crucial turning-point in his spiritual life, even if its importance perhaps grew in his memory with the passage of time. In this connexion, it is worth recalling that Luther's recorded reminiscences of his discovery date from the later years of his life, from the 1530s and early 1540s, and one may deduce from the verbal parallels between the different accounts that it was a story which became something of a set-piece as the years went by and which tended in consequence to take on an increasingly stereotyped form. Secondly, it is clear from all Luther's accounts that this moment of illumination involved a new understanding of

Romans i. 17. More specifically, to judge by the evidence of the 1545 preface and the majority of Luther's other accounts, it appears to have been bound up with the realisation that *iustitia Dei* is to be interpreted passively as the righteousness by which God justifies men through faith, although not all modern scholars would accept this and there is the complication that in the 1542/3 passage in the *Table Talk* Luther associates his new understanding of Romans i. 17 with his discovery of the distinction between law and gospel. Thirdly, it is clear that the question of the date of the 'tower-experience' is inseparable from the question of its content.

It seems to me that there are two—or just possibly three—alternative solutions to the problem. The first is that Luther experienced his new understanding of Romans i. 17 relatively early in his time at Wittenberg, and that it was essentially connected not with the emergence of his final reformation theology of justification, but rather with his earlier discovery that the term 'the righteousness of God' can be understood in a passive sense as the external righteousness by which God justifies men in his mercy—a concept which is apparent throughout the lectures on Romans and which is visible in the later stages of the first lectures on the Psalms. In other words, Luther's illumination must have taken place by 1515—very possibly around 1513/14 at some point during the course of the first lectures on the Psalms, as favoured by many older scholars. This view would also appear to fit with Luther's statement in the 1545 preface that his discovery was linked with the resolution of his personal spiritual crisis in the monastery, for although again this cannot be dated precisely the evidence of the lectures on Romans suggests that by that time he had succeeded in overcoming the religious doubts that had tormented him earlier.[64]

On the other hand, if one accepts a relatively early date for the 'tower-experience', then one has to draw a sharp distinction between the 'tower-experience' and the emergence of his mature theology. While there is no reason to question Luther's claim that the 'tower-experience' was a momentous event in his intellectual and spiritual evolution, it is clear that far from representing the moment at which his reformation teaching suddenly came into focus, it marked only the beginning of a protracted process of development. On this view, it probably makes most sense to see it as the turning point at which he finally freed himself from the intellectual and spiritual difficulties created for him by the nominalist theology of salvation in which he had grown up and came to accept the Augustinian view that the righteousness by which man is justified is something extraneous, something which God confers on man, not something that man can achieve by his own efforts or works—a belief which enabled Luther to overcome his personal fear of God's judgment. If one accepts this solution, however, then it is evident that the 'tower-experience' was only an early step in the evolution of his theology. He had a long way to go and several years were to pass before he arrived at his mature position. Thus, though its psychological importance for Luther need not be doubted, it would be a mistake to over-estimate its significance in his intellectual development. It certainly does not represent the point at which he achieved his final 'reformation breakthrough', even though it was unquestionably a breakthrough of a kind.

The second alternative is that the 'tower-experience' did occur several years later, around 1518/19, as Saarnivaara, Bizer and others claim, and that it was closely associated with the final development of his reformation theology. On this view, it represented a moment of illumination when, so to speak, the various pieces of the jig-saw all slipped into place and it may well have been connected with his new understanding of the distinction between law and gospel which is apparent in his writings from around 1517–18.[65] If one accepts this solution, then clearly it is possible to argue that the 'tower-experience' was Luther's 'reformation breakthrough' in a literal sense, since it was associated with the emergence of some of the characteristic elements of his mature teaching. On the other hand, in that case its significance must have been a great deal less than Luther afterwards came to believe: for he had already moved a long way from traditional nominalist theology by 1518 and he had certainly arrived at his passive interpretation of *iustitia Dei* several years earlier, while he also appears to have emerged from his personal religious crisis well before this. It is quite conceivable that Luther did experience some kind of illumination around 1518/19, when he suddenly felt that he was able to see the theological problems that had occupied him for so long in a new light. But a late date would suggest that this was not so much a dramatic turning-point as a final clarification of his ideas.[66]

Both these solutions are psychologically quite plausible—one can imagine Luther having a moment of illumination at either point in his career—but both have their difficulties in view of the evidence. An early date runs counter to the chronology of the 1545 preface with its clear implication that Luther's new insight into the meaning of Romans i. 17 occurred as he was about to embark on his second series of lectures on the Psalms: it would also not fit with the suggestion in the 1542/43 account in the *Table Talk* that his experience was associated with his discovery of the distinction between law and gospel. On the other hand, a late date would appear to conflict with Luther's repeated statements that his new understanding of Romans i. 17 involved the realisation that the righteousness by which God justified man is passive, as well as with the fact that he was certainly familiar with Augustine's *De spiritu et littera* by 1515; nor is it easy to reconcile a late date with the supposition that the 'tower-experience' was connected with the resolution of his personal spiritual crisis. So explicit is Luther's identification of his illumination with the discovery that *iustitia Dei* can be interpreted passively that it seems to me that on balance the arguments in favour of an early date outweigh those in favour of a date around 1518/19. I am therefore inclined to support the traditional view that the 'tower-experience' must have occurred by 1515 at the latest, while recognising that the evidence is by no means conclusive. However, in that case I would wish to argue, in opposition to the traditionalist theory, that it was not associated with the emergence of his reformation doctrine of justification, but belongs to an earlier phase in his intellectual development.

There is a third possibility that ought to be mentioned, although there is no concrete evidence in the sources to support it. This is that Luther, in fact, experienced two moments of illumination— one relatively early, the other around 1518—which in later years tended to get conflated in his memory. Psychologically this has much to recommend it: certainly Luther's thought progressed by stages and it is quite conceivable that the two major advances in his thinking which took place around 1514/15, when he first began consciously to attack scholastic theology, and around 1518/19, when his mature theology began to crystallise, were each preceded or accompanied by a moment of illumination when the way forward suddenly seemed to become clear. However, attractive as such a solution would be as a way round the various difficulties, it is so speculative that it would be unwise to pursue it.

To sum up, then, whichever solution one adopts, it is evident that the 'tower-experience' played a considerably less important role in Luther's overall intellectual development than most scholars have tended to assume or than he himself came to believe in his later years. The development of Luther's theology of justification was a relatively long drawn out process, which extended over several years, and it now seems probable that he did not arrive at his final position until after the outbreak of the indulgences controversy. Unless one adopts my hypothetical third possibility, the 'tower-experience' can only relate to one moment in that process. If one accepts an early date, then it only marks an early stage in Luther's development. It did not represent his 'reformation breakthrough'. If one considers a later date more probable, then it is arguable that it did constitute his 'reformation breakthrough': on the other hand, in that case it only marks the culmination of a process which had been going on for several years. It is probably true to say that, whenever it took place, the importance of the 'tower-experience' for Luther was as much psychological as intellectual. It represented a moment when doubts which had long been troubling him suddenly appeared to resolve themselves and he afterwards looked back on it as a momentous turning-point. But from a historian's point of view it is clear that one should not overemphasise the significance of what was only one incident in his intellectual biography. Equally, it is clear that in order to see Luther's intellectual development in its true perspective it is important not to confuse the problem of the date and significance of his 'tower-experience' with the broader and much more complex problem of the evolution of his reformation theology.

PART TWO

THE ENGLISH REFORMATION

IV

Who Wrote 'The Supper of The Lord'?

The *Short-Title Catalogue* includes in its list of Tyndale's works a pamphlet called 'The Supper of the Lord', which was originally published anonymously on the Continent in 1533, under the fictitious imprint of Nicholas Twonson of Nuremberg.[1] But there are serious objections against accepting Tyndale's authorship. Although the pamphlet was reprinted several times during the reigns of Henry viii and Edward vi, it did not finally appear under Tyndale's name until 1573, when John Foxe included it in his edition of the works of Tyndale, Frith and Barnes. During the sixteenth century it was widely believed that 'The Supper of the Lord' was the work of George Joye, one of the lesser figures of the English Reformation who is now largely forgotten. But although the weight of the evidence seems to support this belief, the glamour of Tyndale's name has prevented the question from being investigated properly.

Since the early nineteenth century Tyndale's authorship has generally been accepted. Christopher Anderson, in *The Annals of the English Bible* (1845), had little hesitation in pronouncing 'The Supper of the Lord' to be Tyndale's.[2] It was reprinted among Tyndale's works by Thomas Russell in his ill-fated edition of the *Works of the English Reformers*,[3] and by Henry Walter in the Parker Society edition.[4] Walter himself was aware that the case for attributing the work to Tyndale was not completely established and he became increasingly undecided about it the more he studied the problem. When he wrote the biographical introduction to the first volume of the Parker Society edition, he accepted the view that 'The Supper of the Lord' was by Tyndale without much question.[5] But by the time the third volume, which contains 'The Supper of the Lord', appeared, Walter had become much more hesitant. In his introductory note to 'The Supper' he went at length into the objections to Tyndale's authorship; but although he avoided making any definitive pronouncement, the tone of his remarks implied that the book was to be accepted as the work of Tyndale.[6] Subsequently, however, his doubts became even more pronounced, and in a brief article in *Notes and Queries*, published while the third volume was still in the press, he put forward the tentative suggestion that the book ought properly to be attributed to Joye.[7] Nevertheless, the difficulties involved in accepting Tyndale's authorship, which Walter pointed out, have largely been ignored by subsequent writers. On the strength of Walter's preface to 'The Supper' and a misreading of his article in *Notes and Queries*, Demaus declared in his life of Tyndale (1872) that 'on the whole, however, it now seems agreed that the work was Tyndale's, this conviction being strengthened by the fact that Joye, whose self-conceit was boundless, does not claim the authorship of it as he certainly would have done had the work been his'.[8] J. F. Mozley, the author of the most recent biography of Tyndale,[9] and Canon Greenslade, in his selection of Tyndale's writings,[10] both take the same view. The only serious support for Joye's claims is to be found in the article on him in the *Dictionary of National Biography* and this is counterbalanced by the authority of the *Short-Title Catalogue*.

Yet in the sixteenth century Joye's claims received as much support as Tyndale's. The work, which had been written as an answer to More's 'Letter Impugning the Erroneous Writing of John Frith', was ostensibly anonymous. It concludes with a brief but unconvincing apology, in which the author excuses himself from giving his name on the specious ground that while More himself was aware of his identity, the public was only interested in the contents of the book. 'I would have thereto put my name, good reader, but I know well that thou regardest not who writeth but what is written: thou esteemest the word of the verity, and not of the author. And as for M. Mocke, whom the verity most offendeth, and doth but mock it out when he cannot soil it, he knoweth my name well enough'.[11] But in spite of this façade of anonymity, contemporaries seem to have had little doubt that 'The Supper of the Lord' was the work of either Tyndale or Joye. More himself gave arguments for attributing it to each of them in the preface to his rejoinder, 'The Answer to the First Part of a Poisoned Book which a Nameless Heretic hath named The Supper of the Lord', where he discussed the matter at some length.[12] However, he refused to decide between them, protesting that it was unreasonable to expect him to be able to distinguish the work of one anonymous heretic from another. Although John Foxe in 1573 included 'The Supper of the Lord' in his edition of Tyndale's works, John Bale attributed it in both editions of his 'Catalogue of British Authors' to Joye.[13] At the time of its appearance the authorities took the same view. In a list of condemned books issued in 1542, it is described as 'The Supper of the Lord, of George Joye's doing'.[14]

The case for attributing 'The Supper of the Lord' to Tyndale rests largely on the testimony of Foxe and More, yet the evidence of neither is conclusive. In the first place, little weight can be attached to the fact that Foxe printed 'The Supper of the Lord' in Day's folio edition of *The Works of Tyndale, Frith and Barnes.* For instead of including it among the rest of Tyndale's works, he published 'The Supper' as an appendix after Tyndale's letters to Frith.[15] At the same time he made it clear that he had no intention of committing himself on the question of its authorship. After the second letter to Frith, the last item which Foxe recognised as indisputably genuine, there is the colophon—'The end of all M. W. Tyndale's Works, newly imprinted according to his first copies, which he himself set forth'.[16] This is followed by a short preface to 'The Supper of the Lord', which implies that Foxe's only reason for including it was hearsay and that he himself was very doubtful whether Tyndale was, in fact, the author. 'Here followeth a short and pithy treatise touching the Lord's Supper compiled as some do gather, by M. W. Tyndale, because the method and phrase agree with his, and the time of writing are concurrent; which for thy further instruction and learning, gentle reader, I have annexed to his works, lest the church of God should want any of the painful travails of godly men, whose only cure and endeavour was to advance the glory of God and to further the salvation of Christ's flock committed to their charge'.[17]

It is also significant that Foxe does not mention 'The Supper of the Lord' in his account of Tyndale's life in the *Acts and Monuments.* He does state there that Tyndale wrote a treatise on the sacraments, but adds that he put it aside and refrained from publishing it, on the ground that the people were not yet prepared for such advanced teaching.[18] The work which he describes must refer to another book of Tyndale's on the sacraments, whose authorship has never been in question, *A Fruitful and Godly Treatise on the Sacraments*:[19] for there is no suggestion in Foxe's memoir that Tyndale composed two works on the sacraments.

The evidence of More's 'Answer to the First Part of a Poisoned Book' is no less equivocal. In his preface, More reproduced at some length the arguments which he had heard on both sides, without committing himself to either: 'But in the meanwhile there is come over another book against the blessed Sacrament, a book of that sort, that Fryth's book the brethren may now forbear. For more blasphemous and bedlam-ripe than this book is, were that book hard to be, which yet is mad enough as men say that have seen it. . . . The man hath not set his name unto his book, nor whose it is I cannot surely say. But some reckon it to be made by William Tyndale, for that in an epistle of his unto Fryth, he writeth that in anything he can do, he would not fail to help him forth. Howbeit some of the brethren report that the book was made by George Jay. And of truth Tyndale wrote unto Fryth that Geo. Jay had made a book against the sacrament, which was yet partly by his means, partly for lack of money retained and kept from the print. Howbeit what George Jay would do therein afterward when his money were come, that could he not, he saith, assure him. Now of truth George Jay hath long had in hand and ready lying by him his book against the sacrament. And now if this be it, he hath enlengthened it of late, by a piece that he hath patched in against me, wherein he would seem to soil mine arguments, which in my letter I made in that matter against the devilish treatise of Fryth. . . . The maker of this book for one cause why he putteth not his name thereto, writeth in this wise, 'Master Mocke, whom the verity most offendeth, and doth but mock it out, when he cannot soil it, he knoweth me well enough'. . . . Now for myself, though I know Tyndale by name, and George Jay or George Joy, by name also, and twenty other fond fellows of the same sect more: yet if ten of those would make ten such foolish treatises and set their names to none, could I know thereby which of those mad fools had made which foolish book?'[20]

On balance the weight of these remarks seems to be on the side of Joye's authorship, and More provides other evidence which supports the case for Joye. Later in the same preface he reports that some of the protestants, who believed that Joye was responsible for 'The Supper of the Lord', were convinced that 'the cause why he set not his name thereto was because he wist well that the brethren did not regard him. And Tyndale had in his letter also declared him for a fool, by reason whereof he thought that if it came out under his name the estimation thereof would be lost'.[21]

Walter stated in his preface to 'The Supper of the Lord' that in spite of his professions of ignorance More took it for granted throughout the rest of his reply that the opponent he had to deal with was Tyndale.[22] But there is no evidence for this. At the end of the preface to the *Answer*, More declared that since his antagonist had not chosen to give his name he would address him as 'Master Masker',[23] and he adhered to this practice scrupulously. Apart from other considerations this enabled him to attack both Tyndale and Joye at the same time all the way through the book, on the pretext that either of them might be the person whom he had to answer.

While the evidence of More and Foxe is therefore quite compatible with Joye's authorship, other direct contemporary evidence endorses it unequivocally. Both in Bale's 'Catalogue of British Authors' and in the proclamation of 1542 against heretical books it is stated quite explicitly that 'The Supper of the Lord' is the work of George Joye.[24]

Such information as we have about the circumstances which led up to the publication of 'The Supper of the Lord' also supports the conclusion that it was the work of Joye, not Tyndale. For there is evidence that Tyndale was at this time opposed to any discussion of the nature of the sacrament, while Joye was only too eager to express his views on the subject.

Frith's work on the sacrament, which precipitated the controversy and which 'The Supper of the Lord' was designed to defend, was written while he was in prison on the charge of heresy. It had circulated only in MS., and Tyndale who was on the Continent at the time did not learn of its existence until after the publication of More's reply. Shortly before the 'Letter Impugning the Erroneous Writing of John Frith' appeared, when Tyndale was still unaware that Frith had already committed himself, he wrote him the letter[25] to which More referred in the preface to his 'Answer to the First Part of a Poisoned Book'. In it Tyndale urged Frith not to make any statement of his views on the sacraments, since this would only reveal the internal divisions among the protestants and bring down on him the hostility of the Lutherans. It would be better, he advised, not to raise the issue until the protestants were in a position to settle it at leisure among themselves: 'Of the presence of Christ's body in the sacrament, meddle as little as you can, that there appear no division among us. Barnes will be hot against you. The Saxons be sure on the affirmative; whether constant or obstinate I remit it to God. . . . George Joye would have put forth a treatise of the matter, but I have stopped him as yet; what he will do if he get money I wot not. I believe he would make many reasons little serving the purpose. My mind is that nothing be put forth, till we hear how you shall have sped. I would have the right use preached, and the presence to be an indifferent thing, till the matter be reasoned at peace at leisure of both parties. If you be required, shew the phrases of scripture and let them talk what they will. For to believe that God is everywhere hurteth no man that worshippeth him nowhere but in the heart, in spirit and verity: even so to believe that Christ is everywhere, though it cannot be proved, hurteth no man that worshippeth him nowhere but save in the faith of his gospel. You perceive my mind; howbeit, if God shew you otherwise, it is free for you to do as he moveth you.'[26]

The whole tone of this letter is cautious and statesmanlike. It fits in with Foxe's story that Tyndale deliberately refrained from publishing a work on the sacraments in case it should hinder the cause of the Gospel; and there can be no doubt that at the end of 1532 Tyndale was opposed to any action which would revive among the reformers the bitter quarrels about the nature of the real presence which had divided the Lutherans and Zwinglians for the past ten years. At the same time, the letter suggests equally clearly that Joye had no such scruples.

It therefore needs to be explained, if Tyndale is to be credited with 'The Supper of the Lord', how he same to reverse his attitude of caution so soon. More, who had seen an intercepted copy of Tyndale's letter to Frith, pointed out that Tyndale had promised in it to do everything in his power to help Frith and he suggested that 'The Supper of the Lord' might represent Tyndale's attempt to fulfil this undertaking.[27] This explanation has been seized upon by the supporters of Tyndale's authorship. Walter went further in his preface to 'The Supper of the Lord', and suggested that Tyndale may in addition have seen Frith's *Answer to More* through the press in Antwerp.[28] But there is no evidence for any of this and no convincing reason why Tyndale should have acted in such a way. For even after Frith had committed himself, it still remained urgently necessary to avoid stirring up an issue which was bound to cause dissension among the protestants.

It is also not clear why Tyndale should have published the work anonymously. With the exception of some of his earlier translations from the New Testament, all Tyndale's other writings appeared under his own name. By 1533 he was too notorious a heretic to believe that he could protect himself in any way by concealing his name. To explain this difficulty, it has been suggested that Tyndale may have been anxious to avoid making Frith's position more difficult by espousing his cause publicly and thereby associating him with a notorious heretic.[29] But there are objections to this argument too: for 'The Supper of the Lord' was so obviously heretical that it would have been bound to incriminate Frith in any case; while the impudence of the insult to More in the final paragraph does not suggest that its author had any desire to placate the authorities.

On the other hand, there is evidence that Joye was in the habit of publishing works anonymously. Shortly afterwards he published without permission an edition of Tyndale's New Testament, which contained certain unacknowledged and questionable alterations of his own. This led to a bitter quarrel between them, in the course of which Tyndale severely criticised Joye for not giving his own name in the edition he had issued and accused him of playing 'boo peep' with his readers, putting his name to some of his books and concealing it in others.[30] Unfortunately Tyndale does not mention any of Joye's other anonymous publications by name. However, he would hardly have dared to make such a charge against Joye, if he was in any danger of having it turned against himself. Joye, in fact, tried to do so but found it almost impossible. In his *Apology to W. Tyndale* he attempted to counter-attack by pointing out that Tyndale had not published his name when he first brought out his translation of the New Testament, but he does not suggest that Tyndale had adopted the same practice in any of his other works.[31] Had he had reason to believe that 'The Supper of the Lord' was an unacknowledged work by Tyndale, he would hardly have hesitated to bring it up against him. Instead More reported, as we have seen, that many protestants were convinced that Joye was in fact responsible for 'The Supper of the Lord', but that he did not dare to give his name because most of them held him in such low esteem.[32]

At the same time it should be noted that no other work on the sacrament by Joye is recorded in the *Short-Title Catalogue*. Yet according to both Tyndale and More, Joye had a treatise ready on the sacrament at the end of 1532, which he was most anxious to have printed. There is some later evidence to suggest that he succeeded in this ambition. In 1535 Edward Foxe, bishop of Hereford, wrote to Thomas Cromwell from Calais that he had George Joye lodging with him there: he claimed that Joye would 'never again say anything contrary to the present belief concerning the sacrament', and that he was now 'conformable in all points as a Christian man should be'.[33] The implication of his remarks must be that in the past Joye had published heretical views on the sacrament which he was now willing to recant.[34] It is, of course, possible that the treatise of Joye to which Tyndale referred in his letter to Frith never appeared in print. But it seems more likely that it should be identified with 'The Supper of the Lord', or rather with a first draft of it, which was subsequently revised to serve as an answer to More's 'Letter against Frith'.[35]

The contents of 'The Supper of the Lord' unfortunately shed only a dim light on the question of authorship. Foxe justified the inclusion of 'The Supper of the Lord' in his edition of Tyndale's works on the ground that 'the method and phrase agree with' Tyndale's, and although it is possible to detect differences between it and his other writings, it is difficult to assess their significance and one may easily exaggerate their importance.

The doctrinal position expressed in 'The Supper of the Lord' is fundamentally the same as that put forward in Tyndale's *Fruitful and Godly Treatise on the Sacraments*. Both are essentially Zwinglian in their eucharistic teaching. They deny that the sacrament of the Lord's Supper is in any sense a sacrifice, since Christ's death was in itself a complete atonement for the sins of the world. They reject any form of bodily presence, even in the Lutheran sense. They insist that the phrase 'This is my body' is only to be taken metaphorically, and that the bread and wine are symbols of Christ's body and blood but do not contain them in any form.[36]

Nevertheless, there are certain differences of attitude to be found in the two works. In the *Fruitful and Godly Treatise* Tyndale put forward the Zwinglian position in its most extreme form. He emphasises that the sacrament is essentially a 'memorial': it was instituted to testify to Christ's sacrifice on the cross and its main purpose is to keep people in remembrance of this. In consequence the general tendency of the treatise is to minimise the importance of the eucharist. The tone in which it is written is depreciatory. In discussing the nature of the sacrament he uses the word 'only' and 'merely' with great frequency. Thus he remarks that 'the sacraments are bodies of stories only; and that there is none other virtue in them than to testify and exhibit to the senses the covenants and promises made in Christ's blood'.[37] Elsewhere to demonstrate their secondary role, he insists that preaching alone is necessary for salvation, and that the sacraments could if necessary be dispensed with.[38]

The author of 'The Supper of the Lord' appears to have a more profound and mystical conception of the sacrament. 'This is no small sacrament', he declares, 'nor yet irreverently to be entreated; but it is the most glorious and highest sacrament, with all reverence and worship, with thanksgiving, to be ministered, used, received, preached, and solemnly in the face of the congregation to be celebrated'.[39] At the same time it is not merely a memorial of Christ's sacrifice: it is also a sacrament of Christian unity, a token of 'the unity and communion of our hearts, glued unto the whole body of Christ in love'.[40] By participating in the Lord's Supper, the Christian shows that he is incorporated in Christ's Church.[41]

On one point, however, there is a considerable difference between 'The Supper of the Lord' and the rest of Tyndale's writings. 'The Supper of the Lord' concludes with an appeal to the magistrate, as head of the Church, to cause the Gospel to be preached purely and to introduce the true form of celebrating the Lord's Supper. 'Would God the secular princes, which should be the very pastors and head rulers of their congregations, committed unto their care, would first command or suffer the true preachers of God's word to preach the gospel purely and plainly, with discreet liberty, and constitute over each particular parish such curates as can and would preach the word, and that once or twice in the week, appointing unto their flock certain days, after their discretion and zeal to God-ward, to come together to celebrate the Lord's Supper'.[42] Such an appeal to the civil authority to intervene in the affairs of the Church has no parallel in the authenticated writings of Tyndale. Contrary to the general opinion, the belief that the magistrate had an *ex-officio* responsibility for the reform of the Church was not an integral part of protestant thought. Luther for a long time insisted that the magistrate was not in any way concerned with matters of faith:[43] even after 1527, when he finally accepted the necessity for electoral intervention in the Saxon Church, he was careful to point out that the elector could only act as a private Christian and not in virtue of any authority conferred on him by his temporal position.[44] Tyndale who, except in his sacramental beliefs, was profoundly influenced by Luther's teaching, seems to have followed him in not conferring any ecclesiastical functions on the king. Even in *The Obedience of a Christian Man* there is no suggestion that the king has any duties in regard to the reform of the Church. If 'The Supper of the Lord' were the work of Tyndale it would represent a complete revision of his earlier attitude towards the relations of Church and State.[45]

In spite of Foxe's assertions to the contrary there are also some remarkable differences of method and phraseology between 'The Supper of the Lord' and Tyndale's other works. As Henry Walter pointed out,[46] 'The Supper of the Lord' does not contain a single example of the references to the original languages of the Bible, especially Hebrew, with which Tyndale's works normally abound; nor does it make much use of the Old Testament. Yet the *Fruitful and Godly Treatise* begins by declaring that 'to understand the pith of the sacraments, how they came up, and the very meaning of them, we must consider diligently the manners and fashions of the Hebrews',[47] and large sections of it are devoted to describing Old Testament covenants and the signs by which they were confirmed, with erudite discussions of Hebrew etymologies.[48] Even in the brief section on the sacraments in the *Answer to More*, Tyndale suggests that the word Mass is derived from the Hebrew *Misach*.[49] By contrast 'The Supper of the Lord' does not contain a single Hebrew quotation and apart from the conventional statement that the Christian sacraments had Old Testament prototypes in the rites of circumcision and the passover, the Old Testament is completely ignored, the main part of the argument being based on the New Testament and the Fathers.

Arguments from style are notoriously unsatisfactory and it would probably be impossible to establish conclusively that 'The Supper of the Lord' differs from Tyndale's normal manner of writing. Nevertheless, it contains a number of usages which seem to me to be more characteristic of Joye than Tyndale. Thus the eucharist is never described explicitly as a 'memorial', as it is in both the *Fruitful and Godly Treatise* and the *Answer to More*.[50] Throughout 'The Supper of the Lord' Augustine is regularly referred to as 'Austin', and this is the characteristic practice of Joye's *Apology to W. Tyndale* and his *Subversion of More's False Fortress*. Tyndale, however, invariably uses the form 'Augustine'. In addition, the author of 'The Supper of the Lord' is in the habit of appealing frequently to the 'Christian reader', and this form of address is hardly ever varied. In the *Apology* whenever Joye addresses the reader it is always as the 'Christian Reader'. While Tyndale was also in the habit of apostrophising his public, he did not adopt a uniform practice; sometimes he refers to the 'Christian reader', sometimes to the 'godly reader', the 'faithful reader' or even just the 'reader'. A closer examination of the works of both Tyndale and Joye would probably reveal other differences of a similar kind.

These discrepancies might not be a sufficient reason in themselves for denying Tyndale's authorship, but taken in conjunction with the other arguments they assume a much greater importance. In the light of the contemporary evidence there can be little doubt that 'The Supper of the Lord' should be attributed to George Joye and not to William Tyndale.

V

Sir Francis Knollys's Campaign Against the *Jure Divino* Theory of Episcopacy

'This Knight being bred a banished man in *Germany* during the Reign of Queen *Mary*, and conversing with Mr. *Calvin* at *Geneva*, was never after fond of Episcopacy'.
Thomas Fuller, *The Church-History of Britain* (1655), Book ix, Section v, 152.

In his Dictionary Dr. Johnson defined a Dissenter as 'One who, for whatever reasons, refuses the communion of the English Church'.[1] In this sense there were very few protestant dissenters in Elizabethan England. Only the numerically insignificant Brownists and Barrowists carried their opposition to the established order to the point of rejecting the Church of England altogether. The great majority of Elizabethan puritans were not only not Separatists, they viewed the very concept of separation with abhorrence.[2] Like all the sixteenth-century protestant reformers, they believed implicitly in the indivisible character of the Visible Church of Christ. While they accepted that for purposes of external organisation the Visible Church was divided geographically into a series of local or 'particular' churches, each of which was autonomous, they regarded it as axiomatic that within each commonwealth or State there could be only one Church which was the Church of Christ and that to separate from 'those assemblyes which', in Cartwright's phrase, 'have Christ for their head'[3] was to commit the sin of schism.

There is, thus, an important historical difference between the character of protestant dissent in the Elizabethan period and later forms of protestant nonconformity. In the late sixteenth century, in contrast to the period after the Restoration, the mainstream of protestant opposition to the established order came from within the Established Church, not from outside it. The object of most Elizabethan puritans was not to break away from the Church of

England, or even to secure for themselves liberty of worship within it except as a temporary expedient, but rather to bring about a more radical reform of the Church of England, along the lines of the Swiss Reformed Churches, than Elizabeth was prepared to allow. In this sense they were not dissenters at heart. Most Elizabethan puritans were as theologically committed to the idea of a comprehensive national Church, embracing all professed Christians in England, as Whitgift or Hooker. What they objected to was not the idea of an Established Church, but the form which establishment took. Given the opportunity, they would have been as unyielding in imposing their own concepts of uniformity on the Church of England as Elizabeth was in imposing hers.

At the same time, the dividing line between Dissent and Establishment in the Elizabethan period is often hard to determine. Although for convenience historians tend to use the label 'Puritan' to describe all those on the protestant side who criticised the Elizabethan Church for whatever reason, in practice it is anachronistic to think in terms of a clear-cut dichotomy between 'Anglican' and 'Puritan' in the sixteenth century.[4] Not only did most English protestants, until the closing years of the century, share the same theological assumptions, but at the beginning of the reign there was little fundamental disagreement even on matters of worship. In the early 1560s criticism of the 1559 Prayer Book came not only from men like Lawrence Humphrey and Thomas Sampson but also from bishops like Jewel and Parkhurst, who would have preferred to see the worship of the Church of England brought closer into conformity with that of the Swiss Churches, and in the Vestiarian controversy of the 1560s many of the bishops were at first reluctant to enforce the provisions of the Act of Uniformity against the Precisians. Later, in the 1570s and 1580s, the divisions began to harden with the rise of the presbyterian movement and the emergence of a new generation of churchmen such as Whitgift and Bancroft, who were prepared to defend the institutions of the Church of England on their own merits and not simply out of deference to the queen. But even in the 1580s the distinction between critics and supporters of the establishment is not always sharply defined. If the hardcore of opposition was represented by the Disciplinarian Puritans whose aim was the presbyterianisation of the Church of England by constitutional means, there was also—besides the Separatists who rejected the Church of England altogether—a substantial body of moderate opinion which tended to be ambivalent in its attitude towards the established order. Whitgift's policies aroused widespread resentment among clergy and laity alike, but probably only a minority of those who objected to his measures to enforce uniformity wished to see the principles of the Book of Discipline put into practice or the Prayer Book replaced by the Genevan service order. Many puritan ministers, who had scruples about wearing the surplice or using the sign of the cross in baptism, would have been satisfied with the kind of changes which had been proposed in the Convocation of 1563 and which were to be revived in the Millenary Petition of 1603. Similarly there were Calvinist theologians like John Reynolds of Oxford or William Perkins of Cambridge, who were intellectually in sympathy with the presbyterians but who were prepared to accept episcopacy as a human institution. Equally among the laity, opposition to Whitgift's policies came not merely from presbyterian sympathisers but also from many conservative protestants who deplored Whitgift's treatment of the puritan ministers but who had no desire to see any radical revolution in the structure of the Church.

One of the most outspoken lay critics of Whitgift's policies in the 1580s and early 1590s was Sir Francis Knollys.[5] Knollys's career illustrates the difficulties of trying to draw a hard and fast distinction between Puritan and Anglican, critics and supporters of the Established Church, in the reign of Elizabeth. Born about 1514, he belonged, like his near contemporary, Lord Burghley, to a generation whose religious and political attitudes had been formed in the reigns of Henry VIII and Edward VI. A staunch protestant he was one of the few laymen of any prominence to have been an exile on the Continent in Mary's reign, although whether he ever visited Geneva, as Fuller claimed, is uncertain.[6] On his return to England at Elizabeth's accession, he was immediately appointed Vice-chamberlain of the Royal Household and a member of the Privy Council—appointments which he owed in large part to the fact that his wife was Elizabeth's first cousin[7]— and he continued to serve Elizabeth loyally in a succession of household offices until his death in 1596. Throughout Elizabeth's reign Knollys stood out as one of the most forthright and persistent champions of the protestant cause on the Privy Council and, although his personal devotion to the queen was never in question, he was one of the few councillors who was prepared to risk incurring Elizabeth's displeasure for the sake of his principles. He was one of the recognised leaders of the protestant party in the House of Commons in 1559;[8] he supported the prophesyings movement in the 1570s and opposed the move to deprive archbishop Grindal of his see on the grounds that it would give encouragement to the catholics;[9] he was a fanatical anti-catholic, like many of his colleagues on the Council, and he was continually pressing for the adoption of more stringent measures against Jesuits and recusants at home and for more active support of foreign protestants abroad.[10] On the other hand, to describe Knollys as a 'Puritan' without careful qualification, as is often done, is misleading.[11] In many respects he was an establishment figure who was deeply committed to what he regarded as the traditional order in Church and State. Despite his running battles with the bishops, he was not opposed to episcopacy as such, only to the manner in which the bishops exercised their authority, and there is no evidence to support Fuller's innuendo that he had imbibed Calvinist ideas of church government from Calvin himself in Geneva.[12] Equally, though he was always ready to intervene on behalf of puritan ministers, there is no evidence that he was opposed in principle to the Prayer Book, which he had helped to pass into law,[13] and he saw nothing incongruous in speaking against puritan measures in the House of Commons when called upon to do so in his capacity as a privy councillor.[14] But above all—and nothing could mark him off more clearly from the Disciplinarian Puritans of the 1580s—he was a fervent supporter of the Royal Supremacy. If his religious outlook was that of an Edwardian protestant, his political ideas had been shaped by the events of the 1530s. As he reminded the House of Commons in 1593, he had been present in parliament sixty years earlier in the twenty-fifth year of Henry VIII's reign, when the main legislation of the Reformation Parliament was enacted,[15] and he remained a thorough-going Henrician in his attitude to the government of the Church until the end of his life. It is this combination of protestantism and Erastianism which provides the key to Knollys's outlook in his later years.

Not only did he believe that protestantism and the Royal Supremacy were mutually interdependent, so that anything which endangered the one constituted a threat to the other, but to a large extent his hostility towards the bishops was inspired by the suspicion that they were secretly conspiring to undo the achievements of the Henrician Reformation.

As he grew older Knollys became increasingly alienated by developments within the Church of England, especially after the appointment of Whitgift as archbishop of Canterbury in 1583. In 1584, when Whitgift launched his first attack on the puritan clergy, Knollys was one of the privy councillors who was most active in challenging the legality of Whitgift's measures and for several months he conducted a bitter personal campaign against the archbishop, accusing him of acting unconstitutionally in suspending preachers, 'zealous in religion and sound in doctrine', for refusing to subscribe his articles, 'whereunto they are not compellable by law', and of seeking 'an absolute power' which 'openeth the highway to the Pope, to her Majesty's utter overthrow'.[16] Unlike the majority of his colleagues on the Privy Council, who gradually came to acquiesce in Whitgift's policies with the passage of time, Knollys never abandoned his hostility towards the archbishop and his repeated protests against Whitgift's treatment of puritan ministers eventually brought down on him the wrath of the queen, who at one point ordered him to desist from any further intervention on their behalf.[17] Elizabeth's reprimand failed to silence Knollys for long. For in the course of 1588 he embarked on a new campaign against the bishops, accusing them of seeking to undermine the Royal Supremacy by claiming that they derived their authority over the inferior clergy *jure divino*, and for the next three years he pursued the matter relentlessly, bombarding Lord Burghley with a succession of letters and memoranda in an effort to persuade him that the bishops should be compelled to acknowledge formally that they derived their authority solely from the queen, and not from any higher source.

Sir Francis Knollys's campaign against the *jure divino* theory of episcopacy is familiar to modern historians through the numerous references to it which occur in Strype's *Life of Whitgift* and his *Annals of the Reformation*, both of which contain important documentary material relating to the affair.[18] In general, Strype's account of the controversy has been accepted uncritically by later writers but a re-examination of the evidence suggests that it stands in need of substantial revision.[19] Strype's basic mistake, which explains much of the confusion in his account, was to assume that Knollys's campaign was chiefly directed against Richard Bancroft's Paul's Cross Sermon of 9 February 1589.[20] As a result he completely misinterpreted several of the documents which he prints, which he rashly concluded were connected with Bancroft's Sermon, when they were not, while he also postdated the beginnings of the controversy by several months. In addition, his account contains numerous errors of detail; documents are misquoted and misattributed, or wrongly dated; in one instance, excerpts from two different letters are cited as if they occur in the same document;[21] in another, different parts of the same letter are quoted in separate places in a manner which suggests that they come from different letters.[22] Fortunately, enough evidence survives to make it possible to reconstruct the history of the controversy in some detail. With the exception of one important set of papers which Strype used in the *Life of Whitgift* and which he was lent in 1711 by Dr. Thomas Brett, the future Non-Juror bishop,[23] all the documents which he cites are still in existence, while these can be supplemented by other MSS. relating to the controversy of which he was unaware. In one important respect, however, the surviving evidence is one-sided: for it consists very largely of letters and papers which were sent by Sir Francis Knollys to Lord Burghley and which are now among the Burghley papers in the Lansdowne collection in the British Library,[24] or at Hatfield, whereas Burghley's replies to Knollys have long since disappeared. As a result, any account of the controversy must reflect the fact that our knowledge of it comes chiefly from Knollys himself and that, whereas Knollys's activities are well documented, we know much less about the reactions of his opponents or even about the part played in the affair by Lord Burghley except for what can be gleaned from Knollys's correspondence.

What precisely triggered off Knollys's campaign is uncertain. Strype based his account on the supposition that it was provoked by Richard Bancroft's famous Paul's Cross Sermon of 9 February 1589, while he also suggested that Knollys was not acting on his own account but was simply a frontman for the Disciplinarian Puritans who supplied him with arguments 'to manage at Court for the party'.[25] However, there is no evidence to support either of these assumptions. In the first place, it can be shown that Knollys had already embarked on his campaign several months before Bancroft delivered his Sermon and that, in fact, Bancroft's Sermon played a much smaller role in the controversy than Strype supposed. Secondly, it is clear from Knollys's correspondence with Lord Burghley that his campaign against the *jure divino* theory of episcopacy was an entirely independent venture in which the leaders of the presbyterian movement were in no way involved.

In part, Knollys's campaign has to be seen as a reaction against the changes which were taking place in the Anglican theory of episcopacy during the 1570s and 1580s.[26] Whereas at the beginning of the reign most Elizabethan churchmen had accepted St. Jerome's view that episcopacy was a purely human institution, which was not introduced into the Church until after the death of the Apostles, and that there was no essential difference between bishops and other ministers, after the outbreak of the Admonition controversy a number of anti-puritan writers began to lay increasing emphasis on the historical antiquity of bishops and to claim that episcopacy rather than presbyterianism represented the traditional form of government used in the Church. The beginnings of this development can be seen in Whitgift's *Answer to the Admonition* (1572) and his *Defence of the Answer* (1574) in which he defended the right of the Church of England to retain the use of bishops on two main grounds: first, that the external government of the Church was a 'thing indifferent', which each particular Church had the right to determine according to its own particular needs and circumstances, and secondly that— contrary to what Cartwright and his associates alleged—distinctions of authority had existed in the Church since the earliest times. In one passage, on which Knollys was later to seize, Whitgift even went so far as to assert that 'this superiority of bishops is God's own institution'.[27] However, the significance of this remark should not be exaggerated, since in general Whitgift based his main argument against the presbyterians on the claim that no set form of church government was prescribed in scripture[28] and he was prepared to concede that all ministers of God's word were

equal '*quoad ministerium*: "touching the ministry",' while insisting that '*quoad ordinem et politiam*: "touching order and
government", there always hath been and must be degrees and
superiority among them'.[29] During the 1580s the historical arguments for episcopacy were developed by such writers as John
Bridges, dean of Salisbury, in his *Defence of the Government
established in the Church of England for Ecclesiastical Matters*
(1587) and Richard Bancroft who, in his Paul's Cross Sermon
of 1589, maintained that the Church had been governed by
bishops continuously since the time of the Apostles or their
immediate successors, although it was not until the appearance of
Hadrian de Saravia's *De Diversis Ministrorum Evangelii Gradibus*
in 1590 that the claim began to be put forward that episcopacy
was instituted directly by Christ. These developments naturally
aroused the suspicions of Sir Francis Knollys who saw in them a
threat not only to the traditional protestant view that episcopacy
was a human institution, but also to the queen's claim to be the
ultimate source of all ecclesiastical jurisdiction, and part of the
purpose of his campaign was to alert Lord Burghley to the dangerous implications of the new theories.

   However, it is significant that at the time when Knollys first
launched his campaign the claim that episcopacy was a divine
institution had only been advanced in the most tentative terms,
and the publication of Saravia's seminal treatise, which was
responsible for the rapid development of the *jure divino* theory in
the 1590s, still lay in the future. It therefore seems probable that
the origins of Knollys's campaign were connected with Elizabeth's
refusal to allow him to continue his opposition to Whitgift's
measures against the puritans and that, whatever its more general
implications, it was primarily intended as a device to enable him
to resume his attacks on the bishops without formally disobeying
the queen. That this is so is suggested by a passage in a letter
which he wrote to Lord Burghley in August 1589, at the height
of the controversy, in which he protested somewhat disingenuously
that no one could accuse him of having failed to abide by the
queen's injunction. 'Yor Lp: shall fynde', he wrote, 'that none of
them [the bishops] shalbe able to prove anye substancyall matter
agaynste me, synce the tyme, that longe since her Majestie at
wynsore did commande me, that I shoulde not deale withe the

purytanns, as then her Majestie called them, because her Majestie did commytt the governmente of Religion to her byshopps onlye, synce the which tyme I have delte no more withe matters of Religion, then dothe appertayne to her Majesties saffetye, consistinge in the true preservacion of her Majesties supreme governmente, the whiche maye best be called matter of her Majesties pollicie, and not matter of Relygyon, althoughe the Jesuytes do call all their treasons matter of Relygyon'.[30]

This passage would seem to imply that, after his confrontation with Elizabeth, Knollys deliberately changed his tactics and began to accuse the bishops of undermining the Royal Supremacy by claiming that they enjoyed their authority *jure divino*, since in this way he could maintain in all sincerity that he was not interfering in matters of religion, but was defending a basic principle of the constitution which it was his duty as a privy councillor to preserve.[31] If this interpretation is correct, it would also explain the fact that throughout the controversy, although Knollys did attack other supporters of episcopacy, including both Bridges and Bancroft, his most persistent criticisms were reserved for Whitgift, whom he repeatedly accused of maintaining the *jus divinum* of bishops in his writings against Cartwright, and why, somewhat surprisingly, in the later stages of the debate he failed to take any account of the much more radical works of Saravia, Bilson and others which appeared in 1590 and the following years.

The beginnings of Knollys's campaign can be dated to the autumn of 1588, several months before Bancroft's Sermon was delivered. For the first document to survive is a long memorandum, written on 4 November 1588 by Dr. John Hammond in answer to two questions which Knollys had put to him concerning the authority of bishops. The original of this letter is now at Hatfield, having been forwarded by Knollys to Lord Burghley.[32] A contemporary copy of it, which had apparently once been in the possession of archbishop Whitgift, was among the MSS. which Strype was lent by Thomas Brett in 1711, and Strype printed it in a much abridged form in his *Life of Whitgift*.[33] Brett's copy, however, appears to have had no date or indication of authorship. Strype therefore assumed erroneously that it was written in the autumn of 1589, while, in keeping with his belief that the Disciplinarian Puritans were behind Knollys's campaign, he suggested—somewhat implausibly, in view of its arguments—that it was the work of either Cartwright or Travers.[34]

The true author, John Hammond, was a prominent civil and ecclesiastical lawyer, whom Knollys was to consult on several occasions during the coming months. Knollys's choice of advisers does, in fact, suggest a much greater degree of political acumen than he is usually credited with: for the two men whose advice he sought during the controversy—Hammond, the civil lawyer, and John Reynolds, the theologian—though strong protestants, were men of moderate views, who were not identified with the presbyterian wing of the puritan movement, and it seems probable that, as a matter of deliberate policy, he avoided any direct association with the Disciplinarians. Of the two, it was Hammond who was to play the more important role in the controversy and during its early stages Knollys appears to have relied very heavily on his advice. From Knollys's point of view Hammond was a particularly valuable ally. He was a person of considerable legal standing: one of the small number of professional civil lawyers, he was a member of the College of Civilians and the High Commission, and a former chancellor of the diocese of London; as an ecclesiastical commissioner, he had played a leading part in the examination of Campion and other Jesuits in the early 1580s; and he was regularly consulted by the Privy Council in the 1580s on matters relating to the Civil Law.[35] In consequence, his opinions could be expected to carry weight with Lord Burghley. On the other hand, despite the fact that he was a civilian, he was a long-standing critic of Whitgift's policies and he had openly attacked the legality of the archbishop's articles in 1584.[36] On the question of church government his views were remarkably similar to those of Knollys himself. Although he appears to have sympathised intellectually with Calvin's theories,[37] as a lawyer he was a firm believer in the Royal Supremacy and he held a strictly Henrician interpretation of the powers of the bishops.

Knollys had apparently requested Hammond's opinion on two issues—'First, whether the name of a bysshoppe, as of an office having superyorytie over many Churches, or over the pastors thereof, be knowne to the Holye Scriptures or not. Second, whether superyorytie commytted to a mynyster of the Worde and sacraments over many Churches and pastors be mayntenable [i.e. permissible] by the Worde of God, or not'.[38] To the first question Hammond gave the standard sixteenth-century protestant reply: 'that the name of bysshops importinge suche superyoritie is not to be founde in the Scryptures. For by the whole course thereof it appearethe that the names of *Episcopus* and *presbyter* imported one function, so as he that was a pastor or elder was also byshoppe, and the bysshope in lyke sorte called elder, and therefore the name of *episcopus*, being no name of dystynction in offyce from the elder, could not importe superyoritie over elders'—a view which he proceeded to support with a detailed examination of the New Testament evidence.[39]

On the second issue Hammond was prepared to argue that, although episcopacy in its modern form was not to be found in the New Testament, it was not forbidden and was therefore permissible. For 'the supreme civyll magystrate in every countrye may appoynte under offycers in the execution of that government which he hathe in ecclesyasticall causes, as well as he may doe in cyvile matters, for the reason is all one in them bothe'. But he was careful to insist that any authority committed to bishops in this way 'is but an humayne ordynance, and may not be intytled to any greater authorytie, nor otherwyse sayd to be God's ordynance, than the offyce of cyvill magistrates be'. As far as England was concerned, he concluded, in a passage which was to supply Knollys with one of his stock arguments in the coming controversy: 'The Bysshopps of our realme do not (so farre as I ever yet harde), nor may not, clayme to themselves any other authorytie then is geeven them by the Statute of the 25 of Kynge Henry the 8., recyted in the fyrst yeare of hir Majesty's raygne, or by other statutes of this lande, neither is it reasonable they should make other clayme, for if it had pleased her Majesty with the wysdome of the realme to have used no bysshopps at all, we could not have complayned justely of any defect in our Churche, or if it had lyked them to lymyte the authorytie of bysshopps to shorter termes, they might not have said they had any wronge. But sythe it hathe pleased her Majesty to use the mynystery of Bysshopps, and to assigne them this authoryte, it must be to me, that am a subjecte, as God's ordynance, and therefore to be obeyed according to St. Paule's rule'.[40]

Hammond's original letter to Knollys of 4 November 1588

ended at this point. But the copy which Strype used included an addendum, or 'A supply to this former part', as Strype terms it, which is not in the MS. at Hatfield and which may have been written at a slightly later date.[41] In this 'Supply', Hammond proceeded to discuss the question whether—even though bishops derived their powers of jurisdiction from the crown—they could be said to enjoy the superior spiritual powers which they possessed in relation to excommunication and ordination by 'Gods immediate institution', or whether this was 'a matter rather so disposed of in their persons, as the rest of their jurisdiction is'. In Hammond's view 'the case' was 'al one'. For the powers which bishops enjoy in excommunication and ordination are powers which belong to the Church as a whole, and the fact that they are assigned to bishops rests solely on human ordinance, not on divine law. In England these powers are conferred on the bishops by 'the laws and policy of this realm'. 'Whereto', he concluded, 'forasmuch as her Majesty giveth life, they must consequently maintain, they do it by her Majesties authority: and so derive it from God: because she is the Lords immediate minister with us. For, if it had pleased her Majesty to have assigned the imposition of hands to the Deans of every cathedral church, or some other number of Ministers, which in no sort were Bishops, but as they be Pastors; there had been no wrong don to their persons, that I can conceive'.[42]

Hammond's letter is important both because it illustrates the extremely Erastian conception of episcopacy held by an Elizabethan ecclesiastical lawyer in the 1580s and also because it provided Knollys with the principal argument which he was to use over the next few years. Throughout the controversy Knollys was to base his main case against the *jure divino* theory of episcopacy on the claim that the English bishops derived their authority from the so-called Ecclesiastical Appointments Act of 1534 (25 Henry VIII c.20),[43] revived in the first year of Elizabeth's reign, and that any suggestion that the bishops received their powers from a higher source than the crown was an infringement of the terms of the Act, which rendered the person so offending liable to the penalties of *praemunire*.

Shortly after receiving it, Knollys forwarded Hammond's letter to Lord Burghley. Burghley's reaction to it is not known, but it was evidently considered important enough for a copy of it to be made and passed on to archbishop Whitgift. During the next few months Knollys continued to press his attack on a number of fronts, although the evidence of his activities is somewhat fragmentary and it is not always easy to fit the details of the story together.

Among the Burghley MSS. in the Lansdowne collection is another paper on the subject of the superiority of bishops, dated 'In Januarie 1588 [9]', which was also forwarded by Knollys to Lord Burghley.[44] This paper is unsigned and its precise significance in the controversy is obscure, since it consists merely of a list of references to authors who maintained the view that episcopacy was a human institution, ranging from St. Jerome to such sixteenth-century protestant writers as Calvin, Musculus, Beza and Lambertus Danaeus.[45] However, there can be little doubt that Hammond was the author of this paper as well, since the authors named in it are virtually identical with those mentioned by Strype as having been quoted in the concluding part of the 'Supply' to Hammond's letter of 4 November 1588, which he did not print.[46]

The date of this paper also suggests the possibility that it may have been connected with another controversy in which Knollys became involved at the beginning of 1589. Among the MSS. which Strype was lent by Thomas Brett, and which have since disappeared, were copies of three other papers relating to the question of the superiority of bishops, which were stitched together with the text of Hammond's letter of 4 November 1588.[47] The first two of these were printed by Strype in the *Life of Whitgift* and consisted of a syllogism by Sir Francis Knollys attacking a sermon delivered by an unnamed preacher on 12 January 1588[9] together with a reply to it by the preacher concerned,[48] while the third, which Strype omitted—'being', as he put it, 'too long, and interrupting the history if it were here inserted'—comprised an answer to the preacher's reply.[49] Because of its subject matter, Strype jumped to the conclusion that Knollys's syllogism was directed against Bancroft's famous Paul's Cross Sermon and he automatically attributed the preacher's reply to Bancroft.[50] In fact, Strype's account is entirely misleading: for, as he should have noted, Knollys's syllogism refers to a sermon preached on 12 January 1588/9, whereas Bancroft's sermon was delivered a month later on 9 February 1588/9.[51] By a fortunate chance a document survives among the Rawlinson MSS. in the Bodleian which is either the original or a contemporary copy of the reply to the preacher's answer to Knollys's syllogism, which was included among the Brett MSS. but which Strype forbore to print on account of its length; and from this it is possible to identify the name of the preacher on 12 January 1588/9 as well as to fill in some of the gaps in Strype's account. This paper is headed 'Short observacions of the answeares, delivered by Do: Bridges, to [yor Honoures *deleted*] Sr ffr. Knowles syllogisme',[52] from which it appears that the preacher was Dr. John Bridges, dean of Salisbury, the author of the *Defence of the Government Established in the Church of England for Ecclesiastical Matters.*

The text of Bridges's sermon does not survive, but it is possible to deduce his general line of argument from his reply to Knollys's syllogism. In his syllogism Knollys had written:

'Major. Whosoever doth maintain, that any subject of this realm hath superiority over the persons of the Clergy, otherwise than from and by her Majesty's authority, he doth injury to her Majesty's supremacy.

Minor. The preacher, upon Sunday the 12th of January, 1588, maintained, that the Bishops of this realm had superiority over the inferior Clergy, otherwise than by and from her Majesty's authority, namely, *jure divino.*

Conclus. Ergo, the preacher therein did injury to her Majesty's supremacy: unless he can better expound this saying than I can imagine'.[53]

In his answer Bridges did not deny that he had claimed that bishops enjoyed their authority *jure divino.* Instead he attempted to defend himself against the charge that the views he had expressed in his sermon were in any way inimical to the Royal Supremacy. Both the major and the minor premise of Knollys's syllogism, he insisted, were 'captiously set down; the cavil being hidden in the word *otherwise*'. For it was quite possible for bishops to 'hold in some superiority, both *jure divino* and *jure humano*'. This could happen in either of two ways. Firstly, there were some powers which bishops possessed, 'as in superiority of ordaining and consecrating Ministers, and excommunicating', where '*jus humanum* and her Majesty's supremacy do approve, maintain, and corroborate *jus divinum*. To which purpose *jus humanum* doth *subservire juri divino*, without any abasement at all thereunto'. Secondly, there were other ecclesiastical matters, which were not purely spiritual but belonged to the sphere of human law, which nevertheless 'so long as they are concordant with the general rule of St. Paul, of *edifying* in order and comeliness, *jus divinum* doth on the other side approve, maintain, and corroborate them. So that both ways they may well be said to be *jure divino:* but especially the former'. At the same time, he vigorously repudiated the charge that in maintaining the view that the bishops' authority was in some sense *jure divino* he was thereby suggesting that they did not derive their superiority over the inferior clergy from the queen. 'For I never avouched any such thing: which had been clean contrary to the chief scope of my sermon; and against all mine own writings, both against the Papists and against these inordinate brethren, impugning her Majesty's laws, and calling in question her Majesty's supreme authority in ecclesiastical matters'. Finally, after declaring that those who had heard his sermon could testify that the charges made against him were entirely groundless, he attempted to turn Knollys's syllogism against the puritans by arguing that it was writers like Cartwright, Fenner, Travers, Penry and the rest who did injury to her Majesty's supremacy. For they 'do maintain, that the Doctors, the Pastors, the seignory of governing Elders, and the Deacons, such as they pretend to be erected in every congregation throughout the realm, have superiority over the persons, either of the Clergy, or of the Laity, *otherwise than from and by her Majesty's authority*, namely, *jure divino*'.[54]

The Rawlinson copy of the 'Short observacons of the answeares, delivered by Do: Bridges, to Sr ffr. Knowles syllogisme' is unsigned, but again there can be little doubt that it was the work of Hammond. From such evidence as survives it is clear that Hammond was the person on whose advice Knollys relied principally during the spring and summer of 1589,[55] and it is therefore likely that he would have referred Bridges's answer to him for his comments. But, in addition, there is considerable internal evidence which points to Hammond's authorship. In the first place, the general line of argument in the 'Short observations' bears a close resemblance to that of Hammond's letter of 4 November 1588 and the 'Supply' to it printed in Strype. Secondly, there is a remarkable similarity between the list of authors cited in the 'Short observations' and those cited in the 'Supply' to Hammond's letter and the Lansdowne paper of January, 1588/9, which suggests very strongly that all three papers must have been written by the same person.[56]

In spite of its title the 'Short observations' is a long document running to $3\frac{1}{4}$ closely written sides of foolscap. It is therefore only possible to summarise its arguments briefly.[57] In forwarding Bridges's answer to Hammond, Knollys had apparently raised the question whether Bridges's view might be considered treasonable. Hammond began his reply with lawyer-like caution by insisting that he was not competent to pronounce on 'what is treason, or not treason, because it is a pointe of another skill[58] then I doe professe'. At the same time he was careful to stress that, since he had not heard Bridges's sermon itself, he could only judge him by what he had written in his answer. However, on the basis of this he was prepared to conclude that Dr. Bridges 'dealeth uniustly with hir Majestie. ffor, as I doe conceave, hee yeldeth not unto hir hir full right in hir supreme auctoritie' (fol. 43).

Hammond then proceeded to attack Bridges's claim that bishops could enjoy their authority both *jure divino* and *jure humano* as being based on a misuse of language. 'I knowe not, howe I may allowe the manner of this speache, nor what warrant hee hathe thus to confounde the termes . . . ffor when question is of any matter, whether it be Juris divini, or Juris humani: I always understoode the question to be made of too opposite kindes which can not concurre in one matter, and that by theis wordes vz. Iuris divini, are ment such as have theire immediate ordinance from God. And vz. Juris humani, such as take theire immediate auctoritie and being from man'. Therefore, it is logically impossible to say that something is both *juris divini* and *juris humani*, 'insomuch as one thing canot proceede immediatly from twoe such distinct auctorities'. Nor is it satisfactory to argue, as Bridges does, that 'by way of approbacion' something may be said to belong to both laws. For normally the purpose of discussing whether something is *juris divini* or *juris humani* is to discover 'whether they be chaungable by civil auctoritie, or not' . . . 'in which case hee showld receave a sleevles answeare that were tolde, that the matter in question were in respect of ye magistrates allowance Juris humani, for so were hee noe whit nearer the resolucion which hee sought, then he was before' (fol. 43).

However, in Hammond's view, Bridges's 'abuse of termes' was 'not the thing, which offendeth hir Majesties auctoritie'. The real point at issue was that 'hee maintaineth that a Bisshops superioritie is in some points de Jure divino, meaning, as I suppose, the immediate ordinance of God, for other definition I knowe not'. Here again, he insisted, Bridges's case rested on dubious logic. For his argument appeared to be that, because ordination and excommunication were divine institutions—'as in truth they bee'—it must follow that 'therefore this superioritie imployd in the execucion of them, is also de Jure divino, & so consequently the immediate ordinance of God'. Such an argument, Hammond contended, if this was what Bridges meant—for he complained with some justification of the obscurity of Bridges's language—involved an obvious logical fallacy. For whereas a practice may be prescribed in general terms in divine law, the particular manner in which it is exercised may be left to human laws to determine. As an example, Hammond cited the maintenance of ministers of the Word and the payment of tithes. In his view, it is 'an immediate ordinance of God' that ministers should be provided with adequate maintenance. But it does not follow from this that the payment of tithes to the clergy is therefore required by divine law, since ministers may be provided for in other and better ways and tithes may be said to have 'theire ground in humane pollicie' only (fol. 43).

Hammond, therefore, suggested that logically Bridges would have been on safer ground if he had maintained that it was 'by the immediate ordinance of God' that bishops 'doe alone ordaine ministers and doe excommunicate': for he could then have argued that 'their superioritie in some functiones is Gods immediate ordinance'. On the other hand, had he done so, he would immediately have laid himself open to attack on historical grounds: 'For I think that the most learned doe agree that in the times of the apostles, these offices were performed by the pastors, and elders in everie church in common, and that the office of a

bishops calling alone was not knowne to the scriptures. or if that
will not be granted yet it cannot be denied that since the times of
the apostles, and when this office began to gather strength, it
extended first but to one church, and in one church had for a
good space, nether ordinance, nor excommunication tyed unto it.
At other times having ordinacion it wanted the other'. Rather
than argue the point at length—'sith . . . I have no leasure to
oppose better reasons of myne owne'—Hammond then proceeded
to quote a long series of extracts from ancient and contemporary
writers, ranging from Jerome and Augustine to Calvin, Musculus,
Zanchius, Beza and others in the sixteenth century, in support of
his contention 'that bishopes are wholie her [Majesty's] creatures,
and not the immedeate creatures of God at all' (fols. 43v–44).

Finally, Hammond dismissed Bridges's attempt to turn Knollys's
syllogism against the Disciplinarian Puritans as 'but a verie
slender shift'. The two cases, he insisted somewhat disingenuously,
were not comparable and did 'not offer lyke wrong to her
majesties autoritie'. For whereas 'D.Bridges in an office merelie
positive, flatlie excludeth her majesties authoritie', the puritans'
claims related to offices which were 'not of mans, but of Gods
immediate creacion . . . wherein on their parte there is no more
offence then if they should say that matrimonie in all persons
were Gods ordinance, and tooke no part of force from positive
lawe'. However, Hammond must have realised that he was
treading on dangerous ground, for he hastily proceeded to explain
in his final paragraph that he was not in any way opposed to
'Bishops receaved by her majestie in place of pastors & elders'—
of whom he thought 'reverentlie'. For he was 'of opinion, that if
the condicion of our times, or the frame of our Realme cannott
admitt that government which was used in the times of the
apostles . . . a moderate government committed to a bishop without impeachment of the purpose of the holie ghost is well to be
allowed'. 'That case of necessitie excepted', however, he shared
the view of Zanchius that the closer the Church approximated to
the simplicity of the apostles the better (fols. 44–44v).

Further light on Knollys's activities during the early months of
1589 is thrown by a letter he wrote to Sir Francis Walsingham
on 20 March 1588/9. From this letter it is clear that, following
Hammond's letter of 4 November 1588, he had launched an

open attack on Whitgift and the bishops at court, accusing them
of maintaining that they enjoyed their authority *jure divino*, and
that, at the same time as he was pursuing his controversy with
Bridges, he was trying to persuade Lord Burghley that the bishops'
interpretation of their authority constituted a threat to the Royal
Supremacy which could only be resolved by formally requiring
them to acknowledge that their powers were derived solely from
the queen. Walsingham was away from court sick during the
spring of 1589[59] and Knollys's letter was designed to inform him
of the state of the controversy, in the hope, no doubt, that he
would lend his weight to Knollys's campaign. Knollys states that
on the previous day he had sent Walsingham a 'wryting...
concerning the superioritie of Bysshops', which may have been a
copy either of Hammond's letter of 4 November 1588, or possibly
of the 'Short observations', if it had been written by that date. He
then goes on to give Walsingham his version of the dispute. 'My
lorde archebysshopp & the reste', he writes, 'do take a dangerous
course agaynste hir Majesties supreme government, ffor they do
clayme a superioritie of government to be knytte to theyre
byshopryckes Jure divino dyrectlye': for, although they admit that
'all the superioritie that they have as bysshops' is derived 'by way
of medyacion of hir Majestie', in the sense that it is the queen
who appoints them as bishops, nevertheless, once they have been
made bishops by the queen, they claim that 'theyre sayd superyoritie' is 'due unto them as knytte unto theyre bysshoprycke
dyrectly Jure divino'. Unfortunately the Lord Treasurer is
'partely perswadid' that they 'do not denye yt theyre superioritie
is houlden by them as a grawnte geeven unto them dyrectlye from
hir Majestie and that hence they do not claim it *jure divino*. But
in fact, Knollys insists, he has clear evidence to the contrary.
'But I must needes saye yt my lord archebysshoppe of Canterburye, & mye lorde Bysshoppe of Wynchester[60] have protested, &
playnely avowed unto me that the bysshops of England have a
superioritie over theyre inferyor bretherne dyrectlye Jure divino',
while the same claims are also to be found in 'the Bysshoppe of
Canterburyes booke agaynst Cartewryghte (when the sayd
bysshoppe was but Doctor Whytegyfte)' which 'dothe manyfestlye
declare the sayd archebysshops opynion in yt behalffe in manye
places of the sayd booke'. However, Knollys suggests that if

Burghley would demand of the bishops in the queen's name whether they claimed their authority *jure divino*, the matter could easily be resolved; for they would hardly dare to insist on their claims, 'oneles it be upon hope yt hir Majestie would yeelde unto them theyre claymed superioritie to the preiudice of hir owne supreme government, & to the lyghte regarde of the opening of the highewaye to poperye to be made by the Jesuites to followe upon the same'.[61]

During the next two months Knollys continued to press his attack, apparently with some success; for, at the end of May, he succeeded in persuading Burghley to agree to a meeting with Hammond to enable the latter to present the case against the bishops. On 22 May Knollys wrote to Hammond to advise him on what course of action to adopt at his meeting with the Lord Treasurer. 'To the end that you may understand mine advice gratis', he wrote, '. . . I do think it best for you, upon your conference, to persuade my Lord Treasurer that first, it will please him to make her Majesty privy of the state of the controversy between the claim of the bishops' superiority over their inferior clergy; that they do not claim it directly from her Majesty's grant, but they claim it as appertaining to their persons by God's own ordinance, as soon as her Majesty hath made them Bishops. And that my Lord Treasurer will inform her Majesty, also, how greatly this claim is prejudicial to her Majesty's supreme government'. He then went on to suggest that Hammond should try to persuade Burghley to urge the queen to make the bishops set down their case in writing and to allow Hammond to reply to it, that thereby the bishops might be driven to revoke their claims— 'or else her Majesty by your answer to their pretended claim may plainly see how injuriously against her Majesty's supreme government the said Bishops do seek by secret means to defraud her Majesty of her supreme government, given her directly and plainly from God, as well over the clergy as over the laity'. Two days later, on 24 May, Knollys forwarded a copy of this letter to Burghley, since, as he put it, 'I do take it necessary to make your Lordship privy of all my doings that may concern her Majesty's safety. . . . For I do know that, if any good shall be done for the preservation of her Majesty's safety against the dangerous deprivation of her Majesty's supreme government, privily sought by the

undermining ambition and covetousness of some of our Bishops,
... it must be done by your Lordship's good mediation, through
your wise and modest government'.[62]

The outcome of Hammond's interview with Burghley is not
known, but it is clear that, if Knollys believed that Hammond
would succeed in convincing him of the need to take positive
action against the bishops, he was disappointed. Burghley's attitude throughout the controversy seems to have been equivocal.
On the one hand, he was probably in basic sympathy with
Knollys's view on episcopacy and Knollys certainly interpreted
some of his letters as giving him encouragement. On the other
hand, Burghley's relationship with Whitgift had changed since
1584 and, whatever his personal feelings in the matter, he clearly
had no desire to be drawn into an open conflict with the archbishop on the issue, which in any case he probably regarded as of
no great importance. As a result his policy appears to have been
to temporise. While he endured Knollys's endless tirades with
remarkable patience, he seems to have taken as little action as he
could beyond passing some of Knollys's memoranda on to Whitgift
and he refused to raise the issue with the queen.

During the summer of 1589 Knollys was away from court,[63]
but he continued to pour out a stream of letters to Burghley from
the country which became increasingly plaintive as the summer
progressed. The first of these was written on 5 July from Oxford,
where he had been attending the assizes in his capacity as Lord
Lieutenant of the county. It is a long letter, which was ostensibly
concerned with various matters that had arisen during the course
of his visit to Oxford, but it is clear that the question which was
uppermost in his mind was that of the queen's supremacy and in
his conclusion he returned once more to the subject of his campaign against the bishops. This time he appealed to Burghley and
the Lord Chancellor, Sir Christopher Hatton, for their support,
'upon whose good allowaunce and backinge I must muche
depende, because I know my great lacke of wisdome, to keep or to
obtayne any credite with her Majestie'. He, therefore, requested
Burghley to show his letter to the Lord Chancellor[64] that 'ther-
uppon it may please yow two, either to incorage me or to discorage
me in my travell in this behalf'. At the same time he reaffirmed
his belief that if 'by your two LLps: perswacions' Whitgift could

be induced to make the bishops acknowledge publicly 'that they have no superioritie over ther inferior brethren, but suche as is to be derived unto them directlye from her Majesties supreame auctoritie and governmente', this would 'greatly advaunce Her Majesties due honor and saffetye, and . . . overthrow the trayterous praquetices of all Jesuytes and semynaryes, that now to prowdlye do come into this Realme'.[65]

Burghley's reply was discouraging and it immediately evoked a long and aggrieved letter from Knollys, dated from his house at Ewelme on 4 August 1589. 'I have receyved your Lps letter of the firste of Auguste', he began, 'wherein I have received verie smale comforte, and smale hope of the good mayntenance of her Majesties saffetye, consisting in the syncere mayntenance of her Majesties supreme governmente agaynste the covetous ambicion of clergie rulers: for your Lp: sayeth, that the questyon is verie dysputable, whereof I wrote unto your Lp:'. He then proceeded to reiterate his complaints at great length and in a rambling fashion, launching first into a bitter attack on 'the nature of covetous ambicion in churche governors' in all ages, as typified by 'the prowde ambicious governmente of the scribes and Pharises' in the time of Christ, before turning once more to the question of 'the superioritie of byshopps', which he now insisted that Christ had settled once and for all when he forbade his apostles to contend for superiority among themselves. 'But', he added, 'here you muste not take me, that I do denye that byshopps maye have anye lordlye auctoritie or dignitie that they have inioyed, so that they clayme it not from a higher auctoritie, then directlye from her Majesties grante'. What had particularly stung Knollys in Burghley's letter was his remark that the question was disputable; and, after protesting that he had no wish 'to contende withe your Lp:', he went on to suggest—almost certainly correctly—'that the cause of your Lps: writinge unto me, that the questyon is verie dysputable, is not for that your Lp: is of the opinion, but rather for that your Lp: woulde brydell and staye me, from runnynge to faste befor your Lp: in the matter of her Majesties saffetie'. Finally, he protested with some asperity than even if Burghley were 'to sett all the byshopps and all their favorers agaynste me, to prove me a distourber of their governmente in their suppressinge of preachers or otherwyse', they would be unable—as has already been quoted—'to prove anye substancyall matter agaynste me, synce the tyme, that longe since her Majestie at wynsore did commande me, that I shoulde not deale withe the purytanns, as then her Majestie called them'.[66]

Knollys's next letter, written from his estate at Rotherfield Grays on 15 August, was more cheerful. In the interval Burghley had sent him a paper written by an unnamed divine at court in answer apparently to a paper by Hammond 'touchinge superioritie of byshopps'.[67] In an accompanying letter Burghley had made some critical comments on the views expressed by the divine and Knollys interpreted these as a mark of encouragement. 'My verie good Lo:', he writes, 'I have perusede yor courtlye, learned devine his wrytinge, whiche you sente unto me, And I am glad that yor Lp: did myslike his answer to the beginninge of my booke'. In forwarding the paper to Knollys Burghley had apparently not disclosed the identity of its author, but Knollys was confident that he knew who it was. 'And I do know but one chapleyne of her Majesties, that I can gesse, that wolde write with suche audacitie, agaynste the playne truethe of the scripture. ffor he sayethe by waye of collection, that because St Paule did apoynte Tymothie and Tytus to ordayne elders in everie congregacion, that therefore he takes it proved, that they had superioritie over other elders. Althoughe the scripture sett downe by St Paule dothe make no mencion, that either Tymothie or Tytus were byshopps, or that they had superioritie over other elders'. If such proofs are allowed, it is no wonder, Knollys added scornfully, that the bishops' claim of superiority may be alleged to be disputable. He was therefore returning the divine's paper to Burghley with the request that he should send it to 'the grave, learned man aforesayde'—i.e. Hammond—to be answered.[68]

Unfortunately, Knollys does not state in his letter whom he suspected the author of the paper to be. However, a possible clue to the writer's identity is provided by a letter written by Matthew Hutton, the newly appointed bishop of Durham, to archbishop Whitgift on 10 October 1589. In this letter Hutton gave Whitgift a report of a conversation that he had had sometime previously with Burghley and Walsingham at a private dinner in the Lord Treasurer's apartments at court, 'where we three only did dine together'. At this meeting various topics were discussed, among them 'the *antiquity* and *lawfulness* of a Bishop'. According to Hutton, when he was asked about the authority of bishops, he had answered by citing Titus i and II Timothy v and he had argued that, although it was true that the terms *Episcopus* and *Presbyter* were sometimes used interchangeably in the New Testament, nevertheless it was 'certain that there was an office in the Apostles time, which Titus and Timothy did exercise, which was distinct from the office of them who had only authority to preach and minister the sacraments, but not to appoint Priests, and censure offenders'.[69] In view of Hutton's emphasis on the cases of Timothy and Titus and the fact that his meeting with Burghley and Walsingham had clearly taken place several weeks before the date of his letter to Whitgift, possibly about the time that Burghley forwarded 'the courtly, learned divine's paper to Knollys, it seems plausible to assume that he was the divine in question.

If Knollys's letter of 15 August suggests a revival of confidence, the mood did not last. A fortnight later, on 30 August, he concluded a long letter to Burghley and Walsingham, dealing with the capture of a catholic recusant, named Randall, with a bitter complaint about the lack of support he was receiving from Burghley and other members of the Privy Council in the matter of the queen's supremacy. 'But my good lorde, to be playne withe you [he wrote after recounting the details of Randall's arrest] I do stande almoste discoraged to serve her Majestie faythfullye agaynste these popishe traytors, and trayterous recusantes, because I do not fynde myselfe well backed nor countenaunced, in mye standinge in defence of her Majesties righte in her supreame governmente agaynste the fowle claymed superioritie of byshopps, not as undergovernors to her Majestie, but as supreme governors from above her Majestie, to the overthrowe of her Majesties supreame governmente: the which her Majesties supreme governmente, I do wonder and am abashed to see that cheif councellors of this estate do not stande to the defence thereof, agaynste the sayd byshopps'.[70]

Burghley's reply was evidently intended to mollify Knollys: for in a short letter, dated from Ewelme on 18 September 1589, Knollys expressed himself in general agreement with arguments that Burghley had used: 'I have receyved your Lps letter of the xvth hereof, and I muste needes agree with yor Lp: to thinke, that our byshopps and all mynysters of the worde hav their auctoritie which is called, potestas clavium, from the word of God: but to have superioritie one above another, is a posytyve ordenance by wysdome of men to avoyde confucion. And I do thinke also withe your Lp:, that none of our byshopps can mayntayne the contrarie: althoe their claymed superioritie, and their unlawfull urginge of subscription dothe shewe their ambicion, and covetousnes, to the preiudice of her Majesties supreme governmente to manefestlye, whereof I will speake more hereafter'.[71]

However, the fact that Burghley was prepared to state categorically that the bishops derived their superior authority from positive law does not mean that he was any more willing than he had been to take action against the bishops; and it seems probable that the main purpose of his letter was to try to persuade Knollys that his fears were ungrounded, since the bishops did not claim their authority *jure divino*, although Knollys obviously remained unconvinced.

Although Bancroft's Paul's Cross Sermon played a much less significant part in the controversy than Strype attributed to it, it did not entirely escape Knollys's attention. Strype erroneously believed that Bancroft's Sermon was a manifesto of the *jure divino* theory of episcopacy, but, in fact, this is not the case. Although Bancroft himself was later to claim under the influence of Saravia that episcopacy was instituted by Christ,[72] in his Sermon, which was delivered the year before Saravia's tract was published, he confined himself to arguing, as Whitgift and Bridges had done before him, that episcopacy was the traditional form of government which had been used in the Church since the time of the Apostles, whereas the presbyterian system was a newfangled invention.[73] Nevertheless, the general tenor of Bancroft's Sermon was calculated to arouse Knollys's suspicions and at some point in the summer of 1589 he wrote to Dr. John Reynolds of Oxford for his comments on two specific questions arising out of it—first, whether Bancroft could be accused of maintaining the *jus divinum* of episcopacy indirectly, if not directly, and, secondly, whether he was justified in alleging that both Jerome and Calvin appeared to admit that bishops had existed in the Church since the time of St. Mark.[74] On 19 September 1589 Reynolds sent

Knollys a long and scholarly reply, which later came to be highly regarded as a defence of the traditional sixteenth-century view that episcopacy was a human institution.[75] Though a Calvinist in theology, Reynolds, like Hammond, was a moderate and his criticisms of Bancroft were cautiously expressed. On the first point raised by Knollys, he was prepared to agree that Bancroft 'seemeth to avouch the superioritie, wch Bishops have among us over the clergie, to be of Gods owne ordinance; though not by expresse wordes, yet by necessarie consequence, in that he affirmeth their opinion, who impugne that superioritie, to be heresie'. 'Wherein', he continued, 'I must confesse that he hath committed an oversight in my iudgement: and himselfe, I thinke, if he be advertised thereof, will acknowledge it'.[76] He then proceeded to attack Bancroft's argument that episcopacy had existed since apostolic times with a wealth of learned references to the Fathers and to medieval and sixteenth-century writers. Reynolds's answer to Knollys's second question followed logically from this. Bancroft, he insisted, was completely unjustified when 'he affirmeth, that S.Jerom saith, and Mr Calvin seemeth on his report to confesse, that Bishops have had the said superioritie ever since the tyme of S.Marke the Evangelist . . . sith nether Jerom saith it, nether doth Calvin seeme to confesse it on his report.' And after a brief examination of the evidence he concluded 'it is certaine that neither of them doth affirme, that Bishops have so long tyme had such superiorite, as D. Bancroft seemeth to father upon them'.[77] As he had done with Hammond's memoranda, Knollys forwarded Reynolds's letter in due course to Lord Burghley, but again Burghley's response is not known.

Shortly after his letter to Burghley of 18 September 1589, Knollys returned to court and there are no more letters from him to Lord Burghley on the subject of episcopacy for several months. However, it would be wrong to interpret this as meaning that he had abandoned his campaign. At court Knollys would have been in a position to press his arguments on Burghley in person and, although the evidence is fragmentary, it is clear that throughout the whole of 1590 he continued to be preoccupied with the question of the *jure divino* theory of episcopacy and that he was still actively campaigning to have the bishops compelled to acknowledge that they derived their authority solely from the crown.

An indication of Knollys's continued concern with the problem is provided by a letter which he wrote to Lord Burghley in the spring of 1590 on behalf of a puritan minister, named William Hubbock, who had been cited before the High Commission for preaching an allegedly seditious sermon.[78] It is clear from an earlier letter from Knollys to Burghley, dated 29 March 1590, that they had both tried to intercede with Whitgift on Hubbock's behalf, but without success.[79] Two days later, on 31 March, having in the meantime received from Burghley Whitgift's answer to Burghley's letter, together 'with the decree of the greate commyssioners agaynst Mr Hubbocke', Knollys wrote again to the Lord Treasurer to protest against Whitgift's treatment of Hubbock and he took the opportunity to launch a general attack on the archbishop's policies. After reminding Burghley how often Whitgift had opposed parliament's requests for measures to encourage a learned ministry, and 'how greatelye (if not tyrannouslye) the archebysshoppe hathe urged subscription to his owne artycles wthout law', he returned once more to the theme of the bishops' claim to divine right: 'And yor lordshyppe dothe also knowe how playnelye the sayd archbysshoppe in his book intytled, *Doctor Whytguift against Cartwryght*, the sayd archbyssoppe hath claymed in the ryghte of all bysshops a superyorytie belonging to them, over all the inferyor clargye from godes owne ordynance, to the popyshe iniurye of hir Majesties supreme government. Now it is no suffycyent recompence for the archebysshoppe to say barelye, yt he dothe not clayme at this present a superyorytie over the inferyor clargye from gods owne ordynance, oneles the sayd archebysshoppe wyll also retracte his clayme of superyorytie from godes owne ordynance sett downe in his prynted booke ... as before is sayd without the which retractacion hir Majesties supreme government can neither be salved, nor preserved (as I do thinke)'. He, therefore, appealed to Burghley 'to have a zealous care of hir Majesties saffetye', and he urged him that the only way 'to avoyde hir Majesties extreme danger, so vyolentlye intended & labored by the pope & the kynge of Spayne & by theyre confederates now in this dangerous tyme', was 'to abate the ambytion and covetousnes of bysshops' by making them acknowledge that they had no superiority over the inferior clergy except such as was granted to them from the queen, in accordance with the statute of 25 Henry VIII, revived in the first year of Elizabeth. 'By which statute the bysshopps are barred from offending of hir Majesties prerogatyve royall, and from offending of the lawes & customes of the realme'. 'Whereby', he went on to assert—putting forward a novel constitutional doctrine, of which Elizabeth would have disapproved profoundly—'the sayd bysshops are not onelye subiecte to the supreme government of hir Majestie: But also subiecte and answerable to the councellors of estate in yt behalffe'.[80]

There are interesting parallels between this letter and a paper which Knollys drew up a few weeks later, a copy of which survives among Robert Beal's papers in the Yelverton MSS. The paper, which is headed 'A true Declaracion of some partes of the misgovernment of the Churche of England by the Bysshoppes at this day, written the.16.day of May. 1590', consists of two lengthy quotations—the first from the statute, 25 Henry VIII c.20 (the Ecclesiastical Appointments Act of 1534), to which he had referred so frequently in the course of the controversy, and the second from Whitgift's *Defence of the Answer*—each of which is followed by brief comments by Knollys. In his comments on the first passage, Knollys argues that by this Act it is manifest that the bishops have no superiority over the inferior clergy 'otherwyse then is lymyted unto them by Statute', and that 'whosoever offendethe in any parte of the sayd Statute' is liable to the penalties of *praemunire*. From which it follows, he maintains, that all bishops and their under-officers who have deprived preachers 'by vertue of theire offyce as Bysshops, without a good and lawfull commission from hir Majestie are fallen into the penalty of the premunire, by offending of the prerogatyve royall of hir Majestie, and by offending of the Lawes and Customes of this realme'. The passage from Whitgift is of particular interest for the study of the controversy, since it contains the statement that 'this superioritye of bysshops is gods owne instytucion', and it is clearly the passage that Knollys had chiefly in mind whenever he accused Whitgift of maintaining the *jus divinum* of bishops in his writings against Cartwright.[81] Not surprisingly, Knollys's comment on it is that 'this Clayme of superioritye of Bysshops aforesayd to be gods owne instytucion, is dyrectlye agaynst hir Majesties prerogatyve royall in hir supreme government', and therefore it 'must necessarilye be retracted, as repugnant to hir Majesties supreme government, and to hir Majesties prerogatyve royall'. However, he then went on to put forward the curiously Henrician suggestion that in order 'to avoid this ambytious and covetous preiudice to kinges and princes' the latter should 'appoynt a temporall magistrate to be his and theyre deputyes or vicegerent yt may examyne and take accompte of all the decrees and doinges of bysshops, in theyre courtes, or otherwyse, whereby the pre-rogatyve royall and the supreme government of kinges and princes may be saffely preserved and mayntened'.[82]

This paper presents something of a mystery, since the circum-stances in which it was written are not known and there is no evidence to show what use, if any, Knollys made of it. From its contents it would appear to have been written while the issues raised by Hubbock's case were still very much in his mind, and it may represent an attempt by Knollys to marshal more clearly the arguments that he had used in his letter of 31 March. At the same time, in view of its date, it is possible that it may be con-nected with a draft letter from Knollys to queen Elizabeth, which is preserved among the Burghley papers in the Lansdowne MSS. and which is endorsed 'the. 22. of May. 1590'.[83] This letter contains the well-known passage in which Knollys apologises for 'myne oulde error, to saye, that I have not heretofore (in wayghtye matters) used suche temperancye of speache as wyser men have done to your Majestie, nether have I suppressed myne abundant affections (in so wayghtye cases) as wyser men have done & should doe'. Strype consequently assumed that this letter was written by Knollys in order to make his peace with the queen and he inter-preted it as evidence that 'in the month of May, the Queen was displeased with him for meddling in this matter of the constitution of her Bishops; and, as it seems, commanded his absence'.[84] But Strype's interpretation is almost certainly incorrect. In the first place, the letter is only a draft and there is no evidence that it was ever sent to the queen. Secondly, it contains no reference to Elizabeth's having commanded him to absent himself from court. Thirdly, an alternative reading of the text suggests that Knollys's primary purpose in writing the letter was not to apologise for his past errors but rather to try to persuade the queen to allow him to state his case against the bishops before her. For he goes on to write—admittedly, in the deferential language which Elizabeth expected from her courtiers—'Nowe to avoyde theise myne oulde errors, I do most humbly crave at your Majesties handes at this present, that it wyll please you yt my lorde Treasorer may be placed to be a faythefull reporter, & true dealer, betwene your Majestie and me, and also betwene me and suche, as I shall accuse for iniuring of your Majesties saffetye, and of your Majesties supreme government'. The last words suggest that far from apologising for his attacks on the bishops, Knollys was still hopeful of persuading the queen that the bishops constituted a threat to the Royal Supremacy. It therefore seems likely that the letter was composed—possibly in conjunction with the paper of 16 May— as a fresh move in his campaign against the bishops, Knollys's object on this occasion being to petition the queen directly for permission to lay his case before her, but that, following his usual practice, he took the precaution, before sending it, of submitting it to Burghley for his approval. If this interpretation is right, there can be little doubt that the letter was never dispatched, since Burghley would almost certainly have vetoed it.

That Strype was wrong in suggesting that Elizabeth had reprimanded Knollys in May 1590, for meddling with the question of episcopal authority is shown by the fact that he continued to campaign actively against the *jure divino* theory during the later months of that year. In August he was provoked to a fresh outburst by the publication of a tract in defence of episcopacy, entitled *A Reconciliation of all the Pastors and Clergy of the Church of England*, by Anthony Marten, one of the Sewers of the Queen's Chamber.[85] Marten's pamphlet was not a work of great consequence in itself and it is doubtful whether in other circumstances it would have attracted Knollys's attention, especially as he seems to have ignored completely the much more important *De Diversis Ministrorum Evangelii Gradibus* of Hadrian de Saravia, which had appeared only a few weeks earlier and on which Marten drew in the concluding pages of his book. But it is clear that Knollys's anger was aroused by the fact that as a Sewer of the Queen's Chamber Marten was a member of the Royal Household and therefore, in a sense, one of his own subordinates.

On 14 August 1590 Knollys wrote an indignant letter to Lord Burghley in which he complained that 'upon Wednysday last

Mr Martyn the Sewer, presented to me a booke of his owne making, wherein he pretendethe a reconcyliacion of the clargie, but indeede the booke is none other, but a parrasytycall promoter of the ambytious & covetous government by the claimed superyorytye of bysshops'.

'Now I do fynde', he continued, 'yt Mr Martyn hathe had craftyer councell in the penning of his booke, then is conteyned in his own heade, although I do thinke the penning thereof to be his owne doing: but when he dothe come to showe the reasons of the presbytery men, yt are adversaryes to the bysshops claimed superyorytie, The answers yt he makethe to these reasons, are the answeres, yt Doctor Whytegyft dothe make agaynst Cartewryght'.[86] He then went on to accuse Marten of maintaining that the authority of bishops was 'godes institucion first' and only 'in a second degree . . . from the Queenes Majesties authorytie & allowance'—a view which, Knollys insisted, 'smellethe of treason agaynst hir Majesties supreme government'.[87] After repeating the familiar charges against the bishops, Knollys therefore put forward a new proposal—that Burghley should persuade the queen to allow the controversy to 'be dyscussed by the common consent of the most learned unyversitye men, to whome the bysshops must needs geeve place for the matter of true learning: because' (he suggested somewhat naïvely) 'the chieffe devynes of the unyversitye are not yet corrupted wth worldly promotions, nether are they parcyall as yet, nor towched wth ambytion & covetousnes, as the bysshops claymed superyorytie must needes be'.[88]

Burghley appears to have ignored Knollys's letter of 14 August for on 8 September Knollys wrote again to protest against Marten's book. He began by reminding Burghley—as if any reminder were needed—how 'my chieffest study hathe bene of longe tyme to seeke out the true preservacion of hir Majesties saffety specyally towching the mayntenance of hir Majesties supreme government'. Then, after repeating yet again his claim that the bishops derived their authority from the statute of 25 Henry VIII and that anyone who offended against the terms of the statute was liable to the penalties of *praemunire*, he proceeded to argue that 'because Mr Martyn the Sewer, an ordynarye servant to hir Majestie, hathe rashelye in his late prynted booke, dedycated by him unto hir Majestie, in favour of the superyorytie

of bysshops, so foolysshlye advanced the sayd superyorytie of
bysshops, That he dothe justyfye largelye & plentyfullye the sayd
superyorytye of bysshops to be first from godes owne ordynance,
& in a second degree hee claymethe the same superyorytie, (also
for the bysshops,) from hir Majesties grawnte and allowance, But
by clayming of the sayd superyorytye of government fyrst &
pryncypally from godes owne ordynance, & not pryncypally &
dyrectlye from hir Majesties grawnte, nor from hir supreme
government, Therfor Mr Martyn aforesayd is fallen into the
penalty of the premunire, as also Doctor Whytegyfte is lykewyse,
by clayming longe synce in his prynted booke agaynst Cartewryght, that the superyorytie of bysshops is godes owne instytucion,
& not an humayne ordynance, whereof hir Majestie is the supreme
governor'. Finally, he informed Burghley in no uncertain terms,
'I do thinke it highe tyme for the preservacion of hir Mapesties
saffetye, that my sayd opynion may fourthewth come to tryall
whether it be true or false'.[89]

If Knollys's letter was intended as an ultimatum to Burghley, it
had little effect. For two months later he returned to the subject
in a pessimistic letter, dated 9 November 1590. In the meantime
he had written an answer to the arguments put forward in
Marten's book and he now forwarded this to Burghley for his
perusal, since, as he states, 'I dare not presume to sett fourthe
anythinge towchinge hir Majesties saffetye wthout yor lordshippes
good consent to the same'. He therefore begged Burghley 'to
take the paynes to reade over my sayd wryting before I proceede
anye further therein, for wthout yor lordshyps good allowance
thereof, I do meane to surcease & stay from further wrytyng in
that behalffe'.[90] The tone of this letter suggests that he hardly
expected Burghley to approve of what he had written and
that he was becoming resigned to the abandonment of his campaign.

In fact, the end came shortly afterwards. Although the details
are not clear, it is evident that at some point during the next few
months Elizabeth finally lost patience with Knollys and ordered
him to desist from pursuing the matter any further. By May 1591
Knollys was in a state of despair. On 14 May he poured out his
feelings in a long letter to Burghley. After describing how he had
been present the previous day at a meeting of the Star Chamber,

when the case of Cartwright and his fellow prisoners was discussed for the first time, he went on to relate how, when he was asked his opinion on a point of procedure, he had not dared to speak his mind freely, 'bycawse I dowted, whether hir majestie wold allowe me to speyke my conscyence in hir majesties behalffe agaynst the uniust claymed superyorytye of bysshops, dyrectly ympunging of hir majesties supreme government as I do take it, and as I have offrd before hir majestie to prove it, and as I am not aferde in the starre chamber, by the help of lerned cownsayle to prove it (yf hir majestie woll gyve me leave)'. 'Indeed', he continued, 'your Lp. dothe see what a strayte I am dryven into: for it is a deadly greaffe unto me to offend hir majestie, specially publyklye, and yet I had rather dye than to ympugne hir majesties safetye by anye pleasyng speache'. He therefore begged Burghley to show his letter to the queen—'to the ende that hir majestie may gyve me leave to speyk myn owne conscyence frelye in the behalffe of hir majesties safetye in this case aforesayde, or els that yf so motche grace can not be obtayned of hir majestie for me, Than my desyre is that to avoyd hir majesties offence with the offence of my conscyence also, that it woll please hir majestie to make me a pryvate man, that I may so be scylent, and avoyd hir majesties offence, the which offence I am desyrous to flee even as from a serpent'. The pathos of this letter is underlined by Knollys's final sentence—'Althoe wrytyng dothe hinder my syghte, yet I durst not wryte otherwyse than wth myn owne hand in this case'.[91]

If Burghley showed this letter to the queen—which is perhaps unlikely—Elizabeth took no notice of it, for Knollys remained in office until his death five years later. But from this time on—to judge by his few surviving letters to Burghley—he appears to have tried fairly scrupulously to observe Elizabeth's injunction not to attack the authority of the bishops; and, although he continued to protest on occasion against the treatment of Cartwright and his fellow ministers,[92] there are no further references to the *jure divino* theory of episcopacy during the remainder of 1591 and the whole of 1592.

Knollys's suspicions of the bishops, however, remained unaltered and at the beginning of 1593 he returned to the attack for the last time. The occasion was provided by a debate in the House of Commons on a motion by James Morice, Attorney of the Court of Wards, for leave to introduce two bills attacking the *ex-officio* oath and other aspects of Whitgift's ecclesiastical government.[93] In the course of the debate Morice came under heavy attack from several of Whitgift's supporters in the House. Angered by these attacks, Knollys intervened on Morice's behalf and delivered a long harangue, in which he repeated his familiar argument that the bishops derived their authority from the statute of 25 Henry VIII and that anyone infringing this act was liable to the penalties of *praemunire*, while he also questioned the bishops' right to hold their courts in their own names, instead of in the name of the queen.[94] The next day, 28 February, Morice was summoned before the Privy Council and ordered to be confined to the house of Sir John Fortescue, the Chancellor of the Exchequer. Significantly, Knollys was not one of the councillors present on this occasion but on the same day he wrote to Burghley in Morice's support. The ostensible purpose of his letter was to send Burghley 'a booke of suche collections, as I have gathered, spetyallye towchinge hir Majesties supreme government', but he took the opportunity to defend Morice against his critics in the House of Commons. The queen's supreme government, he complained, 'begynnethe now to be impungned in oure lower house of parlement by the cyvilians, and also spetyallie by Mr Dalton, the lawier, and chieffelie impugninge a speeche yt Mr Morrys, the atturney of the courte of wardes, dyd use yesterdaye, agaynst certen abuses now used in the government of the clergie', and he accused the civilians of wishing to 'have a kynde of monarchye in the sayd clergie government, as is in the temporaltye, The which clergie government they would have to be exempted from the temporall government, Saving they speake not agaynst the prynces government towching the supremacy'. At the same time, he assured Burghley 'that in myne opynyon Mr Morrys did speake bothe modestlie, & wyselye, & warylie, & trulye towching the abuses in the government of the clergie at this present'. But, somewhat disingenuously, he omitted any reference to his own part in the debate.[95]

Reports of Knollys's speech, however, inevitably reached Burghley and at the end of April, shortly after the dissolution of parliament, Knollys wrote a long letter to the Lord Treasurer to explain his conduct. After thanking Burghley for his good offices in helping to obtain the award of the Garter for him from the queen, he proceeded to give him an account 'of my dealing in this parlemente tyme agaynst the undue claymed superyorytie of Bysshops over theyre inferior bretherne'. He explained at some length how in his speech, after reciting the statute of 25 Henry VIII, he had challenged the right of the bishops to hold their courts in their own names—'Whereunto I was answered, That the bysshops do keepe theyre courtes nowe by prescryption'. Such an answer, he protested to Burghley, was unsatisfactory: for it was contrary to the royal prerogative for anyone to hold a court without a special licence from the crown, and, in fact, the bishops 'in Kynge Edwardes dayes' obtained an act of parliament to enable them to hold their courts in the king's name. But this statute was repealed under Mary and was not revived at Elizabeth's accession. The bishops would have done wisely he insisted, if they had followed the example of their Edwardian predecessors and sought a similar statute to authorise them to hold their courts in the queen's name; but since they had not done so, and since it was unlawful for anyone to hold a court except by grant from the crown, he could not understand how they could claim to hold their courts in their own names by prescription. Finally, he returned for the last time to the issue which had obsessed him for so long. Reminding Burghley that 'yor lordshyppe sayd unto me, that the Bysshops have forsaken they're clayme of superyorytie over theyre inferyor bretherne latelye, to be by godes owne ordynance, and yt nowe they do onely clayme superyoritie over theyre inferyor bretherne from hir Majesties supreme government', he demanded: 'If this be true, Then it is requysyte & necessarye, yt my lorde Archebysshoppe of Canterburye yt nowe is, do recante or retracte his saying in his booke of the great volume agaynst Cartewryghte, Where he sayeth in playne woordes (by the name of Doctor Whytgyfte) That the superyoritie of Bysshops is godes own instytucion, which saying dothe Impunge hir Majesties supreme government dyrectlye, & therefore it is to bee retracted playnelye & trulye, ffor chryst playnely confessed yt his kingdome was not of this worlde, and therefore he gave no worldlie rule or prehemynence unto his apostles'.[96]

This letter represents Knollys's final outburst on the subject of the *jure divino* theory of episcopacy. He still had three more years to live. But he was now nearly eighty and in failing health; and, although it is clear from his two letters to Burghley in the spring of 1593 that he had abandoned none of his suspicions of the bishops, from this time on he appears to have reverted to his policy of silence, for no letters survive on the subject from the last three years of his life. From his later letters to Burghley, Knollys emerges as a sad and defeated old man. Although, as the award of the Garter showed, he had not lost Elizabeth's personal favour, his campaign to have the bishops compelled to acknowledge that they derived their authority solely from the crown had ended in complete failure. Elizabeth had forbidden him to pursue the matter any further; Burghley had failed to support him; Whitgift's position had been greatly enhanced by the exposure of the Classical Movement and he was now virtually unassailable; while the *jure divino* theory of episcopacy itself, against which Knollys had argued so strenuously, was gaining ground rapidly in the early 1590s under the influence of Hadrian de Saravia's *De Diversis Ministrorum Evangelii Gradibus*, although paradoxically Knollys's later letters to Burghley contain no reference either to Saravia's work itself or to any of the tracts which followed it.

Knollys's lack of success has dogged him beyond the grave. Modern historians have, in general, refused to take his campaign seriously and they have tended to dismiss it as the obsession of a cantankerous old puritan, who, in Conyers Read's phrase, was 'virtually in his dotage'.[97] But such a judgment is not altogether fair. Although it is true that the question of the bishops' authority became something of a King Charles's head with Knollys and it is difficult not to feel a certain sympathy for Burghley, who must have found Knollys's endless stream of letters a constant source of embarrassment, nevertheless his campaign did touch on important theological and constitutional issues. Throughout the formative years of the English Reformation there had been a general consensus among English protestants that episcopacy was a purely human institution, while the same principle was embodied in the theory of the Royal Supremacy as it had been propounded in the reign of Henry VIII. Knollys could, therefore, claim considerable historical justification for his assertion that the *jure divino* theory of episcopacy constituted a threat not only to traditional protestantism, but also to the Royal Supremacy: for, if followed to its logical conclusion, it involved an implicit denial of the Henrician doctrine that the crown was the exclusive source of the jurisdictional authority of the bishops. In practice, so long as the crown and the episcopate remained as closely allied as they did throughout the greater part of the seventeenth century the threat was only hypothetical. But almost exactly a hundred years later the prophetic nature of Knollys's warnings was to be revealed at the time of the Non-Juring schism, when the Non-Jurors refused to recognise the right of crown and parliament to deprive archbishop Sancroft and his colleagues of their sees on the ground that they held their authority in the Church *jure divino*.

How far Knollys, with his Erastian views, can properly be classified as a puritan must remain a matter of debate; but there is a certain irony in the fact that it was Knollys, the so-called puritan, who was defending the traditional Tudor order in Church and State, whereas it was Whitgift and his colleagues of the Establishment who were the innovators with their claim that episcopacy was in some sense a divine institution. But such ironies are characteristic of the history of dissent.

VI

The Philosopher of the 'Politic Society':
Richard Hooker as a Political Thinker

Forty years ago Hooker's reputation as a great political philosopher appeared to be beyond dispute. Writing in 1928, J. W. Allen could say, 'not merely as a controversialist but as a political thinker, he was incomparably the greatest Englishman of the sixteenth century and on the Continent he had few compeers',[1] and it is a verdict that most historians until recently would unhesitatingly have endorsed. Today Hooker's standing as a political thinker is much less certain. The past forty years have seen the appearance of a number of studies which, in a variety of ways, have profoundly modified the traditional interpretation of his political thought. While some old problems have been resolved and some long-standing myths have been exploded (one hopes) for ever, new issues have arisen—especially in the last twenty years—which have challenged the accepted assumptions of a generation ago, and it is arguable that the nature of Hooker's achievement as a political philosopher is more open to question at the present day than at any time in the past. The announcement of a new critical edition of Hooker's works, therefore, provides an appropriate opportunity to review the developments that have taken place in the study of his political ideas in the present century and to attempt a reappraisal of his significance in the history of political thought.

The treatment of Hooker's political ideas illustrates the difficulties that have hampered the progress of Hooker scholarship in the twentieth century. In spite of the advances that have been achieved in certain fields—notably in bibliography and biography, where the researches of literary historians, such as R. A. Houk, David Novarr, and, above all, C. J. Sisson,[2] have done much to elucidate the problems of the posthumous books and to establish the facts behind Walton's fictions—Hooker has always been in many respects an inadequately studied figure. While he has never been neglected in the popular sense, he has tended to fall into the category of thinkers who are more written about than studied, and both as a theologian and as a political theorist he can hardly be said to have attracted the degree of scholarly investigation which his eminence demands. Although his name figures in all the textbooks, the number of serious historical studies of his thought which have appeared in the twentieth century has been remarkably limited, and little detailed research has been done, even in recent years, either into his political theory or into his theology in general. As a result, there has been a tendency for much modern writing about Hooker to be uncritical in character and lacking in depth and for the same stereotyped judgments to be repeated from writer to writer.

At the same time, the study of Hooker's thought has also been handicapped by the 'politic use' that has been made of him in the past. For over two centuries his political philosophy was interpreted very largely through the distorting lens of Locke's *Second Treatise*, and although the manner in which Locke deliberately exploited Hooker's reputation in order to give a semblance of respectability to his own revolutionary arguments is now generally recognised, it is a tribute to Locke's effectiveness as a political propagandist and to the all-powerful influence of Whig historiography in the eighteenth and nineteenth centuries that until as recently as the 1920s and 1930s Hooker was universally regarded as an exponent of the theory of social contract, and few myths have proved more difficult to dislodge than the belief that Hooker's views were, in all essentials, identical with those of Locke. In a similar fashion, the historical understanding of Hooker has also been hampered by the influence of Anglican hagiography. Not only has a large proportion of the general books written about Hooker in the present century been the work of Anglican churchmen—many of them High Churchmen, who have attempted to interpret him from their own ecclesiastical standpoint—but in a more subtle way the traditional Anglican image of Hooker has exercised a profound influence on the way in which he has been treated by secular historians. Thus, it is a remarkable commentary on the power of Anglican tradition that until the publication of Sisson's *The Judicious Marriage of Mr. Hooker* in 1940, Walton's picture of the 'dove-like', if henpecked, Hooker was accepted unquestioningly by most historians, halo and all. Again, secular historians have tended, in general, to accept the conventional Anglican view of Hooker as a great irenical figure, whose mind was above the ephemeral party conflicts of his own time, ignoring or playing down the essentially polemical character of the *Laws*, just as they have tended, in general, to accept Hooker's claim to be regarded as the first major apologist for the Church of England, overlooking his debt to predecessors such as Whitgift. It is, perhaps, also because of the unconscious influence of Anglican hagiography that until recently Hooker's intellectual greatness as a philosopher was assumed to be self-evident, and it is only in the past twenty years that historians have begun to question the logical consistency of his thought.

The primary task of Hooker scholarship in the twentieth century has therefore been to break away from the stereotypes of the past. Admittedly, it is a task that has not always been clearly recognised or actively pursued. It is significant, however, that the most important developments in the interpretation of his thought have come about in the main through the realisation that there was a large element of myth in the traditional interpretation of Hooker and that it was necessary to start by reexamining the preconceptions of earlier historians. While it does not follow that all the criticisms that have been levelled against the traditional conception of Hooker are necessarily justified, and some of the new views that have been put forward are highly contentious, there can be little doubt that the iconoclasm of a handful of twentieth-century historians has done much to advance the understanding of his thought.

As a broad generalisation, one can say that the modern interpretation of Hooker's political theory has evolved through three, or perhaps four, main phases. At the beginning of the twentieth century he was still regarded primarily, as he had been in the eighteenth and nineteenth centuries, as the forerunner of Locke and one of the originators of the doctrine of social contract. Typical of the prevailing attitude among English historians in the early years of the century is Sir Sidney Lee's comment in the third volume of the *Cambridge Modern History*, published in 1904: 'Hooker . . . made a contribution of first-rate importance to the theory of government, both civil and ecclesiastical. He anticipated the great Whig doctrine of the seventeenth century, that government had its origin in a primary contract between the governor and the governed, and he endeavoured to prove that the constitution of the Anglican Church rested on such an implied contract, from which there was no right of withdrawal'—a view which hardly differs from that expressed by Hallam eighty years earlier.[3] On the other hand, although at the beginning of the century Hooker's name was frequently mentioned in works dealing with the history of political thought and his importance was beginning to be recognised by continental historians, such as Jellinek and Tröltsch,[4] his ideas were rarely discussed in detail, and it was not until the 1920s that his writings began to attract the serious attention of historians of political thought both in England and on the Continent. In Germany, for example, a number of writers began to take an interest in Hooker's religious and political ideas in the years immediately following the First World War, among them Wilhelm Pauck, whose pioneering study of Bucer's social theory, *Das Reich Gottes auf Erden* (1928), included a pertinent section on Hooker's theory of Church and State.[5] In England, too, interest in the study of Hooker's political ideas was given a new momentum by the writings of such scholars as Norman Sykes, R. H. Murray, and J. W. Allen,[6] whose chapter on *The Laws of Ecclesiastical Polity* in his *History of Political Thought in the Sixteenth Century* is one of the most perceptive short surveys of Hooker's political theory to have appeared in the past fifty years. However, with the notable exception of Allen, who attempted to set Hooker firmly in the context of his own age, most writers on Hooker in the 1920s continued to see him primarily as a precursor of the seventeenth century, both in his views on the origins of government and in his ideas of natural law.

This traditional way of looking at Hooker was largely undermined in the 1930s by the writings of A. P. d'Entrèves, whose *Riccardo Hooker: Contributo alla teoria e alla storia del dirrito naturale* (1932) constitutes a landmark in the development of the modern study of Hooker. In the first place, it was the first full-scale monograph to be devoted to the study of his political philosophy and the first attempt to set his ideas in their historical tradition, and it is still perhaps the best book on the subject, although unfortunately it has never been translated into English.[7] Secondly, it entirely altered the perspective from which Hooker was normally viewed by emphasising the essentially medieval character of his thought. Not only did d'Entrèves challenge the prevailing orthodoxy that Hooker was to be seen primarily as a social contract thinker, pointing out that it was anachronistic to interpret him in terms of Locke and that it was very doubtful whether Hooker could properly be said to have held a theory of social contract at all,[8] but he also suggested that it was equally anachronistic to interpret Hooker's conception of natural law in terms of Grotius and the seventeenth century. In d'Entrèves's view, Hooker's contribution to the development of the concept of natural law—which he regarded as the most important aspect of Hooker's political theory—could be properly understood only if it was seen not as the precursor of the 'rationalist' theories of the seventeenth century but rather as the culmination of the medieval scholastic tradition of natural law 'as a part of the eternal order which God has imposed upon Creation'.[9] D'Entrèves was by no means the first scholar to emphasise Hooker's debt to Aquinas and medieval scholasticism, but he was the first to analyse it in detail and to make it the key to his interpretation of Hooker. While he did not deny that Hooker's ideas formed an important link between the medieval and the modern world and that he was —to quote from *The Medieval Contribution to Political Thought* —'a Janus-like figure, facing two different if not opposite worlds',[10] for d'Entrèves, Hooker's essential significance as a thinker lay in the fact that he came at the end of the medieval tradition, that in his aims and his outlook he looked backward to the thirteenth century rather than forward to the seventeenth.

The next two decades saw the publication of several studies of Hooker's political ideas but little fresh development in the interpretation of his thought. Gottfried Michaelis's Göttingen doctoral dissertation, *Richard Hooker als politischer Denker*, published in 1933, was, in fact, written before the appearance of d'Entrèves's book, and it might be said to epitomise the early twentieth-century German view of Hooker. Although like d'Entrèves he stresses Hooker's debt to Aquinas in his treatment of natural law, for Michaelis the real interest and importance of Hooker lies in his role in the development of the theory of social contract. While emphasising that the ingredients of Hooker's thought were not original and that he was building on the foundations laid by a succession of late medieval and sixteenth-century writers, he argues with Jellinek against Gierke in favour of the view that Hooker rather than Althusius has the best claim to be regarded as 'the first representative of the classical social contract doctrine',[11] while, like Sir Sidney Lee, he makes the concept of social contract the key to the understanding not only of Hooker's theory of government but also of his theory of Church and State (86ff.). However, if Michaelis undoubtedly exaggerates the degree to which Hooker can properly be regarded as a social contract thinker, his book contains a useful analysis of Hooker's ideas, and for the most part it has been unjustly neglected by English-speaking scholars.

In 1935 C. W. Previté-Orton published his important British Academy lecture on Marsilius of Padua, in which he argued on the basis of internal parallels that Hooker's thought owed much to the influence of Marsilius, especially in the later books[12]—an idea since taken up and developed by a number of writers on Hooker. Of even greater significance for the study of Hooker's political ideas in England was the publication in 1939 of d'Entrèves's volume of Oxford lectures, *The Medieval Contribution to Political Thought*, the last two chapters of which were devoted to Hooker. These two lectures consisted largely of a *résumé* of the arguments of his *Riccardo Hooker*, and in themselves they added little to what he had said before. However, they played an influential role in helping to make d'Entrèves's ideas better known among English-speaking scholars, and by treating Hooker in the same context as Aquinas and Marsilius of Padua they served to reinforce his picture of Hooker as an essentially medieval figure who stands at the end of the medieval tradition of political thought.

During the period immediately after the war two further studies of Hooker's political ideas appeared in England, but neither can be said to have advanced the understanding of his thought. E. T. Davies's *The Political Ideas of Richard Hooker* (1946) was essentially a work of popularisation, designed to present Hooker's ideas to the intelligent layman—useful but largely derivative, while it suffers, like most works of popularisation, from a tendency to oversimplification. More scholarly in its pretensions but equally derivative was F. J. Shirley's *Richard Hooker and Contemporary Political Ideas*. Although not published until 1949, it was mainly written before and during the war and draws heavily on the work of Michaelis, largely without acknowledgement.

By 1950 Hooker's reputation as a political thinker appeared to be firmly established. He was generally recognised as the most important English political theorist of the sixteenth century, while the work of d'Entrèves appeared to have reinforced the traditional English and Anglican conception of Hooker as a great systematic philosopher. In 1952, however, the basic significance of Hooker's achievement was suddenly called in question by the appearance of two studies, both of which independently cast doubt on the validity of Hooker's claim to be regarded as a great logical thinker. The first, a short but provocative essay in *The Cambridge Journal* by H. F. Kearney,[13] went so far as to dismiss Hooker's claims to greatness altogether, arguing not only that he was 'too much caught up in the ephemeral problem of his time to be considered great' but that there was a fundamental inconsistency in his argument arising from his failure to reconcile the dichotomy between a 'rationalist' and a 'voluntarist' conception of law (303–4). According to Kearney, although Hooker started off by discussing law in terms of reason, like St. Thomas, he ended by virtually identifying it with the will of the crown, like Marsilius and Thomas Hobbes. 'It may be argued therefore with justice', Kearney concluded, 'that though Hooker begins with Aquino, he ends with Padua' (307). The same words might have been used with equal appropriateness by Peter Munz to describe the principal theme of his book, *The Place of Hooker in the History of Thought*, also published in 1952. Although working along different lines from Kearney, being chiefly concerned with the problem of Hooker's theory of Church and State, Munz also arrived at the conclusion that Hooker's argument was flawed and that although he started off as a Thomist he ended as a disciple of Marsilius of Padua. According to Munz, it was Hooker's tragedy that he set out with the aim of expounding a theory of Church and State based upon the principles of Aquinas but was unable to reconcile these principles with the realities of the Tudor political situation. As a result, he was forced imperceptibly to shift his ground, and when he came to justify the Royal Supremacy in Book VIII, he found himself increasingly tending to adopt the political arguments of Marsilius of Padua, with their Averroistic implication that the State was a purely secular institution. Munz suggests that it was Hooker's failure to reconcile these two opposing tendencies in his thought that accounts for the incomplete state of the last three books, for as the work progressed he became increasingly aware of the inconsistencies in his position, and in consequence the work slowed down and was still unfinished at the time of his death.[14]

The attacks of Kearney and Munz represent the most important development in the interpretation of Hooker's political theory since the publication of d'Entrèves's *Riccardo Hooker*. The only serious attempt that has been made to defend Hooker's theory against the charge of inconsistency is to be found in an article entitled 'The Coherence of Hooker's Polity: The Books on Power', by Arthur S. McGrade, published in 1963.[15] In this article McGrade rightly insists that the arguments of the later books can only be properly understood if they are interpreted, as Hooker himself intended, in the light of the general principles enunciated in the first four books. However, his argument is primarily directed against Kearney's thesis that Hooker moved from a rationalist to a voluntarist or positivist conception of law, and while he effectively disposes of Kearney's arguments, he does not discuss the more fundamental issues raised by Munz.

This lack of response to the attacks of Kearney and Munz may indicate a waning of interest in Hooker as a political theorist, which may itself be simply a reflexion of the fact that the study of the history of political thought has been becoming increasingly unfashionable in English, and perhaps American academic circles as well, over the past two decades. Certainly, it is significant that, apart from McGrade's article, the only noteworthy contribution to the discussion of Hooker's political ideas that has appeared since 1952 is Christopher Morris's admirably balanced chapter in his book *Political Thought in England: Tyndale to Hooker*, published as long ago as 1953.[16] Perhaps equally significant is the fact that neither of the two most recent works on Hooker has been concerned, except marginally, with his political ideas, although each in its own way touches on the problem of his intellectual consistency. J. S. Marshall's *Hooker and the Anglican Tradition* (1963) is, in effect, a forceful reassertion of Hooker's claim to be regarded as a great systematic thinker, since he argues that Hooker's conscious purpose in writing the *Laws* was to produce a theological *summa*, modelled on the *Summæ* of Aquinas.[17] However, Marshall overstates his thesis, and the general credibility of his interpretation is marred by his pronounced Anglo-Catholic bias and his misunderstanding of the realities of Tudor religious history. A much more cogent study is Gunnar Hillerdal's *Reason and Revelation in Richard Hooker*, published in 1962. Although Hillerdal is concerned primarily with Hooker's theological ideas and not with his political philosophy, his work has interesting parallels with that of Munz. For, like Munz, he raises the question whether Hooker was successful in reconciling two opposing traditions of thought—in this case, his Aristotelian-Thomist philosophy of reason and his protestant theology of grace and predestination. Hillerdal argues that Hooker was unable to do so and that, although he attempted to gloss over the logical contradictions inherent in these two positions, in fact the argument of the *Laws* is constructed around two basically inconsistent conceptions of grace and reason.

The philosophical and theological issues dealt with by Hillerdal are not directly relevant to the interpretation of Hooker's political ideas and, in consequence, lie outside the scope of this essay. Nevertheless, there can be little doubt that the general problem that Hillerdal raises—the problem of the logical coherence of Hooker's thought—is, in the different form in which it is presented by Munz and Kearney, the most important issue that confronts the student of Hooker's political ideas today. Was Hooker the great systematic philosopher and apologist for the Church of England that most modern scholars have assumed? Or was he, in fact, intellectually inconsistent, his argument flawed by fundamental logical contradictions? In other words, is *Of the Laws of Ecclesiastical Polity* to be regarded as a masterpiece or as a failure—a failure, perhaps, on a grand scale, but a failure none the less, because in it Hooker was forced to compromise his principles in order to meet the realities of the system which he was trying to defend?

In attempting to answer these questions, it is necessary to make a distinction between Hooker's purposes and his method of argument. As the rest of this essay will try to show, an examination of the logical structure of Hooker's argument suggests that his theory was more consistent than his recent critics have allowed. On the other hand, throughout the *Laws*, Hooker was continually arguing to a brief, and he cannot easily be acquitted of the charge of subordinating his political ideas to the needs of the immediate controversy. In assessing Hooker's significance as a political philosopher, therefore, it is important to take account not only of the questions of the logical consistency of his ideas but also of the motives that governed the writing of the *Laws*.

Any discussion of Hooker's political ideas must start from the fact that *Of the Laws of Ecclesiastical Polity* is only incidentally a work of political theory. It is not in any formal sense a treatise on the principles of government, like Bodin's *De Republica*, nor is it a discourse on the nature of the English constitution, like Sir Thomas Smith's *De Republica Anglorum*, although much of Hooker's argument is taken up with questions of political philosophy and constitutional practice. Nor is it primarily—as Marshall, for example, has recently argued[18]—a work of theology, an exposition of the principles of Christian doctrine, although again in the course of the book Hooker deals at length with theological issues. Essentially it is a work of apologetic, a defence of the constitution and practices of the Church of England against the attacks of its puritan critics. It is, as Christopher Morris has rightly said, a *livre de circonstance*, which has its roots in the controversies of the Elizabethan Church.[19] As such, it is primarily a work of polemic, designed to serve the same purpose as Whitgift's writings against Cartwright and the Admonitioners in the 1570s and the writings of Bridges, Bancroft, and a succession of Anglican divines in the 1580s and 1590s, whose aim was the refutation of Puritanism and the defence of the Elizabethan Settlement.

Most modern commentators on Hooker have tended to underplay the polemical purpose of the *Laws*, but this is a mistake. It is true that, as a work of propaganda, it is conceived on a grand scale and that both in its style and in the range of its arguments it is greatly superior to most sixteenth-century works of controversy. Hooker's aim was to produce a reasoned justification for the

Elizabethan Church, and the fact that his book is still regarded as a classic, while other equally significant works of the period are largely forgotten, is a measure of his success. Nevertheless, neither Hooker's aims nor the types of argument which he used differed substantially from those of other Anglican apologists of the day. It is conventional to praise Hooker for his moderation and fair-mindedness in debate, and it is true that, by comparison with Bancroft or the overbearing Whitgift, both his language and the manner in which he conducts his argument are commendably temperate: he never descends to the sort of vituperation which disfigures so much sixteenth-century polemical literature. Nevertheless, although Hooker's moderation is in keeping with what we know of his character, it is also a conscious literary device. When Hooker appeals to the Puritans at the beginning of the Preface to 'think not that ye read the words of one who bendeth himself as an adversary against the truth which ye have already embraced; but the words of one who desireth even to embrace together with you the self-same truth, if it be the truth' (Pref. i. 3),[20] he is simply adopting the language of literary convention, and it is important not to be misled by such remarks or by the solemn manner in which he delivers them into mistaking the true purpose of the *Laws*. Like Whitgift and Bancroft, Hooker had two principal objectives in writing the *Laws*, the defence of the *status quo* and the refutation of Disciplinarian Puritanism; and it is an indication of the essentially partisan character of the work that at no point in his argument, even when dealing with more obvious abuses such as pluralism and nonresidence or the lack of preaching ministers, was Hooker ever seriously prepared to concede that the Puritans might be justified in their criticisms of the Elizabethan Church.

Nor, in spite of his apparent moderation, was Hooker any more fair-minded to his puritan opponents than Whitgift or Bancroft. Hooker's Preface has often been praised by Anglican writers for its masterly insight into the nature of Elizabethan Puritanism.[21] In fact, it is a skilful exercise in denigration which sets the tone for the rest of the work.[22] Hooker's aim throughout the Preface was to discredit the puritan cause, partly by exposing the novelty of the Calvinist system of discipline and partly by impugning the motives of the Puritans themselves. The manner in which he set about the task is made clear in the famous description of the institution of the Genevan discipline with which the Preface begins (ch. ii). Hooker's account of Calvin is a calculated piece of misrepresentation, a deliberate attempt to undermine Calvin's reputation among his readers. While professing the greatest respect for Calvin as a person and as a theologian, Hooker, in effect, accuses him of perpetrating a pious fraud, for he implies that Calvin's original reasons for instituting his system of discipline were pragmatic and that he only put forward the claim that it was of divine origin in order to induce the inhabitants of Geneva to accept it the more readily.

Hooker adopts similar smear tactics in order to undermine the credit of the Puritans. He accuses them of setting up their own private judgment above the authority of the Church (Pref. vi). Following Bancroft—on whose Paul's Cross Sermon he drew heavily in chapter iv—Hooker attempts to drive a wedge between the puritan clergy and their lay supporters by suggesting that the latter are principally motivated by the desire to lay their hands on the wealth of the Church and that 'the chiefest thing which lay-reformers yawn for is, that the clergy may through conformity in state and condition be apostolical, poor as the Apostles of Christ were poor'.[23] He hints ominously that among the consequences that are likely to follow from the establishment of the puritan discipline are the destruction of the Queen's Supremacy, 'the overthrow of all learning', the decay of the universities, and even, he suggests, without a shred of evidence, the abolition of the common law and its replacement by Scripture as 'the only law whereby to determine all our civil controversies' (viii. 2–4). As a final smear, he resurrects the hoary sixteenth-century bogey of Anabaptism as an example of the dangers to which the unfettered exercise of private judgment in matters of religion can lead.[24] If Hooker is at his most tendentious in the Preface, it is important to bear in mind that the motives which he imputes to the Puritans throughout the book are necessarily suspect and that, in particular, for his own polemical purposes he deliberately exaggerates the biblicism of the orthodox disciplinarians, making it out to be more extreme than was, in fact, the case.

The arguments that Hooker uses in order to defend the Church of England against the demands of the Puritans for the establishment of the presbyterian system of discipline are also very similar to those of earlier Anglican apologists. In general, modern scholars have tended to ignore the question of Hooker's debt to previous Elizabethan writers, partly on the mistaken assumption that Hooker's predecessors, such as Jewel and Whitgift, contributed little that was positive to the defence of the Church of England. In fact, Hooker's debt to them was considerable. Hooker was by nature an eclectic, and although—apparently as a matter of deliberate policy—he never refers to contemporary Anglican writers (with the exception of Jewel) by name, whereas there are frequent references to the works of his puritan opponents as well as to the writings of older classical, patristic, and medieval authors, there can be little doubt that Hooker drew heavily on the works of his contemporaries. Apart from the echoes of Bancroft that are apparent in the Preface, there are clear traces of the influence of Jewel in his defence of custom and tradition in Book v[25] and of the influence of Saravia in his treatment of episcopacy in Book vii.[26] Further research would probably reveal evidence of extensive borrowings from the works of lesser figures such as John Bridges and Robert Some. Hooker's outstanding debt, however, was undoubtedly to Whitgift, whose writings provided the basis for his attack on the general grounds of the puritan position in Books ii, iii, and iv. Indeed, it is hardly an exaggeration to say that the whole argument of the *Laws* is largely an elaboration of the principles enunciated by Whitgift in his *Answer to the Admonition* (1572) and his *Defence of the Answer* (1574). It was Whitgift's writings that provided the main theoretical foundation for the Anglican defence of episcopacy in the 1570s and 1580s, and it was he who first developed, in relation to the question of church government, the two concepts that lie at the heart of Hooker's own defence of the Elizabethan Church: first, the concept that there is a fundamental distinction to be drawn between matters of faith, which are essential to salvation and which are clearly laid down in Scripture, and 'external' or 'outward' matters of religion, which are 'not commanded or prohibited in scripture' and are therefore to be regarded as 'things indifferent'; and second, its corollary, that each individual Church has the right to determine its own external forms of worship and church government 'according to the state of times, places, and persons'.[27]

What distinguishes Hooker from his contemporaries is, first of all, his attempt to give a broader philosophical foundation to these two concepts by relating the concept of 'things indifferent' to the traditional medieval theory of the hierarchy of divine law and by treating the Church as a species of 'politic society', entitled to the same degree of autonomy in nondivine matters as other forms of civil society, and secondly, his method of argument. In comparison with other sixteenth-century works of controversy, the most striking feature of the *Laws* is the manner in which Hooker presents his case against the Puritans. Instead of adopting the normal sixteenth-century procedure of taking one or more works by his opponents and answering them individually in laborious detail, page by page and sentence by sentence—a method which makes so much sixteenth-century polemical literature so tedious to read and which accounts for the oblivion into which writers such as Whitgift have sunk—Hooker set out to construct a systematic reply to the arguments of the Puritans, starting from first principles, with a general attack on the basic assumptions underlying the puritan 'platform', before proceeding to a detailed refutation of their specific charges against the practices and constitution of the Church of England. Significantly, although Cartwright is the writer whom he cites most frequently, Hooker does not concentrate his attack on any one puritan author but draws his examples from a wide range of puritan pamphlets, including the *Admonitions to Parliament*, the writings of Walter Travers and Edward Dering, Dudley Fenner's *Counterpoison* and *Defence of the Godly Ministers*, John Udall's *Demonstration of Discipline*, and the Marprelate Tracts.

The seventeenth-century church historian Thomas Fuller described Hooker's style as 'long and pithy, drawing on a whole flock of several clauses before he came to the close of a sentence'.[28] The same metaphor might be applied to Hooker's method of argument. The *Laws* was conceived by Hooker as a carefully structured whole. The argument is built up step by step, with each section designed to follow on logically from what had gone before. Although only the first four books were published in 1593, it is evident from the descriptions that Hooker gives of the plan of the whole work in the Preface that the eight books were designed from the outset as a logical entity and that the first four books were written with the arguments of the later books in mind.[29] Hooker himself gives an illuminating description of his method of argument at the beginning of Book 1 : 'For as much help whereof as may be in this case, I have endeavoured throughout the body of this whole discourse, that every former part might give strength unto all that follow, and every later bring some light unto all before. So that if the judgments of men do but hold themselves in suspense as touching these first more general meditations, till in order they have perused the rest that ensue; what may seem dark at the first will afterwards be found more plain, even as the later particular decisions will appear I doubt not more strong, when the other have been read before' [1.i.2].

As A. S. McGrade has pointed out, this passage has an important bearing on the problem of Hooker's intellectual consistency, for it indicates that Hooker himself regarded the whole work as a coherent entity and that he placed great emphasis on the need for his arguments to be studied in their entirety. At the same time, it also implies that the arguments of the *Laws* are of two kinds: in the first four books Hooker is concerned with what he terms 'general meditations', that is, with the discussion of broad issues of general principle; whereas in the last four he is chiefly, though not exclusively, concerned with 'particular decisions', with the refutation of the particular charges levelled by the Puritans against the Elizabethan Church.[30] On the other hand, as McGrade rightly insists, it is essential for the understanding of Hooker's overall purpose that the later books should be studied in conjunction with the first four. Hooker intended his two types of argument to be complementary, and his discussion of 'particulars' in the last four books presupposes the general conclusions previously established in Books I–IV. Consequently, Kearney's criticisms of Hooker fall to the ground, for he makes the mistake of treating Hooker's pronouncements on law in the greater books as if they can be discussed without reference to the general principles enunciated in Book I.

In fact, there is a case for suggesting that Hooker's argument in the *Laws* falls into three distinct parts, rather than two, since Book I is in many ways quite different in character from the other three books of 'general meditations'. Books II, III and IV are each concerned with refuting certain general propositions put forward by the Puritans in support of their claims, and the arguments that Hooker uses in these three books are not noticeably different from those of Whitgift and other Anglican apologists of the period. Book I, on the other hand, consists of a general philosophical disquisition on the nature of laws and 'politic societies' which has no parallel in contemporary Anglican polemic and which is deliberately couched in noncontroversial language, although it prepares the way for the anti-puritan arguments of the later books. Thus the structure of the work can best be understood if it is seen as being divided into three constituent parts: Book I, consisting of a general philosophical introduction to the whole work; Books II–IV, which are directed against the basic general propositions underlying the puritan platform; and Books v–viii, which are concerned with defending the polity and practices of the Church of England against the detailed charges brought by the Puritans. On the other hand, the fact that Hooker was deeply concerned with the logical structure of his argument and that he planned the *Laws* as a coherent whole does not in itself prove that his arguments are consistent. What it does mean is that any discussion of the problem of Hooker's consistency must take account of the fact that he intended his arguments to be treated as a unity and that, in particular, he intended that the later books should be read in close conjunction with the first four.

Both Hooker's aims and his method of argument are extremely important for the understanding of his political ideas. Hooker's primary concern in the *Laws* was the justification of the existing constitution of the Church of England, and to a greater or lesser degree all his arguments are directed to that end. His political arguments are no exception. They are an integral element in the whole work, and they can only be properly understood if they are seen as part of the intellectual weaponry that he employs against the Puritans.

The implications of this for the study of Hooker's political philosophy are most important. In the first place, it means that the nature of the political issues that he discusses in the *Laws* is largely determined by the overall purposes of the work. He was not writing a general treatise on political philosophy, and it is significant that he does not concern himself with some of the most important political problems of the day. In particular, he virtually ignores the most hotly debated issue of the late sixteenth century —the question of the right of resistance. The explanation for this omission, which has sometimes puzzled historians, is almost certainly to be found in the fact that he did not consider the issue germane to his argument. Conversely, those subjects which he does choose to discuss are usually introduced for polemical reasons in order to further his attack on Puritanism. Thus Hooker's discussion of natural law, which is generally regarded as one of the most significant aspects of his political thought, has an important role in the development of his general argument against the Puritans, for it was intended to provide a philosophical basis for the traditional Anglican concept of 'things indifferent'. Similarly, Hooker's insistence on the principle that laws derive their validity from consent is designed, in part at least, to lend support to his argument that the laws of the Church of England are binding on the Puritans because they have been established by the consent of the Church as a whole. Secondly, it is necessary to bear in mind, when studying Hooker's political ideas, that his conclusions were largely determined in advance. As a political theorist he was not engaged in a work of abstract, philosophical speculation; he was seeking to justify the *status quo*. Hooker accepts the existing constitution of Church and State in England as given, and even when he appears to be discussing political questions in general terms, as in Book I and at the beginning of Book VIII, in reality the underlying purpose of his argument is to provide a theoretical justification for the English system of monarchy and, in particular, for the Royal Supremacy.

What distinguishes Hooker, then, as a political thinker is not the originality of his conclusions, for in essentials he was as conservative in his political outlook as most Elizabethan Englishmen. Nor is it even the originality of his theoretical arguments, for, in point of fact, there is little in Hooker that had not been said before. Rather, it is the extraordinary range of his learning and his ability to combine different strands of thought into a coherent whole. Hooker's outstanding characteristic as a thinker is his eclecticism. As a theologian, he was well versed not only in the writings of the Fathers and the sixteenth-century Protestant Reformers, but also in the works of the leading scholastics of the thirteenth and fourteenth centuries. Moreover, for the purposes

of the immediate controversy he appears to have read most of the
puritan pamphlets published between 1570 and 1590, as well as
some, at least, of the principal tracts written by Anglican apologists
in reply. Similarly, as a philosopher he was steeped in the writings
of Aristotle and Aquinas, and he drew heavily on both of them
for his political ideas. Here again, however, his eclecticism is
apparent. For if Aristotle and Aquinas are the two most obvious
influences on his political thought, he also had an extensive knowledge of sixteenth-century political literature, and he was familiar
with the writings of the protestant monarchomachs, some of
whose ideas on the origins of government he borrowed while
rejecting their conclusions. Nor was Hooker's reading confined to
works of theology and philosophy, for one of the most notable
features of the *Laws* is the extent of his knowledge of contemporary English legal and constitutional theory.

It is hardly surprising that Aristotle should have been a major
influence on Hooker's philosophical thought, since Oxford was
still a stronghold of Aristotelianism in the second half of the
sixteenth century. A more difficult problem, which still requires
further investigation, is the source of Hooker's interest in Aquinas.
However, although more research is needed into the question of
the influence of scholasticism in the late sixteenth century, there is
a growing body of evidence which suggests that Hooker's concern
with scholasticism was by no means as exceptional as has often
been assumed. D'Entrèves has pointed out that the works of most
of the leading scholastic theologians were available to him in his
own college library at Oxford. There is in existence a catalogue
of the library of Corpus Christi, made in 1589, only a few years
after Hooker had ceased to be a fellow, which shows that the
college possessed copies of works by Alexander of Hales, Bona-
ventura, Albertus Magnus, Aquinas, Scotus, Ockham, and
Gerson, and there is other evidence to show that the writings of
Aquinas and Scotus were being read and discussed by some of
Hooker's closest associates at Oxford in the early 1580s.[31] At the
same time, it is becoming increasingly apparent, as the result of
recent research into the history of universities in the sixteenth and
seventeenth centuries, that the study of scholasticism survived the
Reformation even in protestant countries and that there was a
widespread revival of interest in the writings of the scholastic

theologians in England, as well as on the Continent, in the later years of the sixteenth century.[32] In the present state of research, Hooker's position in relation to this movement is obscure, and it would be interesting to know to what extent he was himself a pioneer or was simply following in the footsteps of others. Even in his study of scholasticism, however, his eclecticism is apparent. If he considered Aquinas 'the greatest amongst the School-divines' (III.ix.2) and drew more heavily on him than on any other scholastic writer, he also had a high appreciation of Scotus, whom he described as 'the wittiest of the school-divines' (I.xi.5). Hooker, in other words, was far from being a doctrinaire Thomist. He used St. Thomas when it suited him, but he viewed the *Summa Theologia* with the same critical detachment with which he viewed the rest of his sources, and it is important not to exaggerate the extent of Aquinas's influence on his thought. Throughout the *Laws*, Hooker borrowed freely from a wide range of writers, and his debt to Aquinas was certainly no greater than his debt to Aristotle or Whitgift.

Hooker's treatment of political questions follows the general pattern of the argument of the *Laws*. In Book I he is concerned with 'generalities'—with the nature of law in general and the problem of the origins of 'politic societies'. In Book VIII he is concerned with 'particulars'—primarily with the defence of the Royal Supremacy against the implied criticisms of the Puritans, but also, incidentally, with the nature of the king's 'power of dominion' in the secular as well as the ecclesiastical sphere. However, since there is considerable overlap between the arguments of Book I and Book VIII, for purposes of discussion it is more convenient to consider Hooker's political ideas under three heads. First, his theory of law, and in particular his concepts of 'the Law of Reason' and 'Human' or positive law. Second, his theory of the origins of society and government and his conception of constitutional monarchy as the best form of civil government. And third, his theory of Church and State, as expressed in his defence of the Royal Supremacy. At the same time, in examining Hooker's political ideas it is necessary to bear in mind bishop Paget's comments on the importance of the word 'presupposes' in Hooker's vocabulary,[33] for Hooker's political ideas are closely interwoven, and just as the arguments of the whole work were built up stage by stage, so the 'particular decisions' of Book VIII 'presuppose' the 'general meditations' of Book I. Equally, it is important to remember that the *Laws* is a work of ecclesiastical controversy and that, even at his most general, Hooker's political arguments have a purpose to fulfil in the overall structure of the book.

This is particularly the case with Hooker's theory of law, which is the basis not only of his political philosophy but also of his whole *apologia* for the Church of England. Hooker's theory of law plays a key role in the general argument of the *Laws*, since it was designed to provide a philosophical justification for the two basic principles on which the standard Elizabethan defence of the established order in the Church of England rested, the concept of 'things indifferent' and the claim that each national Church had the right to regulate its own external forms of worship and government. The primary purpose of Hooker's argument was to show that the Puritans were in error in holding 'that Scripture is the only rule to frame all our actions by' (Pref.vii.4), and that in consequence the principal reason that they put forward for opposing the existing laws and ceremonies of the Church of England— the fact that they were not in accordance with what was laid down in Scripture—was entirely without foundation. In fact, for polemical purposes Hooker deliberately went out of his way to exaggerate the degree of authority which the Puritans attributed to the Bible, by accusing them of holding 'that one only law, the Scripture, must be the rule to direct in all things' (II.i.2) and of making 'the bare mandate of sacred Scripture the only rule of all good and evil in the actions of mortal men' (II.viii.5). In practice, the Disciplinarian Puritans never adopted such an extreme position. Although there are passages in Cartwright's writings which can be construed in this sense, Cartwright always recognised a clear distinction between the authority of Scripture in the Church and its role in the sphere of man's temporal life. While he held that 'in all our actions, even civil and private, we ought *to follow the direction of* the word of God', he held that 'in matters of the Church and which concern all there *may be nothing done but by the word of God*' and, in practice, he did not deny the validity of either human reason or civil laws in the temporal sphere.[34] Moreover, even in the Church he was prepared to allow that some things were not prescribed in Scripture but were 'left to the order of the Church, because they are of that nature which are varied by times, places, persons, and other circumstances, and so could not at once be set down and established for ever', although he was careful to qualify this by adding, 'and yet so left to the order of the Church, as that it do nothing against the rules aforesaid'.[35] Thus the real issue in debate was not, as Hooker tried to suggest in order to prejudice his readers against the Puritans, whether Scripture was the sole law to be followed in all things, but how far the authority of Scripture extended in matters of religion —whether, in other words, precise rules were laid down in the Word for the external government and worship of the Church, or whether the authority of Scripture was binding only in matters of faith.

Hooker's argument was basically an extension of Whitgift's. What he set out to demonstrate was that although Scripture was sovereign in its own sphere and, contrary to what the Church of Rome taught, everything necessary for salvation was clearly revealed in the Word, nevertheless Scripture was not the only law that God had provided for mankind. Starting from the Aristotelian premise that everything in nature has 'some fore-conceived end for which it worketh' and that in order to achieve this end it is necessary that the operations of every creature should be governed 'by some canon, rule or law' which directs it to the attainment of its own end (I.ii.1), Hooker argues that God has laid down different laws for all his creatures, which determine the order of their being. The first law, which Hooker terms 'the *first law eternal*' (iii.1) in order to distinguish it from the eternal law that God has laid down for his creatures, is that law by which God himself is governed; for 'God . . . is a law both to himself, and to all other things besides' (ii.3). This law differs from all other laws in that it is not imposed by a superior being on an inferior, but is imposed by God on himself by 'his own free and voluntary act': it is 'that order which God before all ages hath set down with himself, for himself to do all things by' (ii.6). By contrast, the essence of all other laws consists in the fact that they are laws that God has imposed on his creatures, either directly, in the sense that he has laid them down himself, or indirectly, in that he has conferred on his creatures the power to make laws for themselves, as in the case of human laws. It is for this reason that Hooker sees all other forms of law—irrespective of whether their precepts are eternally binding or not—as forming part of what he terms the '*second law eternal*', which is the eternal order of the universe which God has set down 'to be kept by all his creatures, according to the several condition wherewith he hath endued them' (iii.1).

This '*second law eternal*' Hooker divides into five main categories 'according unto the different kinds of things which are subject unto it'. First, '*Nature's Law*', by which he means the physical laws of the universe which govern the behaviour of 'natural agents'; secondly, the 'law *Celestial*', by which angels are ruled; thirdly, 'the law of *Reason*', 'which bindeth creatures reasonable in this world'; fourthly, '*Divine* law', which is that law which God has revealed to men in Scripture; and fifthly, '*Human law*', which comprises the laws that men make for themselves on the basis of the law of reason or divine law (iii.1).

What distinguishes man from all other creatures is the fact that he is subject not to one law only but to several different kinds of law, according to the different aspects of his being. As a natural agent, he is subject to the same physical laws as other natural creatures; as a rational being, he is subject to the moral precepts of the law of reason; while as a member of a civil commonwealth or a Church, he is subject to the particular human laws imposed by those societies.[36] At the same time, man is also a spiritual being, with a higher end than mere temporal felicity in this life, and it is for this reason that God has laid down certain supernatural laws in Scripture, which men could never find out by 'the light of nature' alone, in order to lead them to salvation (i.xi.4–6). It is this function of revealing to man the truths necessary for salvation that Hooker sees as the primary purpose of Scripture. While he does not deny that Scripture contains many other precepts besides those specifically relating to salvation, he insists that 'the principal intent of Scripture is to deliver the laws of duties supernatural' (xiv.1) and that the existence of Scripture does not mean that other laws are to be regarded as superfluous (xvi.5). Thus, for Hooker, the essence of his argument against the Puritans is embodied in the principle that 'wisdom hath diversely imparted her treasures unto the world' and that, accordingly, 'we may not so in any one special kind admire her, that we disgrace her in any other; but let all her ways be according unto their place and degree adored' (II.i.4).

From the point of view of Hooker's political theory, the two most important aspects of his theory of law are his concept of the law of reason and his concept of human or positive law. As has frequently been pointed out, Hooker's theory of natural law, like his concept of the hierarchy of laws in general, is closely modelled on that of Aquinas, whom we quotes on a number of occasions.[37] However, one should perhaps not lay too much emphasis on the significance of Hooker's debt to Aquinas, for although Hooker undoubtedly made extensive use of St. Thomas, Aquinas's views on natural law were hardly unique, and his ideas were largely an elaboration of the official teaching of the medieval Church. Like Aquinas—and, indeed, like most late medieval theologians and political theorists—Hooker sees the law of reason, 'which men commonly used to call the Law of Nature' (I.viii.9), as the universal moral law which God has laid down for all men and which all men are capable of understanding through the faculty of reason. For Hooker there are four main characteristics of the law of reason: first, it is divine, since God is its author (iii.1); secondly, it is universal, for it is binding on all men as they are rational beings and not simply on Christians (iii.1), as is borne out by the fact that the knowledge of its precepts 'is general, the world hath always been acquainted with them' (viii.9); thirdly, it is ascertainable by the power of reason, 'for the Laws of well-doing are the dictates of right Reason' (vii.4), and it is through the faculty of reason that men arrive at a knowledge of the principles of natural law, although as Hooker is careful to insist, this does not necessarily mean that every human being has a perfect understanding of the precepts of natural law, since manifestly this is not the case, but simply that 'there is nothing in it but any man (having natural perfection of wit and ripeness of judgment) may by labour and travail find out' (viii.9); and fourthly, it is the basis of all human or positive laws, which are deductions or extrapolations from the law of reason (iii.1).

There are differences between Hooker's treatment of the law of reason and the popular medieval and sixteenth-century conception of the law of nature, but these are largely of a technical, philosophical character and are due to the fact that, like Aquinas,

Hooker attempts to explain man's understanding of the principles of natural law in terms of Aristotelian epistemology. The popular medieval belief was that the knowledge of the law of nature was innate in mankind, since God had implanted or engraved its precepts in the hearts or minds of men. It is interesting to observe that Hooker himself sometimes appears to conform to this view, as when he adopts the language of popular usage and speaks of men as carrying 'written in their hearts the universal law of mankind' (ɪ.xvi.5), or when he describes the law of nature as 'an infallible knowledge imprinted in the minds of all the children of men' (ɪɪ.viii.6). However, in his main discussion of the law of reason in Book 1, he rejects the idea that the knowledge of the principles of the law of nature is innate in mankind, arguing, like Aristotle, that at birth the mind or soul of man is a *tabula rasa*—'as a book, wherein nothing is and yet all things may be imprinted' (ɪ.vi.1)— and that men only grow to knowledge by degrees. Instead, he follows Aquinas in putting forward the view, which again is essentially Aristotelian in origin, that as 'in every kind of knowledge some such grounds there are, as that being proposed the mind doth presently embrace them as free from all possibility of error, clear and manifest without proof' (viii.5), so the precepts of natural law comprise a series of self-evident propositions which man is capable of discovering for himself through the light of reason.[38] At the same time Hooker also follows Aquinas in holding that the precepts of the law of nature fall into different categories, for while 'the main principles of Reason are in themselves apparent' (viii.5), other, more specific maxims of the law of nature are known by deduction from these first principles.[39]

One difficulty, which is implicit in all theories of natural law but is posed in an acute form by Hooker's rejection of the concept of innate ideas, is how one can know for certain what 'the dictates of right reason' really are. Hooker, in effect, suggests three answers at different stages of his argument. As a theologian he puts forward the conventional medieval and sixteenth-century view that God has provided confirmation for the precepts of the law of nature in Scripture, in order that 'the rule of divine law should herein help our imbecility, that we might the more infallibly understand what is good and what evil' (ɪ.xii.2). But he also holds that there are two natural ways by which men can discover what the laws of reason are. The first and safest method is to go back to first principles and endeavour to determine by abstract reasoning what the causes of goodness are. This 'is the most sure and infallible way, but so hard that all shun it' (viii.2). Hooker, therefore, suggests that there is a second method. This is to seek to discover empirically what all men have thought the principles of the law of nature to consist of, for 'the most certain token of evident goodness is, if the general persuasion of men do so account it'. In Hooker's view, the fact that a proposition is universally held to be true is an almost infallible indication that it must be. 'Wherefore although we know not the cause, yet thus much we may know; that some necessary cause there is, whensoever the judgments of all men generally or for the most part run one and the same way, especially in matters of natural discourse. ... The general and perpetual voice of men is as the sentence of God himself. For that which all men have at all times learned, Nature herself must needs have taught; and God being the author of Nature, her voice is but his instrument. By her from Him we receive whatsoever in such sort we learn' (viii.3). The implication of this is that it would be impossible for all men to agree unless God had caused this to happen and that God himself must, therefore, be the author of all universally held propositions. This argument is also of interest because it suggests that Hooker's approach to natural law was closer to that of Grotius and the seventeenth century than d'Entrèves would allow.[40] Although Hooker would not admit—any more than Grotius himself did—that the law of nature could exist if God had not first laid it down, nevertheless, by suggesting that one possible way of ascertaining the principles of the law of reason was to try to discover what all men believed to be true, Hooker was, in effect, advocating the same empirical method that Grotius was to adopt as the basis of his inquiry into the principles of the law of nature in the *De Iure Belli et Pacis*.[41]

The view has sometimes been put forward that Hooker's theory of the law of reason represents a departure from the teachings of the earlier Protestant Reformers and that in emphasising the concept of the law of nature he was consciously going back to an older tradition of thought which had largely been lost sight of at the Reformation.[42] However, this is an exaggeration. The sixteenth-century Reformers did not, as one school of modern historians has maintained, either reject or even substantially modify the traditional medieval concept of natural law.[43] On the contrary, as J. W. Allen rightly pointed out in his chapter on the *Laws* (188), the theory of natural law was held just as strongly, if perhaps not always so consistently, by Protestants as by Catholics in the sixteenth century, and it is a mistake to assume that it had no place in protestant teaching. It is true that the protestant doctrine of original sin entailed an even lower view of human nature than the modified Augustinianism of the medieval Church, with its semi-Pelagian concept of free will, and it is notorious that Luther and the other early Reformers often spoke in extremely disparaging terms of human reason and Aristotelian philosophy. But it is necessary to set these remarks in their proper context. When Luther denounces reason as 'the devil's whore' or when he pours scorn on the 'pig-philosophers' and 'pig-theologians' of the later middle ages, what he is attacking is not the use of reason as such but the application of human reason to questions of faith, which in his view lie beyond the scope of reason.

Basic to protestant theology was the Ockhamist distinction between faith and reason, and it was this distinction, coupled with the belief that man's spiritual faculties are utterly vitiated by the Fall, which led the early Reformers to insist that human reason was entirely inadequate to deal with matters of faith and that the only authority to be followed was that of Scripture. On the other hand, this did not mean that they denied the validity of reason in the temporal sphere. On the contrary, it is one of the basic assumptions of Luther's political theory that the temporal and spiritual orders are completely distinct and that in the temporal order God has placed man under the rule of reason and natural law, which he sees as the basis of all human laws.[44] Similarly, all the Protestant Reformers took it for granted that the knowledge of natural law was not confined to Christians but was to be found among all men, and in proof of this they appealed— as Hooker himself did—to the evidence of Romans ii.14, where St. Paul declares that 'the Gentiles, which have not the law, do by nature the things contained in the law'.[45] Against this it has to be admitted that the Reformers, in general, took the view that the knowledge of natural law had been partially obscured in men's hearts as a result of the Fall and that, in consequence, men were rarely capable of grasping the principles of the law of nature in their entirety without divine aid. This was not in itself a new doctrine, however; it was essentially the position of the medieval Church, and it was not interpreted as meaning that the precepts of the law of nature were no longer valid. Instead, the Reformers tended to argue, again in medieval fashion, that it was for this reason that God had confirmed the commandments of natural law in Scripture, especially in the Decalogue, in order that men might be reminded of its teaching—a view which, as we have seen, Hooker himself held.[46]

Thus there is no substantial difference between Hooker's conception of natural law and that held by all the leading Reformers. Basically, they all agreed that natural law represented the divine moral law which God had imposed on all men from the beginning of the world and that knowledge of it was common to all peoples. At the same time they also held that natural law was the basis of all secular law and that Christian rulers were under the same obligation to observe the law of nature as they were to observe the revealed law of God. Where Hooker differs most significantly from the orthodox Reformers is in the much greater degree of respect that he shows for the power of human reason. Unlike them, he does not envisage the possibility of any conflict arising between reason and revelation in ordinary circumstances. Rather, he sees them as operating in close harmony, the purpose of Scripture being to 'perfect' the light of man's 'natural understanding ... that the one being relieved by the other, there can want no part of needful instruction unto any good work which God himself requireth' (I.xiv.5). Hooker also went out of his way, apparently deliberately, to flout orthodox protestant opinion by suggesting that it would not be possible to interpret Scripture at all without the aid of human reason (III.viii.11). On the other hand, Hooker did not have an eighteenth-century belief in the unlimited power of natural reason. In the first place, he insisted that everything that he said 'concerning the force of man's natural understanding' must always be understood with the qualification 'that there is no kind of faculty or power in man or any other creature, which can rightly perform the functions allotted to it, without perpetual aid and concurrence of that

Supreme Cause of all things' (I.viii.11). Secondly, he admitted that man's knowledge of the law of nature was corrupted by the Fall; this is one of the reasons why he considers that human laws are necessary, since, as a consequence of the Fall, men are no longer naturally inclined to obey the law of reason voluntarily (x.3–4). Thirdly, Hooker did not believe that all men have the same capacity for understanding the precepts of the law of nature. Certain categories of people, he held, have no knowledge of the law of reason whatsoever and need to be guided by other men: children, who are too young to understand it; 'innocents', who 'are excluded by natural defect'; and madmen, who have temporarily lost the use of their reason (vii.4). But even among the rest of mankind, who have 'the light of reason' to guide them, there are different degrees of understanding of the law of nature, for its precepts are not all equally easy to discern. 'The first principles of the Law of Nature are easy; hard it were to find men ignorant of them. But concerning the duty which Nature's law doth require at the hands of man in a number of things particular, so far forth hath the natural understanding even of sundry whole nations been darkened, that they have not discerned no not gross iniquity to be sin' (xii.2). Thus it is significant that when he comes to discuss the making of human laws, Hooker specifically recommends that 'none but wise men' should be employed in devising such laws, since 'men of common capacity and but ordinary judgment are not able (for how should they?) to discern what things are fittest for each kind and state of regiment' (x.7).

Hooker's theory of 'human' or positive law follows logically from his concept of the law of reason.[47] For him, as for most medieval thinkers, human laws are necessary for two main reasons: first, because, as a result of man's fallen nature, men are incapable of observing the precepts of the law of nature in its entirety of their own volition and they therefore need to live under the compulsion of positive law; and second, because the law of reason only lays down general principles and does not provide for all the contingencies of human life and, in particular, for the needs of 'politic societies'. Human laws, therefore, are of two kinds: first, those which embody the principles of natural law but give them the sanction of positive law, which Hooker terms 'mixedly' human 'because the matter whereunto it bindeth is the same which reason necessarily doth require at our hands, and from the law of reason it differeth in the manner of binding only'; and second, those which he terms 'merely' human, because they 'make that a duty now which before was none' and relate to matters which are not laid down precisely in the law of nature but are left to men's discretion to regulate as they think fit. To illustrate the first category, he cites the instance of laws forbidding polygamy and marriage within the prohibited degrees, both of which are condemned by the law of nature; as an illustration of the second, he cites the case of laws relating to inheritance, which may legitimately vary from society to society (I.x.10). Human laws may thus be said to differ from the laws of reason in three major respects: first, they are coercive, for they carry the sanction of positive force, and any breach of them will be punished by the authority that has appointed them; secondly, they are of only local validity, for they are binding only on the society that has made them and not on all men, except in the case of the law of nations, which Hooker treats separately (x.12–13); thirdly, in so far as they are 'merely' human, they are mutable, for if circumstances change, they can be altered. Theft, for example, is always punishable, since it is contrary to the law of nature, but the punishments imposed for it may vary, for 'the kind of punishment is positive, and such lawful as men shall think with discretion convenient by law to appoint' (x.6).

The two most significant aspects of Hooker's theory of human law are, first of all, his insistence that all human laws derive their ultimate validity from consent, and secondly, his application of the concept of human law to the sphere of ecclesiastical law. Hooker's theory of human law is closely linked to his theory of 'politic societies', and just as it is one of the basic axioms of his theory of government that all government (except in the special case of rulers who derive their authority directly from God) ought to be founded on the 'consent of men', since no man has a natural right to exercise political authority over his fellow men, so equally it is one of the fundamental principles of his theory of law that laws can only derive their validity from the consent of the people who are to be governed by them.[48] 'Laws they are not therefore which public approbation hath not made so' (I.x.8). Consent, however, may be expressed in a variety of ways, and he is careful to insist that it is not necessary that all individuals should 'personally declare their assent by voice sign or act'. Laws, he points out, may be said to have the consent of the people if they are passed by their representatives, acting in their name, as in the English parliament. Similarly, the edicts of absolute monarchs are binding on their subjects—'whether they approve or dislike it'—because absolute monarchs enjoy their authority either by divine appointment or by consent of the people. For the same reason, Hooker holds that men have a duty to observe the laws and customs established by their predecessors: 'And to be commanded we do consent, when that society whereof we are part hath at any time before consented, without revoking the same after by the like universal agreement. Wherefore as any man's deed past is good as long as himself continueth; so the act of a public society of men done five hundred years sithence standeth as theirs who presently are of the same societies, because corporations are immortal; we were then alive in our predecessors, and they in their successors do live still' (I.x.8).

Essentially, Hooker's theory represents a sophisticated version of the traditional English constitutional doctrine that the king had no power to make laws without the consent of his people. However, his discussion of the concept of consent also has a direct bearing on the controversy with the Puritans. By stressing the principle that men are bound by the laws made on their behalf by their representatives as well as by those made by their predecessors, Hooker was, in effect, reinforcing his general contention that the Puritans had a duty to conform to the laws of the Established Church, since such laws had been instituted by the public consent of the whole people.[49]

Of equal significance for Hooker's attack on Puritanism was his application of the concept of human law to the external laws of the Church. One of the key arguments he uses against the Puritans is the idea that the Visible Church, and the 'particular' local churches of which it consists, must be viewed from two different aspects. It is not only a spiritual society, it is also a species of 'politic society'. It is, as he puts it, 'both a society and a society supernatural'. As such it is governed by two different kinds of laws. As a 'society supernatural' it is bound by 'a law supernatural, which God himself hath revealed concerning that kind of worship which his people shall do unto him'. As a 'natural society', however, it requires external laws of government, like other forms of 'politic society' (I.xv.2–3). These external laws are not laid down in Scripture but are left to the discretion of each individual Church to determine as it shall think fit, an argument that he develops in detail in Book III. 'Touching things which belong to discipline and outward polity, the Church hath authority to make canons, laws, and decrees, even as we read that in the Apostles' times it did. Which kind of laws (forasmuch as they are not in themselves necessary to salvation may after they are made be also changed as the difference of times or places shall require' (III.x.7). The external laws of the Church in matters not relating to salvation are, therefore, in essentially the same category as other human laws, for they possess the same characteristics as other forms of human law. They are positive; they are mutable; they are made by the consent of the Church as a whole; and they are binding on all the members of the particular Church which has established them, unless and until they are abrogated by the consent of that Church.

The interlocking character of Hooker's political ideas is illustrated by the close connexion between his theories of government and society and his theory of law. In his view, the first point of distinction between the laws of reason and human laws lies in the fact that, whereas the former 'do bind men absolutely even as they are men, although they have never any settled fellowship, never any solemn agreement amongst themselves what to do or not to do' (I.x.1), the latter are the products of human society. His investigation of the nature of law, therefore, led him on naturally to consider the nature of 'politic societies' and the problem of how they came into existence. Hooker's principal ideas on the subject of society and government are to be found embedded in his discussion of the nature of human law in the famous tenth chapter of Book I. However, he subsequently elaborated these ideas in chapter ii on 'the power of dominion' in Book VIII, and it is necessary to consider the arguments of the two books in conjunction.[50]

Hooker's theory of society and government may be described in very general terms—like that of Aquinas, from whom, however, he differs significantly on many points—as an attempt to reconcile

Aristotle's concept of the State as a natural institution with the traditional Augustinian doctrine of the Church that government is a consequence of the Fall. For Hooker, there are two main reasons why society and government are necessary. The first is to be found in the fact that men have a natural need to live in society. Although he does not actually quote Aristotle's dictum that 'man is a political animal', he does maintain, like Aristotle, that men cannot live on their own and that 'therefore to supply those defects and imperfections which are in us living single and solely by ourselves, we are naturally induced to seek communion and fellowship with others' (I.x.I). On the other hand, he also accepts the traditional medieval and sixteenth-century protestant belief that government is a necessary consequence of man's fallen nature. In Hooker's view, it is the fact that human nature is corrupt and men no longer capable of living together without strife and envy which makes the existence of government imperative for mankind. For he is prepared to concede—and here he differs from Aristotle—that there is 'no impossibility in nature considered by itself, but that men might have lived without any public regiment'. 'Howbeit', he continues, 'the corruption of our nature being pre-supposed, we may not deny but that the Law of Nature doth now require of necessity some kind of regiment, so that to bring things unto the first course they were in, and utterly to take away all kind of public government in the world, were apparently to over turn the whole world' (x.4).

However, although the general philosophical assumptions underlying Hooker's theory of government and society are Aristotelian, and although there are frequent echoes of the *Politics* in both Book I and Book VIII, Hooker does not attempt to follow Aristotle at all closely in the details of his argument. On many points he either rejects or substantially modifies the teaching of 'the arch-philosopher' in accordance with Christian doctrine or the political thinking of his own age. Where Hooker differs most conspicuously from Aristotle is in his account of the origins of civil society. Hooker holds, like many late medieval and sixteenth-century theorists, that political societies owe their existence not only to man's natural instinct for association but also to some kind of agreement, either formal or tacit, made by men when they first came together to form societies.[51] 'Two foundations there are', he

writes, 'which bear up public societies; the one, a natural inclina-
tion, whereby all men desire sociable life and fellowship; the
other, an order expressly or secretly agreed upon touching the
manner of their union in living together. The latter is that which
we call the Law of a Commonweal, the very soul of a politic body,
the parts whereof are by law animated, held together, and set on
work in such actions, as the common good requireth' (I.x.1). For
Hooker, in other words, the State has a dual origin: in one sense,
it is a natural institution that has its roots in man's basic human
instincts; in another sense, it is a rational construct, since it is the
product of human reason, which leads men to unite together to
form societies.

The concept of human reason plays an important part in
Hooker's theory of the origins of society, as one would expect,
since he sees the formation of society as being the direct result of
the application of the principles of reason to the needs of man's
natural life. Thus he considers that it was through reason that
men first learned to perceive the benefits of living together in
society. In particular, he holds that it was through reason that
men were brought to recognise that the only way whereby the
conflicts and strife engendered by the Fall might be avoided was
'by growing unto composition and agreement amongst themselves,
by ordaining some kind of government public, and yielding themselves subject thereunto; that unto whom they granted authority
to rule and govern, by them the peace, tranquillity, and happy
estate of the rest might be procured'. For men 'knew that no man
might in reason take upon him to determine his own right, and
according to his own determination proceed in maintenance
thereof, inasmuch as every man is towards himself and them
whom he greatly affecteth partial; and therefore that strifes and
troubles would be endless, except they gave their common consent
all to be ordered by some whom they should agree upon: without
which consent there were no reason that one man should take
upon himself to be lord or judge over another' (I.x.4).

Hooker's emphasis on the necessity for some form of 'composition' or 'agreement' among men before government can be
established is the most important principle of his theory of government, for it is the basis on which all his subsequent arguments
about the nature of political authority and the validity of human

laws rest. In his view, consent is the only rational foundation for human government, since no human being possesses a clear and indisputable right to exercise authority over his fellow men. Thus while he does not explicitly reject Aristotle's view that there is 'a kind of natural right in the noble, wise, and virtuous, to govern them which are of servile disposition', he implies that this cannot be proved, and he therefore argues that 'for manifestation of this their right, and men's more peaceable contentment on both sides, the assent of them who are to be governed seemeth necessary' (I.x.4). Similarly, while he is prepared to allow that the law of nature gives fathers supreme authority 'within their private families', he cannot perceive how this authority can extend beyond the limits of the individual family. Consequently, he holds that 'over a whole grand multitude . . . impossible it is that any should have complete lawful power, but by consent of men, or immediate appointment of God' (x.4). According to Hooker, the only valid exception to the principle that power, if it is to be lawful, must be based on the consent of the governed is in the case of rulers who receive their authority directly from God. However, the exception is more important than might appear at first sight. For in Book VIII he suggests that there are two classes of rulers who fall into this category: first, those who are called directly by God, 'which thing he did often in the commonwealth of Israel'; and secondly, those who enjoy their authority by right of conquest, since the latter may be said to owe their position to the direct intervention of divine providence, 'for it is God who giveth victory in the day of war' (VIII.ii.5; Houk, 171, 170).

On the other hand, Hooker was capable, as we have seen, of interpreting the concept of consent very broadly, and the same principles that apply in the case of human laws also apply in the case of the compacts or agreements by which political societies are instituted. Thus he does not posit the necessity for any formal contract or agreement before society can come into existence, since he makes it clear that consent may be given tacitly as well as positively. In his first reference to the idea of a compact, he talks of 'an order expressly or secretly agreed upon' (I.x.1), while later he speaks of power being 'either granted or consented unto by them over whom they exercise the same' (x.4). In a similar fashion, when discussing the nature of royal authority in Book VIII. he suggests that what he terms 'the articles of compact' may be modified in the course of time not only 'by express consent, whereof positive laws are witnesses', but also 'by silent allowance famously notified through custom reaching beyond the memory of man' (vIII.ii.11; Houk, 176). Again, just as in Book 1 he had argued that men are bound by the laws passed by their predecessors even though they have not consented to them themselves, so in Book vIII he argues that subjects are bound by 'the articles of compact' which their ancestors have made with their rulers, either at the time of the first institution of government or by subsequent 'after-agreement', and he refuses to allow that they have any power to alter them unilaterally. Although he holds that initially the 'power of dominion' was vested in the people,[52] he considers that once government has been established and authority conveyed to a ruler, it is to all intents and purposes irrevocable.[53] Hence his insistence that 'such things therefore must be thought upon beforehand, that power may be limited ere it be granted' (vIII.ii.10; Houk, 176). Equally, Hooker was prepared to extend the concept of consent to include absolute monarchies. For he held that no single form of government was enjoined in the law of nature,[54] and while in general he appears to take the view that absolute monarchs owe their authority to right of conquest, he does not rule out the possibility that absolute monarchy might be established by consent.[55] Moreover, he suggests that even monarchies that were originally founded by right of conquest may come in the course of time to acquire the sanction of consent, since they may be transformed by 'means of after-agreement' into 'that most sweet form of kingly government which philosophers define to be "regency willingly sustained and endured, with chiefty of power in the greatest things"' (ii.11; Houk, 176).

Given these assumptions, it is clear that Hooker's outlook differed radically from that of Locke and the majority of seventeenth-century social contract theorists. In the past Hooker has frequently been cited as one of the earliest representatives of the theory of social contract, and the view has even been put forward that he was the first thinker to propound the doctrine in its classic form.[56] It is now generally recognised that not only is this conception of Hooker too simple, but it has its origins in an historical myth, since it can be traced back directly to the way in which

Locke and other late seventeenth- and early eighteenth-century Whig writers and politicians appealed to the authority of Hooker in order to provide the theory of social contract with a respectable pedigree.[57] Although Hooker undoubtedly anticipated certain aspects of the seventeenth-century doctrine of social contract, there are major differences between his concept of a compact of society or government—he does not clearly distinguish between the two—and the fully fledged theory of the social contract which emerged in the seventeenth century, and it is very doubtful whether he can properly be classified as a social contract thinker.

In the first place, Hooker's interest in the idea of compact was philosophical, not political, and his theory lacks the ideological overtones that characterised most seventeenth-century social contract thinking. Historically, the theory of social contract as it evolved in the late sixteenth and early seventeenth centuries was closely associated with the idea of the right of resistance and the doctrine of popular sovereignty. The majority of seventeenth-century social contract theorists—whether they emphasised the idea of a contract of society or the older concept of a contract of government—were concerned to prove that political authority was ultimately derived from the people and that a ruler who broke the terms of his original contract might lawfully be resisted or deposed by his subjects. By contrast, Hooker was primarily interested in the idea of compact as a means of explaining how society and government came into existence, and it is hardly accidental that at no point in his argument does he draw the inference that, because society originates in some kind of 'composition' or 'agreement', subjects are entitled to resist their rulers. Secondly, the manner in which he stated his theory of compact was much more tentative than that of most seventeenth-century contract theorists. Not only was he careful to qualify his theory by insisting that consent might be given tacitly as well as positively, with the result that it is impossible to accuse Hooker of falling into the error of supposing that society and government were founded upon an actual historical contract, but he was also prepared to allow that in certain circumstances governments might be established legitimately without any kind of agreement on the part of the people. His theory also differs from Locke's in two other important respects. First, he was prepared to recognise the validity of all forms of government, including absolute monarchy, since, unlike Locke, he did not consider that it contravened the law of nature. Secondly, as d'Entrèves has emphasised, his theory of compact does not involve Locke's individualistic conception of natural rights—a concept that hardly existed in the sixteenth century.[58]

The main point of difference between Hooker's political philosophy and that of the social contract theorists, however, lies in the fact that what Hooker held was a theory of compact or consent rather than a theory of contract. Whereas the keynote of the theory of social contract, in whatever form the doctrine was expressed, was its emphasis on the contractual nature of political authority and the reciprocal rights and obligations of rulers and subjects, the basis of Hooker's theory was not the idea of contract but the idea of consent. What Hooker was concerned to emphasise in his account of the origins of society and government in Book I was the principle that men could not be subject to any form of government except by their own consent. Although he talks of men 'growing unto composition and agreement amongst themselves' (I.x.4), he does not suggest that such agreements constitute contracts in the legal meaning of the term, nor does he claim that the fact that government originates in consent creates any kind of contractual relationship between rulers and ruled. In Hooker's view, consent was a necessary precondition without which, in normal circumstances, society and government could not come into being: however, in marked contrast to Locke, he held that the institution of government was, for all practical purposes, an irreversible act, and that, once the people had consented to be governed in a certain way, they had no power either to withdraw the authority which they had conferred on their sovereign or to alter the terms on which it was held, except with his voluntary agreement.[59] Correspondingly, Hooker's conception of the political obligations of rulers was fundamentally different from that of the majority of social contract theorists. Although he laid great stress on the responsibilities which rulers owed to their subjects—and, in particular, he held that in a limited monarchy the king had a duty to abide by the laws and customs of the realm—it is clear that like most medieval and sixteenth-century political thinkers he believed that these obligations were of a moral rather than of a legally enforceable character and that only God had the power to punish a tyrannical ruler.[60]

It has been argued by d'Entrèves that, although Hooker cannot be said to have held a concept of the 'contract of society' (*pactum societatis*) in the sense in which this was understood in the seventeenth century, it is possible to find traces in his thought of the older idea of a 'contract of government' (*pactum subjectionis*), especially in Book VIII.[61] But it is doubtful whether this is really the case. It is true that there are passages in Book VIII where Hooker appears to use the language of contract, as, for example, when he talks of 'the articles of compact', made when kings were first instituted, which show 'how far their power may lawfully extend', or when he speaks of 'that first original conveyance, when power was derived by the whole into one' (VIII.ii.11, 9; Houk, 176, 175). However, one should be careful not to read too much into such phrases. Hooker never states that the 'original conveyance' of authority from the people to the prince creates any kind of contractual relationship between the two parties, and it is clear from the context of his remarks that what he has in mind when speaking of 'the articles of compact' is not a formal contract of government of the kind that figures in the writings of some of his more radical contemporaries, such as Buchanan, but rather the ancient laws and customs of the realm, which it is the duty of monarchs to observe. These laws and customs derive their validity partly from immemorial usage and partly from positive law.[62] Hooker's concept, in other words, is closer in spirit to the traditional medieval conception of fundamental law than it is to the idea of a *pactum subjectionis*, for although he holds that the ancient laws and customs are binding on rulers, he does not recognise the existence of any sanctions that can compel rulers to observe them other than those of conscience and the fear of divine judgment.

Hooker's theory of compact can thus be summed up as a theory of how society and government came into existence rather than a theory of contract in the seventeenth-century sense of the term. For, although his views on the origins of government undoubtedly foreshadow those of the seventeenth-century social contract theorists, the idea of contract—whether in the sense of a contract of society or a contract of government—plays no part in his thought, and it is, in fact, entirely alien to his political philosophy. On the other hand, it is equally important not to exaggerate the novelty of his theory of the origins of 'politic societies'. The idea that society or government was founded on some kind of agreement or compact was coming to be held by a growing number of political theorists in the second half of the sixteenth century, and most of the arguments which Hooker puts forward in the *Laws* can be paralleled in other works of the period, notably in the writings of some of the protestant monarchomachs and the late sixteenth- and early seventeenth-century Jesuits.

One writer whose theory of the origins of civil society has particularly close affinities with Hooker's is George Buchanan, the Scots humanist and Reformer, whose *De Jure Regni apud Scotos* was published in Edinburgh in 1579 and in London in 1580. Although Hooker never refers to Buchanan by name, the *De Jure Regni apud Scotos* was one of the most famous political pamphlets of the late sixteenth century, and it is difficult to believe that Hooker was not familiar with its contents or that he did not borrow from it, consciously or unconsciously. Many of the most distinctive features of Hooker's theory are also to be found in Buchanan's dialogue, and the arguments of I.x.1–5 in particular appear at times to follow Buchanan very closely. Like Hooker, Buchanan attributes the origins of political societies to two factors: first, man's natural instinct for association, which he shares in common with many of the beasts and which leads him instinctively to shun solitude and to seek the fellowship of his own kind;[63] and secondly, 'that light infused by God into our minds', which 'some call Nature, others the Law of Nature', which teaches men to perceive the utility of joining together to form civil societies (7). Like Hooker, too, Buchanan lays great emphasis on the divine character of the law of nature, so that he can argue simultaneously—very much as Hooker does—that society is created by the voluntary agreement of men, who recognise the practical advantages of mutual cooperation, and that it is God who is the only 'Author of humane Society', since it is 'that Divine Law rooted in us from the beginning', which is 'the cause . . . of men's incorporating in political Societies' (8). Buchanan also anticipates Hooker in suggesting that at the beginning, when society was first instituted, kings were not bound by any laws but 'the lust of Kings stood instead of Laws', and that it was 'the insolency of Kings' which compelled men to recognise the need to have fixed laws and to constrain their rulers to observe them (13).[64] On the other hand, Buchanan differed fundamentally from Hooker in the use to which he applied his theory. The primary purpose of the *De Jure Regni apud Scotos* was to justify the right of subjects to resist tyrannical rulers, and, in contrast to Hooker, Buchanan specifically argues that not only is the king under the law but that 'there is then a mutual paction betwixt the King and his Subjects' which entitles the latter to take up arms against a ruler who breaks the terms of the covenant or contract under which he holds his authority (65–6). Such views were entirely contrary to Hooker's traditionalist conception of political authority. It is, therefore, scarcely surprising that Buchanan's name is never mentioned in the *Laws*. If Hooker was influenced by Buchanan, as seems probable, he would hardly have been prepared to acknowledge that some of his leading ideas were derived from such a notorious exponent of the doctrine of the right of resistance.

In theory, Hooker held that not only were all forms of government equally valid but that, in principle, they were all equally divine, since God's sanction could be given in various ways and the ruler who was appointed directly by God, the absolute monarch whose power was founded on right of conquest, and the ordinary ruler who derived his authority from popular consent could each be said to exercise his office by divine right.[65] However, it would be wrong to infer from this that Hooker regarded all forms of government as being equally good or that he was indifferent to the details of political organisation. In practice, as he made clear when he turned to the discussion of 'particulars' in Book VIII, he had no doubt that the best form of constitution was one where the law, in Aristotle's phrase, was king. 'Happier that people whose law is their king in the greatest things, than that whose king is himself their law. Where the king doth guide the State, and the law the king, that commonwealth is like an harp or melodious instrument, the strings whereof are tuned and handled all by one, following as laws the rules and canons of musical science' (VIII.ii.12; Houk, 178).

In Hooker's view, the two basic foundations of good government were popular consent and the sovereignty of the law, the latter being in practice the more important. However, he was careful to qualify his remarks on the sovereignty of law by insisting that the powers of government should not be restricted excessively. 'I am not of opinion', he writes, 'that simply always in kings the most, but the best limited power is best: the most limited is, that which may deal in fewest things; the best, that which in dealing is tied unto the soundest, perfectest, and most indifferent rule; which rule is the law; I mean not only the law of nature and of God, but very national or municipal law consonant thereunto' (viii.ii.12; Houk, 177–8). For Hooker this ideal was represented by the type of limited monarchy which was to be found in England, 'wherein though no manner person or cause be unsubject to the king's power, yet so is the power of the king over all and in all limited, that unto all his proceedings the law itself is a rule' (ii.13; Houk, 178), and 'where the people are in no subjection, but such as willingly themselves have condescended unto, for their own most behoof and security' (ii.7; Houk, 173).

Hooker's theory of the English constitution is of particular interest, because it represents an attempt to combine his own philosophical belief in the consensual origins of society and government with the traditional constitutional doctrines of the English Common Law. For a sixteenth-century theologian, Hooker displays an unusual knowledge of contemporary legal and constitutional ideas, which has often been attributed to the influence of his years at the Temple, although it is perhaps more likely that it reflects the personal influence of his friend and former pupil, Sir Edwin Sandys.[66] Whatever the sources of his legal knowledge, one of the impressive features of Book viii is the extent to which Hooker appears to have absorbed the principles of the common law and the expert manner in which he tosses off legal maxims, as if he had been studying the Year Books all his life. The one unorthodox element in Hooker's constitutional thinking lies in his insistence that in monarchies of the English type the king's 'power of dominion' is derived originally by 'conveyance' from the people, and that, in consequence, 'kings, even inheritors, do hold their right to the power of dominion, with dependency upon the whole entire body politic over which they rule as kings' (vm.ii.9; Houk, 175)—a claim that appears at first sight to be more in tune with the theories of Buchanan and the author of the *Vindiciæ contra Tyrannos* than with those of Bracton and Fortescue. In practice, however, Hooker had little difficulty in reconciling his belief in the popular origins of political authority with the orthodox conception of the English monarchy embodied in the common law. Although he laid considerable emphasis on the concept of the king's 'dependency' upon the people, he took care to make it clear that this 'dependency' consisted simply in the fact that the king's powers were originally derived by grant from the people. It did not imply that his authority was subject to popular control or that the people had any right to withdraw the authority which they had conferred on him. Moreover, in the same section of Book vm, he specifically went out of his way to dissociate himself from the arguments of the *Vindiciæ* by insisting that in hereditary monarchies the natural heir succeeded to the throne automatically on the death of his predecessor by right of birth, without any form of election, and that the ceremony of coronation was not to be construed as an act of investiture by which the new king received power from the people (ii.8–10; Houk, 173–6).

In other respects, Hooker's theory corresponds very closely to the traditional medieval and Tudor view of the English constitution. In the first place, he regards it as axiomatic that the basic principle of the English system of government is that the king is under the law—'*Rex non debet esse sub homine, sed sub Deo et lege*' in Bracton's famous dictum, which he quotes (vm.ii.3; Houk, 169). In Hooker's view the essential difference between absolute monarchy and monarchy of the English type lies in the fact that whereas 'kings by conquest make their own charter' and are subject only to divine law and the law of nature (ii.11; Houk, 176), in England the powers of the crown are circumscribed by law, and both the extent of the king's authority and the manner in which it may be exercised are determined by the positive laws and customs of the realm. 'The axioms of our regal government', he writes, 'are these: "Lex facit regem"': the king's grant of any favour made contrary to the law is void; '"Rex nihil potest quod jure potest"' (ii.13; Houk, 178). Secondly, it is clear that underlying Hooker's conception of royal authority is the traditional medieval and sixteenth-century distinction between *gubernaculum* and *jurisdictio*, between the king's 'absolute' and his 'ordained' power.[67] Although Hooker does not discuss the constitutional powers of the king in detail, except in relation to the Church, which is the main concern of Book VIII, he does hold that there is a clear distinction between those things which the king may do in virtue of his supreme power and those which he may not. In civil matters, he writes, 'the king, through his supreme power, may do great things and sundry himself, both appertaining unto peace and war, both at home, by commandment and by commerce with states abroad, because so much the law doth permit. Some things on the other side, the king alone hath no power to do without consent of the lords and commons assembled in parliament: the king of himself cannot change the nature of pleas, nor courts, no not so much as restore blood; because the law is a bar unto him; not any law divine or natural . . . but the positive laws of the realm have abridged therein and restrained the king's power' (ii.17; Houk, 182–3). Thirdly, as this passage shows, Hooker holds the conventional belief that the power of making laws belongs not to the king alone, but to the king in parliament, which represents the whole community of the realm, and that, in consequence, the king has no power either to introduce new laws or to alter those that are already in existence without the consent of his subjects.[68] On the other hand, he clearly recognises—and here again his views are merely a reflexion of contemporary constitutional doctrine—that if parliament alone can pass laws, it is an essential part of the royal prerogative that kings possess the power to veto legislation put forward in parliament, 'which not to give them, were to deny them that without which they were but kings by mere title, and not in exercise of dominion' (vi.11; Houk, 244).

From this it is clear that Hooker's conception of sovereignty was essentially medieval and traditional in character. Although he undoubtedly knew the writings of Bodin,[69] his preoccupation with the English constitution appears to have led him to ignore the philosophical issues concerning the nature of sovereignty which Bodin had raised in the *De Republica*. Whereas for Bodin the two essential criteria of sovereignty are, first, that the sovereign is by definition above the law and cannot be legally bound by positive laws, although he is subject to the law of nature and divine law, and, second, that the sovereign is the ultimate source of positive law, since it is his sanction that gives it its effect, Hooker's conception of sovereignty is quite different. For Hooker, sovereignty —'dominion' or 'power supreme'—is simply that power which a king exercises over his people. While this entails the idea that the king has no external superior on earth, it is perfectly compatible both with the notion that the king is under the law and with the idea that the king has no power to make new laws without the consent of his subjects.[70] It might be argued that for Hooker, sovereignty in Bodin's sense of the term does not reside in the king but in the whole body of the people, since he holds that the people are the original source of the king's power of dominion and that their consent is necessary for legislation. It is difficult, however, to maintain that this is, in fact, the case. Although Hooker argues that the king holds his dominion 'with dependency upon the whole entire body politic', the people in Hooker's theory cannot be said to possess sovereignty in Bodin's meaning of the term, since they have no power to alter or withdraw the authority which they have conferred on the king. Nor can they be regarded as the ultimate source of positive law, since they cannot legislate without the king's assent. In practice, the assumptions underlying Hooker's conception of sovereignty are the exact antithesis of those of Bodin. Whereas Bodin's theory is founded upon the principle that the sovereign must by definition be above the law, Hooker still adheres to the traditional Aristotelian and medieval ideal that the law itself should be sovereign.

Hooker's conception of sovereignty is also traditional in another sense. Although he never discusses the question of resistance directly, implicit in his whole argument is the conventional medieval and sixteenth-century assumption that the king is answerable only to God and that, while he has a moral obligation to observe the law, if he fails to do so, his subjects have no right to take action against him. 'For concerning the dealings of men who administer government', he writes in Book II, 'and unto whom the execution of that law belongeth; they have their Judge who sitteth in heaven, and before whose tribunal-seat they are accountable for whatever abuse or corruption, which (being worthily misliked in this Church) the want either of care or of conscience in them hath bred' (i.1). Unfortunately, Hooker did not develop this theme in Book VIII, except possibly in chapter vi, but it is clear from that passage and from the general tenor of his remarks throughout the book that he shared the orthodox belief of most Tudor Englishmen that rebellion was always wrong and that he was not prepared to countenance it under any circumstances.[71] Hooker, as we have seen, did not hold a contractual theory of government, and in the context of the sixteenth century there was nothing inherently incompatible between the idea that the king was under the law, or even between Hooker's claim that political authority was originally derived from the people, and the standard Reformation doctrine that subjects had no right to resist their rulers, however tryannically they might behave.

Hooker's principal purpose in Book VIII was not to explain or defend the English constitution but to justify the Royal Supremacy, and it is this aspect of his political theory which has emerged as the main focus of controversy in recent discussions of his thought. Criticism of Hooker's theory of Church and State is not a new phenomenon. In the past he has frequently come under attack from churchmen and historians alike for his alleged Erastianism, and to many modern Anglicans his forthright defence of the Royal Supremacy and his assertion of parliament's right to legislate for the Church have been a source of continuing embarrassment. In the past twenty years, however, the question of Hooker's treatment of the problem of Church and State has taken on a new significance as a result of the arguments put forward by Peter Munz in his study *The Place of Hooker in the History of Thought*.

Munz's study raised two issues, in particular, that are of fundamental importance for the overall interpretation of Hooker's political thought. First, it raised the general question of Hooker's intellectual consistency, arguing that, contrary to popular belief, Hooker did not have a single, coherent theory of Church and State, but that he shifted his ground in the course of writing the *Laws*. Secondly, it raised in a more extreme form than either d'Entrèves or Previté-Orton had done the question of Hooker's debt to Marsilius of Padua. According to Munz, as a logical edifice the *Laws* is essentially a failure, for although Hooker's original aim was to formulate a theory of Church and State which would be in accordance with the philosophical principles of Aquinas, in practice this proved to be an impossible under-taking, since he was unable to reconcile St. Thomas's hierarchical conception of the relationship between grace and nature, Church and State, with the facts of the Tudor constitution. In conse-quence, like other Tudor political theorists, he found himself increasingly drawn towards the Averroistic arguments of Marsilius of Padua, with their logical implication that there was a funda-mental dichotomy between the natural ends of the State and the spiritual ends of the Church, and that the State, as a purely secular institution, was entitled to exercise complete control over the earthly existence of its members, including the external life of the Church.[72] In fact, Munz claims, Hooker was never happy with this solution. While he borrowed heavily from Marsilius, especially in Book VIII, he hesitated to follow his arguments to their logical conclusion. It was for this reason that he left the last three books unfinished at the time of his death, since he was conscious of the contradictions between his Thomism and his Marsilian theory of the State but did not know how to resolve them (107–11).

Munz's argument, though ingenious, rests on too many un-proven assumptions, and it is doubtful whether it will stand up to close examination. In the first place, his description of the alter-native theories of Church and State open to Hooker is too schematic, and in his efforts to establish a medieval pedigree for Hooker's political ideas he largely ignores the influence of the Reformation on the development of political theory in the six-teenth century. Secondly, his argument is based on a fundamental misinterpretation of the character of Tudor political theory. Like many modern scholars, Munz tends to overestimate the influence of Marsilius of Padua on English political thought in the sixteenth century, and his use of the term 'Tudor Averroism' to describe the philosophy underlying the theory of the Royal Supremacy is seriously misleading.[73] While references to Marsilius are not un-common in English works of the sixteenth century and it is well known that an English translation of the *Defensor Pacis* was published in 1535 under the auspices of Thomas Cromwell, in general Tudor writers used Marsilius eclectically, as they used other late medieval authors, such as Gerson, and it would be rash to assume that they swallowed his ideas in their entirety. In practice, Marsilius appears to have been quoted chiefly for his historical arguments—in particular, for his attacks on the papacy and his views of episcopacy—and it is significant that the one explicit reference to the *Defensor Pacis* in the *Laws* is to be found not in Book VIII but in Book VII, where Hooker cites him as an exponent of the theory, which he himself had once held but had since abandoned, that bishops were not introduced into the Church until after the death of the Apostles.[74] While there are undoubtedly parallels between the arguments used by Tudor writers to justify the Royal Supremacy and the arguments of the *Defensor Pacis*,[75] there is no evidence to support Munz's contention (89-96) that the Tudor theory of the Royal Supremacy was 'Averroistic' in the sense that it was founded on an essentially secular conception of the State. On the contrary, the whole Tudor argument for the Royal Supremacy was based on a fundamentally theocratic conception of kingship. However the Royal Supremacy may have been exercised in practice, in theory, at least, it was taken for granted, as much in Elizabeth's reign as in the reigns of her father and brother, that the monarch was the divinely appointed head of the Church, and that he was responsible not merely for the temporal welfare of his subjects but also for the care of their spiritual needs and the advancement of true religion.[76] Given this strong Tudor commitment to the ideal of 'the godly prince', much of Munz's argument falls to pieces, for it cannot be maintained that Hooker was under any intellectual pressure to shift his ground because of the need to justify the Royal Supremacy in terms of an essentially secularist philosophy of the State.

Equally, it is difficult to detect any evidence that Hooker did, in fact, shift his ground in the course of writing the *Laws*. Contrary to what Munz contends, a close examination of Hooker's arguments suggests that there is no fundamental inconsistency between the standpoint he adopts in Book VIII and that of the earlier books, but rather that his defence of the Royal Supremacy follows logically from his previous discussions about the nature of the Visible Church and its character as a 'politic society'. Thus, while Hooker's treatment of the Royal Supremacy differs in certain important respects from the conventional arguments put forward by Tudor propagandists, these differences stem directly from his conception of the nature of political authority and are a testimony to the internal consistency of his ideas.

The basis of Hooker's justification of the Royal Supremacy lies in his conception of the Church as a 'politic society', which he had elaborated in the earlier books, especially in Books I and III. As we have seen, this concept formed one of the two main pillars of his defence of the Church of England against the criticisms of the Puritans. Together with the concept of 'things indifferent', it provided the theoretical foundation for his claim that every national Church was an autonomous institution, which had the right to establish its own laws in relation to the external government and worship of the Church. In essence Hooker's theory was not new. It was a refinement of the argument, which had been used in the Henrician formularies of the 1530s and 1540s to justify the breach with Rome and was later employed against the Puritans of the 1560s and 1570s by Parker and Whitgift, that the Visible Church on earth was divided into a series of local churches, each of which was independent and each of which was free to follow its own customs in matters of external rites and ceremonies.[77] However, Hooker restated this theory in a more sophisticated form by applying to the Church some of the political concepts that he had developed in relation to civil societies.

Theologically, Hooker's conception of the Church as a 'politic society' was founded on the traditional Protestant distinction between the Invisible and the Visible Church. Like most sixteenth-century protestant theologians, he takes as his starting-point the idea that the Church is to be defined in two ways. Viewed in its primary sense as Christ's 'body mystical', it is a purely spiritual society, whose existence can only be apprehended intellectually and whose membership is known only to God, since God alone knows who truly belongs to Christ's Church. However, the Church is also to be viewed as a visible society, which has existed on earth since the beginning of the world, and in this sense it is 'a sensibly known company' whose members are united by outward profession of faith in Christ (III.i.2–3).

What distinguishes Hooker's doctrine of the Church from that of almost all his protestant contemporaries is his extremely comprehensive definition of the membership of the Visible Church. For Hooker the Visible Church must be taken to comprise all those who outwardly profess Christianity, including even heretics and notorious sinners (iii.i.7–13; cf. v.lxvii.6). Since men cannot know who is saved, it is not for them to judge who does or who does not belong in Christ's Church. As he puts it in Book v, 'in the eye of God they are against Christ that are not truly and sincerely with him, in our eyes they must be received as with Christ that are not to outward show against him' (lxviii.8). In Hooker's view only explicit atheism or public denial of Christ excludes one from the Church altogether. 'That which separateth therefore *utterly*, that which cutteth off *clean* from the visible Church of Christ is plain Apostasy, *direct* denial, utter rejection of the whole Christian faith as far as the same is professedly different from infidelity' (lxviii.6). The importance of this principle was that it enabled Hooker to argue against his puritan opponents that even Roman Catholics and excommunicated persons were to be regarded as being in some sense members of the Visible Church, even if it was wrong to communicate with them (iii.i.10–13; v.lxviii.9), while it also provided the basis of his claim that in a Christian country such as England all members of the commonwealth were also by definition members of the Church (viii.i.2; Houk, 155–6).

For Hooker the Visible Church, like the Invisible, is a unity in the sense that all Christians on earth are united 'in outward profession of those things, which supernaturally appertain to the very essence of Christianity, and are necessarily required in every particular Christian man' (iii.i.4). He holds, however, that this unity is purely spiritual, and that for the purposes of external organisation the Visible Church on earth is divided into a series of autonomous local churches, a concept that he illustrates with his famous simile of the sea: 'as the main body of the sea being one, yet within divers precincts hath divers names; so the Catholic Church is in like sort divided into a number of distinct Societies, every of which is termed a Church within itself' (i.14). If Hooker's analogy is hardly convincing, the reasoning behind his argument is clear. For Hooker the Visible Church has two aspects: it is both a spiritual fellowship of all those who profess faith in Christ, in which sense it is a worldwide community that embraces all Christians, and it is also a temporal organisation, a group of men joined together for the exercise of Christian religion and worship. In this latter sense it is not one society but many, for as a temporal organisation, the Church exists wherever a body of men are associated together on a permanent basis for the practice of the Christian religion. 'A Church', he writes, 'as now we are to understand it, is a Society; that is, a number of men belonging unto some Christian fellowship, the place and limits whereof are certain' (i.14). Hooker's purpose in developing this argument was to justify the autonomy of the Church of England, and it is, therefore, hardly surprising that he applies this definition exclusively to national churches. In Hooker's view the natural unit which comprises an autonomous Church is the entire Christian community in any country or State, and he does not consider the possibility that his definition taken on its own might apply equally well to the 'gathered' churches of the Separatists and the Anabaptists.

Apart from enabling him to justify the autonomy of the Church of England, the importance of this definition of a Church as 'a Society' or 'a number of men belonging unto some Christian fellowship' was that it allowed Hooker to apply to the Church as an external organisation his concept of a 'politic society'. For Hooker the Church as a temporal institution possesses a dual character, 'being', as he had put it in Book i, 'both a society and a society supernatural' (xv.2). In one sense it is a spiritual community of men who are united with God and with other Christians throughout the world in the fellowship of faith; in this sense it is 'a society supernatural', governed by the divine law which God has revealed in Scripture. But it is also a temporal association, a group of men who have joined together for a specific purpose, and viewed in this way it is a human society, not basically different in character from other forms of 'politic society'.[78] The advantage of claiming that in so far as it was a temporal association of men, the Church constituted a species of 'politic society' was that it permitted Hooker to argue that each national Church must by definition possess many of the same attributes as other types of 'politic society', in particular the power to make laws for its own external government. Thus, while he is careful to insist that the Church has no power to alter the laws that God has laid down in Scripture concerning matters of doctrine (i.xv.2; iii.x.7), he holds that in the purely temporal sphere of ecclesiastical organisation the Church has the same powers as other forms of 'politic society' to legislate for its external needs. 'All things natural', he writes in Book VII, 'have in them naturally more or less the power of providing for their own safety: and as each particular man hath this power, so every politic society of men must needs have the same, that thereby the whole may provide for the good of all parts therein. . . . The Church therefore being a politic society or body, cannot possibly want the power of providing for itself; and the chiefest part of that power consisteth in the authority of making laws' (xiv.3).

In the first seven books Hooker employed the argument—that the Church was a 'politic society'—in an extremely comprehensive manner, in order to justify the right of the Church of England not only to determine its own external order of worship but also to retain its episcopal form of church government. Hooker's treatment of the problem of episcopacy is of considerable interest, because in certain respects it foreshadows his justification of the Royal Supremacy in Book VIII. Although in common with a growing number of Anglican divines in the 1580s and 1590s he was prepared to defend episcopacy on historical grounds, arguing consistently, not only in Book VII but also on a number of occasions in the earlier books, that it was the form of government instituted by Christ and the Apostles,[79] the real basis of his defence of episcopacy was quite different. Throughout the *Laws* Hooker always maintained, as a matter of overriding principle, that church polity was by its nature a 'thing indifferent' and that every 'politic society' possessed an inherent right to determine its own form of government. Thus even in Book VII, where he argued at length in support of Saravia's doctrine that the original institution of bishops could be traced back to Christ himself, through the Apostles, he was careful to qualify this argument by insisting that episcopacy was a matter of positive law. In consequence, bishops could be said to owe their continued existence in the Church since the death of the Apostles to the authority of the Church that had chosen to retain them, rather than to any immutable command of divine law. On the same principle, he had no hesitation in admitting that the Church had power 'by universal consent upon urgent cause' to abolish episcopacy at any time, 'if thereunto she be constrained through the proud, tyrannical, and unreformable dealings of her bishops, whose regiment she hath thus long delighted in, because she hath found it good and requisite to be so governed' (vii.v.8). In other words, in Hooker's view, the ultimate authority to decide how the Church should be governed rested with the Church as a whole, which in this respect enjoyed the same powers as other forms of 'politic society'. In Book viii he was to employ the same argument in a different fashion in order to justify the Royal Supremacy and the right of parliament to legislate for the Church.

Hooker's problem in Book viii was that he was faced with the task of defending the Royal Supremacy on two fronts. He not only had to defend it against the claims of the papacy but he had also to answer the implied criticisms of the Puritans, who, without venturing to attack the Supremacy openly, maintained that Church and State constituted two separate, though related, types of society, each with its own laws and its own form of government. In effect, he met both forms of attack in the same way by developing the argument that in a Christian country such as England Church and commonwealth were united to form a single society and that in consequence there was no logical reason why the same person should not possess supreme authority in both ecclesiastical and temporal affairs.

In support of this claim, Hooker put forward two distinct—though complementary—sets of propositions. First, taking his cue, as so often, from Aristotle, he argued that all 'politic societies' are by their nature concerned with the care of religion. 'For of every politic society that being true which Aristotle hath, namely, "that the scope thereof is not simply to live, nor the duty so much to provide for life, as for means of living well": and that even as the soul is the worthier part of man, so human societies are much more to care for that which tendeth properly unto the soul's estate, than for such temporal things as this life doth stand in need of: other proof there needs none to shew that as by all men the kingdom of God is first to be sought for, so in all commonwealths things spiritual ought above temporal to be provided for' (viii.i.4; Houk, 158). What distinguishes a Christian from a heathen commonwealth is that the former upholds 'that religion which God hath revealed by Jesus Christ', and in this sense it is not simply a 'politic society' but a Church (i.2; Houk, 156). Secondly, he maintained that where the members of a body politic were

Christian, as in England, the same body of people must by definition constitute both Church and commonwealth—'seeing there is not any man of the Church of England but the same man is also a member of the commonwealth; nor any man a member of the commonwealth, which is not also of the Church of England' (i.2; Houk, 156). On the basis of this principle, he was able to argue in opposition to the Puritans that, although in theory Church and commonwealth were distinct, in practice, where the same body of people constituted both, they did not form two societies, but one. 'For the truth is', he writes, 'that the Church and the commonwealth are names which import things really different; but those things are accidents, and such accidents as may and should always dwell lovingly together in one subject' (i.5; Houk, 161). Or again, 'the Church and the commonwealth therefore are in this case personally one society, which society being termed a commonwealth as it liveth under whatsoever form of secular law and regiment, a Church as it hath the spiritual law of Jesus Christ; forasmuch as these two laws contain so many and so different offices, there must of necessity be appointed in it some to one charge, and some to another, yet without dividing the whole, and making it two several impaled societies' (i.4; Houk, 160). On the same principle, he was able to argue against the Catholics that the use of the term 'Church' was not to be confined to the clergy, since it embraced the whole body of believers, that is, all the members of a Christian commonwealth (i.4; Houk, 160).

Although he treated the idea with much greater sophistication than his predecessors had done, Hooker's theory of the identity of Church and commonwealth was not new. The basic concept that Church and commonwealth constituted a single society, under the government of one supreme head, had formed one of the standard ingredients of the Tudor theory of the Royal Supremacy since the 1530s, and the actual argument that there was no one in England who was not also by definition a member of the Church of England had first been employed by Stephen Gardiner in his *De Vera Obedientia* of 1535, while Whitgift had also anticipated Hooker by using the same argument to refute the puritan claim that Church and commonwealth formed two separate societies.[80]

Where Hooker departed from the orthodox Tudor theory of the Royal Supremacy was in his refusal to argue that the king enjoyed his position as Supreme Head or Supreme Governor either *ex-officio* or by immediate appointment from God. Whereas most Tudor apologists for the Royal Supremacy had taken it for granted, first, that the king's authority in the Church was God-given, in the sense that God had entrusted all Christian rulers with the care of the Church in their dominions, and, secondly, that the oversight of the Church formed an integral part of the office of a king, inseparable from the other duties of kingship, neither of these arguments was compatible with Hooker's theory that the original source of political authority in all 'politic societies' was the people and that every 'politic society' had the right to determine its own form of government and to regulate the powers it conferred on its rulers. In consequence—and there could be no better proof of the overall consistency of his political ideas than this—Hooker found himself compelled by the logic of his own arguments to maintain that God had nowhere laid down that kings either should or should not possess supreme authority in ecclesiastical affairs, but that it was, in principle, a matter for men to determine. 'As for supreme power in ecclesiastical affairs', he writes, 'the word of God doth no where appoint that all kings should have it, neither that any should not have it; for which cause it seemeth to stand altogether by human right, that unto Christian kings there is such dominion given' (viii.ii.5; Houk, 171–2). In other words, for Hooker, the Royal Supremacy, like all forms of government, belongs to the sphere of positive law. From this it follows that the Royal Supremacy, like royal authority in general, must ultimately be derived from the consent of the people. Although Hooker does not make this point explicitly, the logical implication of his argument is that in a Christian commonwealth, where Church and commonwealth are one, the people have the undoubted right to confer such powers on their ruler. At the same time, just as he maintained that all forms of government were in some sense divine, so he maintained that in a secondary sense the Royal Supremacy could also be said to enjoy the sanction of divine law, for 'unto kings by human right, honour by very divine right, is due' (ii.6; Houk, 172).

Hooker's general approach to the defence of the Royal

Supremacy was thus essentially pragmatic. Even when, like other Tudor writers, he cited the precedents of the Jewish kings of the Old Testament, he quoted these merely as examples to show that it was lawful for kings to exercise such authority in the Church without drawing the inference that it was necessary that all kings should act in the same way (iii.1; Houk, 187–8). Instead, he based his main argument for the Royal Supremacy on the principle of expediency. For Hooker, just as all government is instituted for the practical purpose of promoting the common good, so the purpose of committing 'the supreme charge of all things' to the care of one man is to avoid the inconveniences which are likely to arise in practice, 'if men are subject unto sundry supreme authorities' (ii.18; Houk, 185). ' "No man", saith our Saviour, "can serve two masters": surely two supreme masters would make any one man's service somewhat uneasy in such cases as might fall out. Suppose that to-morrow the power which hath dominion in justice require thee at the court; that which in war, at the field; that which in religion, at the temple: all have equal authority over thee, and impossible it is, that thou shouldest be in such case obedient to all: by choosing any one whom thou wilt obey, certain thou art for thy disobedience to incur the displeasure of the other two' (ii.18; Houk, 185–6). Consequently, although God has not laid it down as a necessary law that kings should possess supreme authority in ecclesiastical affairs, reason teaches that this is, in practice, the best system of government for a Christian commonwealth.

The other major point of difference between Hooker's theory and the conventional Tudor doctrine of the Royal Supremacy lies in his emphasis on the principle that the king's authority in the Church is limited by law. While it had always been accepted by Tudor theorists that the king's Supremacy extended only to the external government of the Church, and that he had no power to exercise the spiritual functions of the clergy, much less to command anything in matters of faith which was contrary to God's word,[81] Hooker went considerably further than this by insisting that the same constitutional principles applied in Church as in State and that, therefore, even in the sphere of the external government of the Church the monarch's authority is, or ought to be, circumscribed by positive law. 'It hath been declared already in general', he writes, 'how "the best established dominion is where the law doth most rule the king": the true effect whereof particularly is found as well in ecclesiastical as in civil affairs'. From this he proceeded to argue that just as in the temporal sphere the king is bound to act in accordance with the civil laws of the commonwealth, which he has no power to alter without the consent of his subjects, so equally he is bound to exercise his ecclesiastical supremacy in accordance with the positive laws of the Church which again may only be altered with the consent of the whole. 'Whether it be therefore the nature of courts, or the form of pleas, or the kind of governors, or the order of proceedings in whatsoever spiritual businesses; for the received laws and liberties of the Church the king hath supreme authority and power, but against them, none. What such positive laws have appointed to be done by others than the king, or by others with the king, and in what form they have appointed the doing of it, the same of necessity must be kept, neither is the king's sole authority to alter it' (VIII.ii.17; Houk, 182–3).

For Hooker the ultimate authority to make laws for the external government of the Church belongs not to the king alone, or even, as the catholics claimed, to the clergy alone, but to the whole body of the Church, including the laity. It is this argument which underlies his claim that in England the authority to make laws for the Church is vested in parliament together with Convocation (VIII.vi). Hooker bases his justification of parliament's right to legislate for the Church on three main principles, which he had already developed at earlier stages of his argument: first, that in all 'politic societies' the power of making laws naturally resides in the whole body politic, since laws are only valid if they have the consent of the whole; secondly, that in so far as it is a temporal organisation, the Church is a 'politic society'; and thirdly, that in a Christian commonwealth, Church and State constitute a single society. 'It is undoubtedly a thing even natural', he states, 'that all free and independent societies should themselves make their own laws, and that this power should belong to the whole, not to any certain part of a politic body, though haply some one part may have greater sway in that action than the rest: which thing being generally fit and expedient in the making of all laws, we see no cause why to think otherwise in laws concerning the service of God' (vi.6; Houk, 230). From this it follows that in a Christian commonwealth the power of making ecclesiastical laws must by definition belong to the whole body of the people and not simply to the clergy, who constitute only one section of the Church, or to the king acting alone, although Hooker is careful to emphasise that the assent of 'the highest power' is necessary for all ecclesiastical legislation (vi.6–9; Houk, 230–5). But if this is so, then it is only logical that in England the power of making laws for the Church should be exercised by parliament, interpreted in its widest sense as including both king and Convocation: for 'the parliament of England together with the convocation annexed thereunto, is that whereupon the very essence of all government within this kingdom doth depend; it is even the body of the whole realm; it consisteth of the king, and of all that within the land are subject unto him: for they all are there present, either in person or by such as they voluntarily have derived their very personal right unto'.[82]

Given his basic assumptions, the logic of Hooker's argument is unimpeachable: since the Church is a 'politic society' and since, in a Christian commonwealth, Church and State are not two societies but one, parliament must by definition represent the people of the whole realm, not only in their civil capacity as a commonwealth, but also in their ecclesiastical capacity as a Church; *ergo*, parliament has the undoubted right to make laws for the external government of the Church. On the other hand, it was not Hooker's intention to exclude the clergy from all share in the making of laws for the Church. On the contrary, in accordance with his general principle that 'none but wise men' should be admitted to the task of devising laws, he holds that, although the clergy have no power to impose laws on the Church by their own authority, it is only proper that where spiritual matters are concerned, the responsibility for drawing up laws for the Church should be entrusted to the bishops and clergy. 'The most natural and religious course in making of laws is, that the matter of them be taken from the judgment of the wisest in those things which they are to concern. In matters of God, to set down a form of public prayer, a solemn confession of the articles of Christian faith, rites and ceremonies meet for the exercise of religion; it were unnatural not to think the pastors and bishops of our souls a great deal more fit, than men of secular trades and callings'. 'Howbeit', he continues, 'when all which the wisdom of all sorts can do is done for devising of laws in the Church, it is the general consent of all that giveth them the form and vigour of laws, without which they could be no more unto us than the counsels of physicians to the sick: well might they seem as wholesome admonitions and instructions, but laws could they never be without consent of the whole Church, which is the only thing that bindeth each member of the Church, to be guided by them' (VIII.vi.11; Houk, 243). It is a comment that reveals very clearly the extent to which Hooker's theory of Church and State is rooted in the basic principles of his political philosophy.

In the past forty years a succession of scholars have drawn attention to the parallels that exist between Hooker's ideas and those of Marsilius of Padua.[83] In particular, it has often been pointed out that there are many features of his theory of the Church—notably, his emphasis on the autonomy of local churches, his insistence on the principle that in a Christian commonwealth the Church is to be identified with the whole body of the people, and his consequent claim that the power of making laws for the Church resides in the whole body politic and not in the clergy alone—which bear a striking resemblance to the arguments of the *Defensor Pacis*. However, it would be rash to infer that Hooker must have derived any of these ideas directly from Marsilius, in spite of the fact that he refers to the *Defensor* in Book VII. In practice, although Hooker presented his arguments in a more sophisticated form than many of his contemporaries, the main elements of his doctrine of the Church were commonplaces of sixteenth-century thought. The principle that the Visible Church was divided into a series of autonomous local churches had been asserted by all the Protestant Reformers, while in England the same argument had been employed since the 1530s to justify the Royal Supremacy and the independence of the *Ecclesia Anglicana*. Similarly, it was a basic maxim of Protestant theology, as it had been of conciliarist thought, that the Church was to be identified with the *communio fidelium*, and most of the Protestant Reformers accepted in theory, at least, if not necessarily in practice, that the doctrine of the priesthood of all believers implied that ultimate authority in the Church resided in the whole Christian community.

Equally, while Hooker may well have read the *Defensor Pacis*, it is difficult to believe that his political ideas were profoundly influenced by it. Most of the arguments that he puts forward in Book VIII can be paralleled in other Tudor works of political propaganda, and it is unnecessary to posit the influence of Marsilius in order to explain their presence in his thought. On the other hand, if Hooker did borrow from Marsilius, as is possible, it is likely that he regarded him simply as a useful source of polemical arguments, as did many sixteenth-century English writers, and that he paid little attention to the philosophical implications of his thought. In particular, it is impossible to detect in Hooker's thought any traces of the Averroistic leanings that Munz appears to discover in him. At no point does Hooker come close to suggesting that the State is a purely secular institution, which is only concerned with the advancement of man's temporal well-being in this world. On the contrary, his political philosophy is founded on precisely the opposite assumption. For Hooker, it is of the essence of all 'politic societies' that they are concerned with the promotion of man's spiritual welfare and, therefore, with the advancement of religion.[84] What distinguishes a Christian from a heathen commonwealth is that the religion maintained in the one is true, in the other, false; in principle, they both exist to serve the same ends (VIII.i.2; Houk, 155–6). Thus Hooker never envisaged the possibility that it could ever be lawful to subordinate religion to the interests of the State, as he showed by his vigorous condemnation in Book v of 'these wise malignants' who seek to make what he terms 'a politic use of religion' (ii.3–4). Nor is there any evidence to suggest that his views underwent a change in Book VIII, since, in fact, it is in Book VIII that one meets some of his most positive assertions of the principle that 'in all commonwealths things spiritual ought above temporal to be provided for' (i.4; Houk, 158).

For the same reason it cannot be said that Hooker was an Erastian in the modern sense of the term any more than Thomas Erastus himself was. It was never Hooker's intention to justify the right of the civil magistrate—or of parliament—to control the Church in all circumstances. As he himself makes clear, his theory of the Royal Supremacy only applies in a commonwealth where king and people are both Christian. Where, as in the Roman Empire of the first three centuries, the Church exists in the midst of a heathen society and the magistrate is not Christian, the latter can possess no authority in the Church, since Church and commonwealth have 'no mutual dependency' (viii.i.4; Houk, 159). Similarly, he holds that the right of parliament to legislate for the Church of England derives solely from the fact that in a Christian commonwealth the same people constitute both Church and State, so that parliament represents them in their dual capacity. Like all his contemporaries, Hooker regarded the Christian commonwealth as the summit of political evolution, and he did not foresee the gradual secularisation of the State over the following centuries. Had he done so, he would hardly have approved of the continued survival of parliament's right to make laws for the Church long after the conditions which had justified it had ceased to apply.

While Book viii, as it stands, is incomplete and lacks the final polish of the first five books, it is difficult to accept that there is any fundamental inconsistency between Hooker's treatment of the problem of Church and State and the arguments of the rest of the *Laws*. Hooker's defence of the Royal Supremacy, like his justification of parliament's right to legislate for the Church, is firmly grounded on his basic concept that the Church is a 'politic society' and its corollary, the argument that in a Christian society Church and State are one, which is implicit in the earlier books, even if it is worked out in detail only in Book viii. In fact, one of the most notable features of Book viii is the extent to which its arguments continually relate back to ideas that Hooker had developed in earlier parts of the *Laws*: his concept of the Church as a 'politic society' had first been adumbrated in Book i and forms one of the two main pillars of his general defence of the Church of England; his theory of the identity of Church and commonwealth follows logically from his definition of the Visible Church in Book iii; his insistence that the Royal Supremacy is based on human rather than divine law reflects his belief that political authority is derived from the people and that no single, uniform system of government is prescribed for all 'politic societies'. Similarly, his claim that parliament is the proper authority to legislate for the Church is directly related to his general theory that consent is the necessary basis of all laws. The examples could be multiplied endlessly. Thus at every stage in Book VIII one is continually reminded of what Hooker had written at the beginning of Book I. 'I have endeavoured throughout the body of this whole discourse, that every former part might give strength unto all that follow, and every later bring some light unto all before. So that if the judgments of men do but hold themselves in suspense as touching these first more general meditations, till in order they have perused the rest that ensue; what may seem dark at the first will afterwards be found more plain, even as the later particular decisions will appear I doubt not more strong, when the other have been read before' (I.i.2). It is advice that Hooker scholars ignore at their peril.

VII

John Strype as a Source for the Study of Sixteenth-Century English Church History

Because he was not a medievalist John Strype does not find a place in David Douglas's classic study of the golden age of English antiquarian scholarship, *English Scholars 1660–1730*.[1] Yet in terms both of his output and of his influence on the subsequent development of the study of English church history Strype is arguably one of the most important scholars that the age produced. Even today, nearly 250 years after his death, the twenty-five volumes of his works in the Clarendon Press reissue of the 1820s are still a standard source for the study of English church history in the sixteenth century and it is difficult to open a book dealing with any aspect of the English Reformation, which does not have its quota of references to Strype. At the same time, as any one who works on the period knows, Strype's standing as an ecclesiastical historian is ambiguous. If, on the one hand, he is widely quoted, on the other, he is frequently attacked for his mistakes and his works are notoriously full of pitfalls for the unwary. It is therefore perhaps appropriate, in a volume devoted to 'the Sources, Materials and Methods of Ecclesiastical History', to consider, first, what is Strype's value today as a source for the study of the English Reformation and, secondly, the question of his reliability as a church historian. The two questions, one should stress, are distinct, although they are not unrelated.

As a scholar Strype belongs in the antiquarian tradition of the late seventeenth and early eighteenth centuries. He was born in 1643, the youngest son of a prosperous Dutch merchant who had settled in London and married an English wife and who died while Strype was a child.[2] After receiving his education at St. Paul's school and Jesus and St. Catharine's colleges, Cambridge, he took orders in 1666 and almost the entire remainder of his life—from 1669 until his death in 1737 at the age of ninety-four —was spent as minister of the parish of Leyton in Essex, a post which he combined for many years with that of lecturer at nearby Hackney. Strype's father had left him in comfortable circumstances[3] and he was able to devote his life to the study of ecclesiastical antiquities—in particular, to collecting and transcribing records relating to the history of the English Reformation. Although he had been gathering materials for many years, Strype's first historical work, the *Memorials of Thomas Cranmer*, was not published until 1694, when he was already over fifty. But thereafter he emerged as one of the most prolific scholars of the age. The life of Cranmer was followed by the lives of Sir Thomas Smith (1698), bishop Aylmer (1701), and Sir John Cheke (1705). Then in quick succession came the first part of the *Annals of the Reformation* (1709), the lives of Grindal (1710), Parker (1711) and Whitgift (1717–18), his edition of Stow's *Survey of London* (1720) and the three volumes of *Ecclesiastical Memorials* (1721), covering the history of the Reformation in England during the reigns of Henry VIII, Edward VI and Mary—all published in the short space of twelve years. Finally, between 1725 and 1731, when he was in his eighties, he brought out three further volumes of the *Annals*, carrying the narrative down to 1589 and the records to the death of Elizabeth.

Strype's professed aim as an historian was to base his work on original sources. As he put it in the preface to the second edition of the *Annals*, 'My relations of things are not hearsays, nor taken up at second hand, or compiled out of other men's published writings; but I have gone as near the fountain-head as possible; that is, to archives, state-papers, registers, records, and original letters, or else to books of good credit printed in those times; directing more surely to the knowledge how affairs then stood'.[4] Although by modern standards Strype's scholarship was defective, he was an indefatigable collector of records and he had access to all the major collections of his own day, as well as to many smaller private collections. Among the more important collections that he used were the State Paper office, the Cotton library (before the fire), the Petyt MSS. now in the Inner Temple, archbishop Parker's MSS. at Corpus Christi college, Cambridge, and the registers of the archbishops of Canterbury at Lambeth, while in the early years of the eighteenth century he acquired the entrée to the Harleian library, then in process of formation.[5] Apart from those collections that he explored himself, he corresponded with scholars such as Thomas Baker, Ralph Thoresby and bishop Moore, who sent him transcripts of documents, while, as his reputation grew, strangers would write to him volunteering to lend him papers in their possession.[6] In addition, he built up an important collection of original MSS. of his own, which provided him with much of the material that he used.

Strype's two most important coups were the acquisition of the papers of John Foxe, the martyrologist, and of that part of Lord Burghley's papers which had passed into the possession of Burghley's secretary, Sir Michael Hickes, and thence by descent to Hickes's grandson, Sir William Hickes of Ruckholt—both of which he used extensively in his works. Both these collections came into Strype's ownership under somewhat dubious circumstances. The Foxe papers were originally lent to Strype in the 1680s or 1690s by his friend, William Willys of Hackney, the cousin and executor of Sir Richard Willys, 1st baronet, who had married Foxe's great-granddaughter, Alice. Strype retained possession of them and, after the death of the second baronet, Foxe's last surviving descendant, in 1701, he treated them as his own private property.[7] Later, between 1709 and 1711, he sold the bulk of them to Robert Harley and they are now among the Harleian MSS. in the British Library.[8] The history of the Burghley papers is similar, but rather more complicated. Ruckholt, the seat of the Hickes family, was in Strype's parish of Leyton and Sir William Hickes allowed Strype to make extensive use of them. In or about 1682 Strype persuaded Hickes to sell them to the printer, Richard Chiswell (who published the *Memorials of Cranmer* in 1694), who undertook to publish them from transcripts to be prepared by Strype.[9] In the event, the edition was never published and, after Hickes's death in 1703, the MSS. remained in Strype's possession until his own death in 1737, when they were sold by his executors to the antiquary, James West. Eventually, after West's death in 1772, they were purchased by Lord Shelburne, afterwards first marquess of Lansdowne,[10] so that they too, like the Foxe MSS., are now in the British Library.

What gives Strype's works their lasting value as a source for the study of the English Reformation is that he did not simply use this mass of documentary material as the basis for his own narrative: he made a point of reprinting original records wherever possible, with the result that his works are an important repository of the raw materials of Tudor church history. It might be assumed that in the 250 years since Strype's death much of this material would have found its way into print in some other form. But surprisingly this is not the case. Although most of the collections that Strype used are familiar to modern historians, the greater part of the documents that he prints has never been properly edited since his own day. To cite only one example, whereas the Burghley papers at Hatfield have been excellently edited in the *Calendar of the Manuscripts of the Marquis of Salisbury* published by the Historical Manuscripts Commission,[11] no attempt has been made to publish the Burghley MSS. in the Lansdowne collection, for which the only guide is the *Catalogue of the Lansdowne Manuscripts*, published in 1819. Consequently, for many important documents relating to the Tudor period Strype's works are still the most accessible printed source and it is not surprising that scholars frequently tend to quote these documents from Strype instead of going back to the originals in the British Library or elsewhere. In addition, Strype also preserves the texts of some documents which he was lent by private individuals but which have since disappeared.

Unfortunately, by modern standards Strype has considerable deficiencies as an editor and transcriber of documents. In the first place, his treatment of records tends to be haphazard. Following a practice adopted by bishop Burnet in his *History of the Reformation*,[12] he usually prints the longer and more important documents in appendices, which fill a substantial part of each volume. But he also prints many documents in the text. When the records are given in the appendices, they are generally printed more or less verbatim, although on occasion he omits passages either because of the length of the document or because he did not consider it sufficiently interesting to transcribe in full. On the other hand, when he cites a document in the main body of his narrative, his practice varies. Sometimes, particularly if it is short, he prints it in full. On other occasions, he paraphrases it or turns it into *oratio obliqua* or only gives abbreviated extracts, so that—

although the gist of the document may be recorded—it is not in a form which can easily be used by the modern scholar who wishes to quote from it.

Secondly, his system of references is, by modern standards, extremely vague. Although there are exceptions, he usually only cites the collection from which a document comes. For example, an item from the Foxe or Burghley papers may be cited simply as *MSS. Foxii* or *MSS. Burghlian.* or sometimes just as *MSS. ecclesiast. penes me.* However, this is an inconvenience rather than a serious drawback, since it is usually possible, with the aid of the relevant library catalogue, to track down the item that Strype is referring to without too much difficulty.

A much more serious fault is that, although Strype prided himself on the care he took in copying MSS.,[13] in practice his transcriptions are frequently inaccurate and sometimes misleading. As anyone who has had occasion to check Strype's printed version of a document against his original source will know, S. R. Maitland was hardly exaggerating when he wrote, in a devastating critique of the first volume of the Ecclesiastical History Society's edition of the *Memorials of Thomas Cranmer*, of 'Strype's loose, inaccurate, mode of copying, and his great liability to mistake'.[14] Words are often misread; phrases and passages are omitted without any indication that this is the case; occasionally, even, documents are conflated to the confusion of subsequent readers of Strype's works.[15] On the other hand, as Maitland himself pointed out in the same review, part of the explanation for Strype's frequent inaccuracies lies in the fact that in many cases he had made his original notes and transcripts several years before he came to prepare his material for publication, with the result that by that time 'he had in a great degree forgotten what they were about, and whether they were extracts, abstracts, or full copies'.[16] Consequently, as a general rule, one can say that Strype is likely to be more accurate when he is quoting from MSS. in his own possession, such as the Foxe or Burghley papers, than when he is relying on notes and transcripts compiled several years earlier; but even in the case of the Burghley papers I have found from my own experience that mistakes are not infrequent. The conclusion to be drawn from this is that it is always hazardous to assume that the text of a document printed in Strype is reliable and it is advisable, wherever possible, to check Strype's version against the original. Fortunately, this is not such a daunting task as might appear at first sight, for most of the documents Strype used are readily accessible and it is usually possible to identify a specific item without great difficulty.

It is as a general historian, however, that Strype's weaknesses are most pronounced and in some respects more dangerous: for, owing to the enormous prestige which his works enjoyed in the eighteenth and nineteenth centuries, his statements have often been accepted uncritically by later church historians and many traditional misconceptions about the English Reformation turn out on investigation to have been fathered by Strype.

Some of Strype's limitations as an historian are those of his age. In the first place, like most seventeenth-century antiquaries, he was an undiscriminating collector of facts and this is compounded by the fact that he followed the contemporary convention of writing his histories in the form of annals. In Strype's works, the materials are assembled not by topic but by year, with the result that a great deal of miscellaneous information tends to be jumbled together with little attempt at organisation, while conversely no attempt is made to follow an issue through if it involves events falling in different years. While it would be anachronistic to blame Strype for not breaking away from the annalistic tradition, it undoubtedly helped to encourage the magpie element in his nature which led him to treat the accumulation of facts as an end in itself.

Secondly, he was a man of strong prejudices, which are always close to the surface in his writings. Above all, he was a staunch and complacent Anglican. He was sublimely convinced that the English Reformation had been brought about by the direct inter-vention of divine providence and in a sense he saw the function of his books as being to inculcate in his readers a due sense of grati-tude to the Almighty for his benevolence in establishing the Church of England. 'He that readeth and weigheth this history', he writes in the preface to the *Annals*, 'will see great reason to acquiesce in the reformation of our church, and to be a peaceable and thankful member of it; and be convinced what a mighty hand of God overruled in this blessed work, and overthrew all opposition before it'.[17] Not surprisingly he was strongly anti-catholic. More significantly, he tended to be equally anti-puritan. When writing about the controversies of Elizabeth's reign, his sympathies are always with the Establishment, while the Puritans are depicted as innovators and trouble-makers. An interesting study could, in fact, be made of Strype's use of language, for his vocabulary reflects his prejudices. Episcopacy, for example, is 'the ancient wholesome government used in' the Church.[18] Whitgift is 'this vigilant and industrious Prelate',[19] 'our useful Bishop',[20] or 'our careful Archbishop'.[21] By contrast, the Puritans are 'the innovators',[22] 'this faction',[23] 'the malecontent party';[24] Cartwright is 'the great ringleader of disorders and disturbances' in the university of Cambridge;[25] Robert Beal is 'one of the heads and patrons of this disaffected party',[26] and so on.

Strype's biases, however, are so obvious that they can easily be guarded against. A much more serious failing—since his mistakes are not always immediately apparent—is that as an historian he was both careless and given to indulging in speculation. On the credit side, it should be said that Strype frequently uses some such phrase as 'if I mistake not' or 'as I conjecture', when he is putting forward his own suppositions, and sometimes his guesses are right. But often they are wrong—and they are wrong because he was hasty and did not take sufficient care in reading his sources. In his critique of the Ecclesiastical History Society's edition of the *Memorials of Thomas Cranmer*, S. R. Maitland assembled a long list of factual mistakes which were directly attributable to Strype's slipshod handling of Cranmer's *Register*.[27] Many of these mistakes are trivial—such as giving the wrong name or the wrong diocese for a bishop involved at a consecration or declaring that a fact is omitted from the *Register*, when it is clearly mentioned— but, especially when taken together, they indicate how unreliable Strype can be on points of detail.

Some of Strype's errors, however, are more serious, because they came to be widely accepted by later historians and they have bedevilled the subsequent interpretation of sixteenth-century English church history. In many cases these errors are due to the fact that Strype misread or misunderstood his original sources. Since I have mainly used Strype as a source for the Elizabethan period, I would like to cite two classic instances from the *Annals* and the *Life of Whitgift*—his account of the making of the

Elizabethan Prayer Book and his treatment of Richard Bancroft's Paul's Cross sermon.

In the first volume of the *Annals* Strype prints two documents, which have since become famous—*The Device for alteration of religion, in the first year of queen Elizabeth* and the letter, attributed to Edmund Guest, concerning a proposed revision of the Prayer Book.[28] Strype believed—wrongly, as we now know—that the *Device* represented the official programme which was adopted for the settlement of religion at the beginning of Elizabeth's reign and he, therefore, assumed, as a matter of course, that the committee of divines named in the *Device* for revising the Prayer Book was actually appointed and that it was this group which drew up the 1559 Prayer book.[29] To be fair to Strype, he did not originate this idea which can be traced back through Burnet to Camden.[30] But so convinced was he that the *Device* was followed that at a later stage he gives a vivid description of how 'great pains had been used in reviewing of the old Common Prayer Book' and 'in this business the divines, Dr. Sandys, Dr. Bill, and the rest above mentioned, were diligently employed at Sir Thomas Smith's house in Westminster'[31]—a claim for which there is not the slightest evidence, although it was generally accepted on Strype's authority until quite recently. (Incidentally—and this is typical of Strype's capacity for making minor errors—Sandys was not one of the divines named in the *Device*, whom, in fact, he lists correctly on an earlier page.)[32] At the same time, Strype had also come across among the Parker correspondence at Corpus the unsigned and undated letter, commenting on proposals for a revision of the Prayer Book, which he attributed to Edmund Guest, and he, therefore, jumped to the conclusion that Guest must have been added to the committee of divines, named in the *Device*, at Cecil's instigation and 'that the main care of the revisal and preparation of the book lay upon that reverend divine, whom I suppose Parker recommended to the secretary to supply his absence'.[33] The precise significance, date and even authorship of this letter are still a matter of debate among historians and it would take too long to discuss the matter in detail here.[34] What is quite clear, however, from the text of the letter is that, whatever proposals it does refer to, it does not refer to the Prayer Book which was established by the Act of Uniformity. Consequently, there is no evidence to show that Guest—if he was the writer of the letter—was involved in the making of the 1559 Prayer Book, as finally drawn up—much less that he was the principal author of it, as Strype has misled generations of historians into supposing.

The case of Bancroft's Paul's Cross sermon is very similar. In an earlier article some years ago I showed that the origins of the popular belief that Bancroft's sermon represented the first statement by a post-reformation Anglican divine of the *jure divino* theory of episcopacy can be traced back directly to Strype's account of the sermon in the *Life of Whitgift* and the *Annals*: for, although Strype did not go as far as later writers, he was the first person to state that Bancroft had asserted that bishops enjoyed their authority by divine right.[35] Significantly, earlier historians, such as Heylin and Collier, had not interpreted Bancroft's sermon in this way. Strype was led to do so, partly because he had apparently not read the sermon itself, but mainly because he once again carelessly misinterpreted a piece of documentary evidence. In this case, he rashly assumed that a syllogism by Sir Francis Knollys, attacking an unnamed preacher for maintaining that bishops enjoyed their superior authority '*iure divino*', must refer to Bancroft's sermon, when, in fact—as he should have observed—it explicitly referred to a sermon preached on a different date.[36]

What these examples show—and they could be multiplied endlessly—is that it is dangerous to take any statement by Strype on trust or to cite him as an authority unless one can corroborate his remarks from another source. For even when, as is usually the case, his statements appear to be founded on solid documentary evidence, there is always a strong possibility that he may have misinterpreted his sources or introduced some error that was not in the original. Even on minor points of fact, where it might seem reasonable to assume that he would be reliable, there is no guarantee that this is the case and, indeed, there is a considerable statistical likelihood that he will make a mistake. Thus, as a general rule, one should never quote an unverified statement by Strype as authoritative, for his accuracy can never be taken for granted. For the same reason, it is important, when reading older books on sixteenth-century English church history, especially those written in the nineteenth century, to check their sources, for in many cases they contain misstatements which ultimately derive from Strype.

So far my remarks may appear to have been mainly critical. Yet, in summing up, it is important to stress how much the modern historian of the English Reformation owes to Strype. Strype may not have been a very accurate scholar and he may have misled posterity by his mistakes, but more than any other historian he laid the foundations for the modern study of sixteenth-century English church history through his collections of original records and documents and the measure of his achievement is the extent to which his books are still quoted today. Ideally, what is needed is a new annotated edition of Strype, such as S. R. Maitland called for over a hundred years ago,[37] which would correct his errors, provide accurate texts of the documents he cites and give adequate references to the sources he used. However, this would be a formidable undertaking and it is unlikely that, even with the resources of modern scholarship, it will ever be carried out. Meanwhile, even in their present form, his works remain an unrivalled source of documentary material and miscellaneous information relating to the English Reformation, provided that they are handled with proper care.

Notes

LUTHER AND RESISTANCE TO THE EMPEROR

1 Karl Müller, *Luthers Äusserungen über das Recht des bewaffneten Widerstands gegen den Kaiser*, Sitzungsberichte der Königlich Bayerischen Akademie der Wissenschaften, Phil.-hist. Klasse, Jahrgang 1915, Abhandlung 8, Munich 1915.

2 Among the most important contributions to the discussion of the problem since Müller are: Fritz Kern, 'Luther und das Widerstandsrecht', *ZRG*, 37, *KA* 6 (1916), 331–40; Johannes Heckel, *Lex Charitatis: Eine juristiche Untersuchung über das Recht in der Theologie Martin Luthers*, Abhandlungen der Bayerischen Akademie der Wissenschaften, Phil.-hist. Klasse, N.F. 36, Munich 1953, 2 rev. ed., ed. Martin Heckel, Darmstadt 1973, App I 'Luthers Lehre vom Widerstandsrecht gegen den Kaiser', 295–306; Hermann Dörries, 'Luther und das Widerstandsrecht' in *Wort und Stunde*, 3, Göttingen 1970, 195–270, which has now replaced Müller as the standard work on the subject. *Das Widerstandsrecht als Problem der deutschen Protestanten 1523–1546*, ed. Heinz Scheible, Texte zur Kirchen- und Theologie-geschichte 10, Gütersloh 1969, contains a valuable selection of documents relating to the problem, including several of Luther's most important *Gutachten*. For detailed bibliographies of the modern literature on the subject, see Heckel, *Lex Charitatis*, 295 n. 1441; Scheible, *Widerstandsrecht*, 9–13; *Luther und die Obrigkeit*, ed. G. Wolf, Wege der Forschung 85, Darmstadt 1972, 469–82. The latter contains a selection of articles published in the 1950s and 1960s, several of which relate to the question of Luther and the right of resistance to the emperor (see especially those by K-F. Stolzenau, 196–302; E. Weymar, 303–34; and G. Wolf, 335–40).

3 An exception is James Mackinnon, *Luther and the Reformation*, 4, London 1930, 24–8.

4 The most comprehensive modern study of the policies of the protestant princes and cities in the 1520s and early 1530s is Ekkehart Fabian, *Die Entstehung des Schmalkaldischen Bundes und seiner Verfassung 1524/29–1531/35: Brück, Philipp von Hessen und Jakob Sturm*, Schriften zur Kirchen- und Rechtsgeschichte 1, 2 ed. Tübingen 1962. Older but still useful is Hans von Schubert, *Bekenntnisbildung und Religionspolitik 1529/30 (1524–34): Untersuchungen und Texte*, Gotha 1910. Both books contain important chapters dealing with the political history of the debate over the right of resistance to the emperor.

5   For a classic statement of Luther's teaching on non-resistance and the limits of obedience, see *Von weltlicher Oberkeit, WA* 11, esp. 265–8.

6   *WA* 18, 310.

7   *Documents Illustrative of the Continental Reformation*, ed. B. J. Kidd, Oxford 1911, no. 45, 87–8.

8   For a detailed study of Frederick's role in the Indulgences controversy and the legal arguments which he employed on Luther's behalf, see Wilhelm Borth, *Die Luthersache (Causa Lutheri) 1517–1524; Die Anfänge der Reformation als Frage von Politik und Recht, Historische Studien* 414, Lübeck/Hamburg 1970.

9   Ibid., 129–31.

10 See Luther's letter to elector Frederick, 5 March 1522, *WA Br.* 2, no. 455, p. 455.

11 *WA Br.* 2, no. 455, pp. 454–7.

12 Ibid., 456.

13 Ibid., 455–6: 'Dieser Sachen soll noch kann kein Schwert raten oder helfen, Gott muss hie allein schaffen, ohn alles menschlich Sorgen und Zutun'.

14 Cf. *Von weltlicher Oberkeit, WA* 11, 268–9.

15 Cf. his letters to elector John of Saxony, 22 May 1529, *WA Br.* 5, no. 1424, 76–7; 18 November 1529, ibid., no. 1496, 181–3; 24 December 1529, ibid., no. 1511, 209–11.

16 For the proceedings of the Diet of Nuremberg in regard to the Edict of Worms, see Borth, *Luthersache*, 135–43.

17 See Luther's letter to elector Frederick, 29 May 1523, *WA Br.* 3, no. 618, 75–7.

18 All four statements are printed, with a useful historical introduction, in *WA Br.* 12, no. 4222, 35–45; also (without introduction) in Scheible, *Widerstandsrecht*, nos. 1–4, pp. 17–19.

19 See *WA Br.* 12, no. 4222, Introduction, 36. Some of the specific points raised by Spalatin can be deduced from the answers of Melanchthon, Bugenhagen and Amsdorf—for example whether it is wrong for a prince to go to war without the consent of his people (see below, 12–13).

20 Cf. Müller, 4, 6–9; Dörries, 3, 196–8.

21 For Frederick's position at this period, see Paul Kalkoff, 'Friedrich der Weise und Luther', *HZ* 132 (1925), 41–2. Frederick officially maintained in his dealings with the imperial authorities that he was in no way committed to the truth of Luther's teaching, but that his only concern in the matter was to ensure that *dieser nicht ungehört vergewaltigt werde.*

22 The meaning of this obscurely worded passage appears to be that, while it is wrong for a prince to defend his own subjects if they are atacked for the sake of religion, it is permissible for him to go to the assistance of foreigners who may be attacked. To illustrate Luther's meaning, Müller cites the example of Gustavus Adolphus coming to

the aid of the German protestants in the thirty years war (Müller, 7 n. 2).

23 *WA Br.* 12, 39-40.

24 Müller, 7. Dörries describes these conditions as being 'not only ... difficult to fulfil, but incapable of fulfilment'; he suggests—somewhat implausibly—that Luther deliberately couched his rejection of resistance to the emperor in oblique language, leaving the elector to draw his own conclusions, since he was confident that Frederick would understand how his remarks were intended to be interpreted, even though they avoided giving a direct negative (Dörries, 3, 197-8).

25 The words Luther uses at the beginning of this section, *Si autem vellet bellum suscipere pro tuenda ista causa* are ambiguous and it is possible to interpret them as referring to war against the emperor: but, in view of the context in which the paper was written, it seems more probable that Luther was using them here in a wider sense to refer to war in general.

26 This passage is often interpreted as meaning that Melanchthon held the view that princes derived their authority from the people (cf. Müller, 6; Dörries, 3, 199). But it is probably wrong to read too much into this passage. The form of words used by Melanchthon suggests that he was not so much expressing his own thoughts as commenting on a point raised by Spalatin: in other words, what he appears to be saying is that, *if* it is the case that rulers should not go to war without the consent of their subjects, from whom they derive their authority, then clearly the elector should not go to war in this instance, since his people do not support Luther's teaching. H. Lüthje states that this is the only passage in Melanchthon's writings in which the idea that the prince holds his authority from people is to be found; see Hans Lüthje, 'Melanchthons Anschauung über das Recht des Widerstandes gegen die Staatsgewalt', *ZKG*, 47, N.F. 10 (Gotha 1928), 516.

27 *WA Br.* 12, 41.

28 Ibid., 42-3.

29 Amsdorf had been entrusted with the task of collecting the opinions of his colleagues and forwarding them to Spalatin and his own answer, which is dated 8 February 1523, was evidently written after he had received the replies of the others.

30 *WA Br.* 12, 44. For a fuller discussion of the views of Melanchthon, Bugenhagen and Amsdorf, see Dörries, 3, 199-202; for Melanchthon's paper, see also Lüthje, op. cit., 515-16.

31 The treatise was apparently finished in December 1522 (the preface is dated 'New Year's Day 1523'—that is, Christmas Day 1522) and it is likely that Luther borrowed from it, consciously or unconsciously, when he came to write his *Gutachten* for the elector.

32 *WA* 11, 276-7.

33 *WA Br.* 3, no. 814, 416–17. For the problem of the date of this letter, see ibid., Introduction, 415.
34 *Ob Kriegsleute auch in seligem Stande sein können, WA* 19, 643.
35 Ibid., 633–6.
36 Ibid., 640–1. As examples of rulers who are said to be bound by such an oath, Luther cites the cases of the kings of France and Denmark.
37 Ibid., 647–8.
38 Ibid., 649–51.
39 For a detailed history of these negotiations, see E. Fabian, part A.
40 For the details of the 'Pack affair', see Kurt Dülfer, *Die Packschen Händel. Darstellung und Quellen,* Veröffentlichungen der Historischen Kommission für Hessen und Waldeck, 24, 3, Marburg 1958, and Fabian, 33–6 and Excurse 11–14, pp. 338–42. Fabian argues against Dülfer that the real instigator of the whole incident was Philip of Hesse who used Pack's revelations to further his plans to attack the ecclesiastical principalities of Mainz and Würzburg. Fabian demonstrates conclusively that Philip was already planning his campaign against Mainz and Würzburg before Pack made his revelations about the 'Breslau treaty' and he makes out a strong case for suggesting that not only was Philip not Pack's dupe, but that it was he who inspired Pack's revelations (see especially Excurse 12 and 14, pp. 339–42).
41 *WA Br.* 4, no. 1246, 421–4.
42 See the letter from Luther and Melanchthon to elector John, 1 or 2 May (?) 1528, *WA Br.* 4, no. 1258, 449.
43 Luther to elector John, 22 May 1529, *WA Br.* 5, no. 1424, 76–7. Significantly, this letter was written by Luther on his own initiative and not in answer to a request for advice from the elector.
44 The league negotiations of 1529 and the reasons for their collapse are examined in detail in Fabian, op. cit., part A, 1, 2, 'Das Scheitern der Speyerer Bündnispolitik am "Bekenntnis"', 44–92; see also Schubert, *Bekenntnisbildung,* esp. chap. 5.
45 *WA Br.* 5, 77. For the part played by Melanchthon in organising opposition to the Speyer agreement, see Fabian, op. cit., 46–50.
46 *WA Br.* 5, no. 1424, Beilage, 78–81.
47 See *WA Br.* 5, no. 1496, Introduction, 180–1; Schubert, *Bekenntnisbildung,* 184f. For Philip of Hesse's opposition to the clause, see Fabian, op. cit., 54.
48 Scheible, *Widerstandsrecht,* no. 7, 25–9.
49 For the arguments of the Saxon jurists, see Schubert, *Bekenntnisbildung,* 186–7.
50 Ibid., 189–90; see also *WA Br.* 5, no. 1496, Introduction, 181.
51 Scheible, *Widerstandsrecht,* no. 8, pp. 29–39. For similar views expressed by Johannes Brenz, see the letter from Brenz to margrave George of Brandenburg-Ansbach, 27 November 1529, ibid., no. 9, pp. 40–2.
52 See the letter from Philip of Hesse to margrave George of Branden-

burg-Ansbach, 21 December 1529, ibid., no. 10, pp. 43–7. Among the arguments which Philip put forward in this letter are: (1) that the emperor and the princes have mutual obligations towards each other and the emperor has bound himself by oath (namely, in his election capitulation) to observe the laws of the empire, therefore the princes only owe the emperor a conditional obedience and may resist him if he breaks his obligations to them; (ii) the position of the German princes is altogether different from that of the officials of the Roman Empire in the time of the apostles, in that the latter were not hereditary rulers, *sunder schlechte landtpfleger* whom the Roman emperors could remove at their pleasure, therefore Paul's prohibition of resistance does not necessarily apply in the same way to the German princes (compare Philip's letter to Luther, 21 October 1530, *WA Br.* 5, no. 1737, pp. 653–5, see below, 25); (iii) the princes have a Christian duty to protect their subjects against all unjust force not only in temporal but also in spiritual matters (*wir als die dorzu unsern unterdanen eingesezte obrigkait dieselben unsere unterdanen vor unrechtem und unpillichem gewalt in zeitlichen und vil meher in geistlichen, doran die eher Gottes und die seligkait gelegen ist, zu beschirmen schuldigk*).

53 Schubert, *Bekenntnisbildung*, 223–4; *WA Br.* 5, no. 1522, p. 224 n. 3. In arguing for resistance, the Saxon chancellor, Christian Beyer, claimed to be speaking only in his personal capacity and not on behalf of the elector, but it is clear that his views were those of the Saxon government.

54 See his letter to Luther, 27 January 1530, *WA Br.* 5, no. 1522, pp. 223–4, from which it is evident that he had not consulted Luther directly on the question since receiving Bugenhagen's opinion. For John's attitude at this period, see Dörries, 3, 208–9.

55 *WA Br.* 5, no. 1496, pp. 181–3; no. 1511, pp. 209–11. Karl Müller argued that Luther's letter of 24 December 1529 marked a significant turning-point in the development of his attitude to the question of resistance to the emperor in that in it Luther appeared no longer to be opposing resistance to the emperor in principle, but only on the grounds that it was inopportune at the present time (Müller, op. cit., 20–2, 24–9). But this view has rightly been rejected by modern scholars: cf. G. Wolf in Wolf, *Luther und die Obrigkeit,* 337–9; Dörries, 3, 215 n. 42. As Dörries points out, Müller's interpretation is impossible to reconcile either with Luther's letter of 6 March 1530 or with his position at the time of the Torgau meeting in October 1530, and it is clear that too much should not be read into the language of the letter of 24 December 1529, which is concerned with opposing a specific proposal by Philip of Hesse rather than with the general question of resistance to the emperor.

56 *WA Br.* 5, no. 1522, pp. 223–4.

57 The first argument had been used by the Saxon jurists in the joint

memorandum drawn up by Saxony and Brandenburg-Ansbach for the Schwabach meeting of the protestant estates in October 1529: Schubert, *Bekenntnisbildung*, 186-7. Similarly, Philip of Hesse had used the second in his letter to margrave George of Ansbach of 21 December 1529, see above, 20 n. 52.

58 *WA Br.* 5, no. 1536, pp. 258-61; Scheible, *Widerstandsrecht*, no. 14, pp. 60-3. The letter was reprinted on several occasions in the sixteenth century, see *WA Br.* 5, no. 1536, Introduction, 251-8. The letter is discussed in Müller, op. cit., 22-4; Dörries, 3, 209-12.

59 *WA Br.* 5, no. 1536, pp. 258-9.

60 Ibid., 259. Both these arguments and the argument from the emperor's election capitulation were also rejected equally emphatically by Melanchthon in a separate *Gutachten*, dating from the same period, which covers many of the same issues, Scheible, *Widerstandsrecht*, no. 13, pp. 57-60. Scheible considers that in view of the obvious parallels between the two documents Melanchthon's *Gutachten* represents a preliminary study which he prepared for the joint letter of 6 March 1530: ibid., 57 n. 182.

61 *WA Br.* 5, 259-60.

62 Ibid., 259: 'Sunde hebt oberkeit und gehorsam nicht auff, Aber die straffe hebet sie auff, das ist, wenn das Reich und die kurfursten eintrechtiglich den keiser absetzten, das er nimer keiser were'. By *das Reich* Luther presumably meant the estates of the empire assembled in the diet.

63 For a detailed account of the negotiations between the protestant estates following the Diet of Augsburg, see Fabian, op. cit., part A, II 'Der Augsburger Reichstag von 1530 und der Abschluss des Schmalkaldischen Bundes', 92-183.

64 For the attitude of the Saxon government after Augsburg, see ibid., 114f.

65 The text of this paper is printed in Müller, Beilage 2, 89-92; Scheible, *Widerstandsrecht*, no. 15, pp. 63-6. For the authorship of this paper, which is cited in Müller, op. cit., 89, simply as an 'anonymous legal opinion' (*Anonymes Rechtsgutachten*), see Fabian, 117-18. There is some disagreement among scholars as to whether Luther and his colleagues were presented with the full text of the jurists' memorandum or with a paper summarising its main conclusions; the arguments on both sides are discussed in Dörries, 3, 217 n. 45.

66 See Fabian, op. cit., 119.

67 Philip of Hesse to Luther, 21 October 1530: *WA Br.* 5, no. 1737, pp. 653-5. Luther's reply, which was dated from Torgau, 28 October 1530, is in ibid., no. 1740, pp. 660-1. In it Luther avoided giving Philip a direct answer on the question of resistance, stating merely that he had declared his opinion on the matter to the elector (that is, in the Torgau Declaration), *Welche on zweivel E.f.g. unverborgen sein wird.*

68 Contrary to what is suggested by Hans Baron in 'Religion and Politics

in the German Imperial Cities during the Reformation', *EHR*, 52 (1937), 423. Baron attributes to the Saxon jurists the arguments used by Philip of Hesse in his letter to Luther of 21 October.

69 Müller, op. cit., 90–2.

70 25 or 26 October to 28 October.

71 Luther to Wenceslas Link, 15 January 1531: *WA Br.* 6, no. 1772, pp. 16–17; Luther to Lazarus Spengler, 15 February 1531: ibid., no. 1781, pp. 36–7; Luther to Spengler, 18 March 1531: ibid., no. 1796, pp. 56–7; Melanchthon to Joachim Camerarius, 1 January 1531, *Corpus Reformatorum*, 1–28, *Philippi Melanchthonis Opera*, ed. C. G. Bretschneider and H. E. Bindseil, Halle and Brunswick 1834–60, 2, no. 955, cols. 469–70; Melanchthon to Camerarius, 15 February 1531: ibid., no. 957, col. 471.

72 See esp. *WA Br.* 6, no. 1781, p. 36, no. 1796, p. 56.

73 The original MS. in the Weimar archives is in Luther's hand. Müller considered that Luther was the sole author of the Declaration (Müller, op. cit., 32 n. 2). This view has recently been criticised by Fabian on the grounds that the paper was presented in the joint names of Luther and his colleagues and that they must, therefore, be regarded as co-authors of the statement (Fabian, op. cit., 121 and n. 616). But while he is undoubtedly right to emphasise the collective character of the declaration, there is no reason to suppose that Luther was not responsible for the actual wording of the document.

74 In the sixteenth century *weil* could be used both in the causal sense of 'because' and in the temporal sense of 'so long as': see J. and W. Grimm, *Deutsches Wörterbuch*, Leipzig 1854–1971, 14, i, cols. 762f., which cites numerous examples of both usages from Luther's writings. In general, historians have tended to assume that Luther was using it here in its modern sense of 'because'; in other words, that he was saying that the theologians would not oppose resistance if it was permitted by the temporal laws, '*because* the Gospel does not teach anything contrary to the temporal law': compare Müller, op. cit., 33; Kern, op. cit., 334; Mackinnon, *Luther and the Reformation*, 4, 28. But although both usages are to be found in Luther, it is clear that *weil* must mean 'so long as' in this passage: this view is supported, though more tentatively, by Gottfried Krodel in *Luther's Works*, American Edition, St. Louis and Philadelphia 1955– , 49, Letters II, ed. and trans. Gottfried G. Krodel, 432 and n. 29. In practice, Luther never had maintained that temporal laws could not be in conflict with divine law and it would have been contrary to his basic principles to do so.

75 *WA Br.* 5, Beilagen, 662; Scheible, *Widerstandsrecht*, no. 16, p. 67.

76 *WA Br.* 5, 662; Scheible, *Widerstandsrecht*, 67–8. For the importance of this supplementary advice, see Dörries, 3, 218–21. In the subsequent negotiations over the formation of the Schmalkaldic League, the Saxon government apparently relied exclusively on the

Torgau Declaration and deliberately suppressed all mention of the theologians' second paper (ibid., 220–1).

77 For discussions of its significance, see Müller, op. cit., 32f.; Dörries, 3, 216f.

78 See above, 26 n. 74.

79 See *WA Br.* 6, 36, 56.

80 See below, 34, 37. In a passage in the *Table Talk*, dated between 18 August and 26 December 1531, Luther specifically rejected the argument that the princes were public persons, insisting that they were private persons in relation to the emperor, though he added that the matter should be discussed by the lawyers. *WA TR* 2, no. 2285a, p. 404: 'Principes Germanicos esse publicas personas dicunt, ideo ipsos adversus caesarem defendere posse suos, si post concilium executio fuisset caesari a papa mandata. Ego autem dico: Nequaquam. Principes enim erga caesarem dico esse privatas personas. Sed iuristis afferamus illa discutienda'.

81 *WA Br.* 6, no. 1772, p. 17.

82 See above, 25 n. 71.

83 For the politics of Nuremberg during the Reformation, see Baron, in *EHR*, 52 (1937), esp. 415–22, 614–21.

84 The Nuremberg pastors appear to have been divided on the issue, Andreas Osiander being in favour of resistance (ibid., 421–2). Baron's account underestimates the strength of the theological opposition in the city to resistance to the emperor in 1529–31.

85 *WA Br.* 6, 16–17, 36–7.

86 Ibid., 37.

87 Ibid., 17.

88 Compare *WA TR* 2, 404–6, nos. 2285a (part of which is quoted above, 28 n. 80), and 2285b. Equally ambiguous is Luther's attitude in his *Warnung an seine lieben Deutschen* (*WA* 30, 3, 276–320) which was published about March or April 1531 but was begun, if not finished, the previous October. It is sometimes claimed that in this tract Luther came out openly in support of resistance: but although he states that he will not blame those who resist if war should break out, since it is the catholics, not the protestants, who will be responsible for causing the war, he studiously refrains from actually advocating resistance, insisting that it is his duty as a preacher not to counsel war, but rather to advise men to seek peace and avoid war, as he has always done in the past, see esp. 278–83.

89 *CR* 3, no. 1458, cols. 126–31. Scheible prints only the second part of the paper which deals with the question of resistance to the emperor, *Widerstandsrecht*, no. 20, pp. 89–92.

90 For the political background to this memorandum, see Franz Lau and Ernst Bizer, *A History of the Reformation in Germany to 1555*, trans. B. A. Hardy, London 1969, 123f.

91 *CR* 3, cols. 126–8.

92 Ibid., col. 128. The natural law argument had been used as early as
1532 by Melanchthon (despite his rejection of it in 1530) in a letter to
Heinrich von Einsiedel, 8 July 1532: *CR* 2, no. 1066, cols. 603–4.
After 1536 it was used quite explicitly by the Wittenberg reformers in
several of their individual or collective *Gutachten* justifying resistance;
see, for example, *CR* 3, no. 1067, cols. 631–2 (1537 or 1539,
Melanchthon only); Scheible, *Widerstandsrecht*, no. 21, pp. 92–4
(November 1538); *WA Br.* 8, no. 3369, pp. 515–17 (July ? 1539). In
the later 1530s this argument seems to have been particularly favoured
by Melanchthon, who was responsible for drawing up most of the
collective *Gutachten* on resistance of these years: see Lüthje, op. cit.,
530–3.

93 *CR* 3, cols. 128–9.

94 Ibid., cols. 129–30.

95 Müller op. cit., 68.

96 See his treatise, *De officio principum, quod mandatum Dei praecipiat
eis tollere abusus Ecclesiasticos* (1539), printed in *CR* 3, no. 1520,
cols. 240–58, under the year 1537, and the *Gutachten* of the Wittenberg theologians of 1536, also composed by Melanchthon: *CR* 3,
no. 1511, cols. 224–9.

97 *CR* 3, cols. 128, 131.

98 Scheible, *Widerstandsrecht*, no. 21, pp. 92–4, Luther, Jonas, Bucer and
Melanchthon to elector John Frederick and Philip of Hesse, 13/14
November 1538 (written by Melanchthon); *WA Br.* 8, no. 3369,
pp. 515–17, Luther, Jonas and Bugenhagen to elector John Frederick,
July ? 1539 (probably written by Bugenhagen or Jonas); Scheible,
Widerstandsrecht, no. 23, pp. 98–100, Bugenhagen, Cruciger, Maior
and Melanchthon to the heads of the Schmalkaldic league, May/early
June 1546.

99 For the political background, see Lau and Bizer, *Reformation in
Germany to 1555*, 141f.

100 Müller op. cit., 69–70; *WA Br.* 8, no. 3297, Introduction, 364–5.

101 *WA Br.* 8, no. 3297, pp. 366–7.

102 Dörries, 3, 246 n. 117. Dörries points out that the argument that the
emperor may be resisted since he is not acting as emperor, *sonder als
ain geschworner und hauptman des bapsts*, appears in an anonymous
theological *Gutachten*, printed in Scheible, *Widerstandsrecht*, no. 18,
p. 80. Scheible dates this paper as c.1530, but the date is uncertain.

103 *WA Br.* 8, p. 367.

104 Ibid., 367–8. Virtually the same arguments as Luther used in this
letter appear in a passage in the *Table Talk*, dated 7 February 1539
(that is, the day before the letter to Ludicke); but there the order is
reversed and Luther places his main emphasis on the constitutional
position of the princes and he appears to attach rather less importance
to the argument that the emperor is not acting *pro sua persona* but as
the *feudatarius* of the pope, *WA TR* 4, no. 4342, pp. 235–9; see also

Müller, op. cit., 75–6; Dörries, 3, 253–4. For his comment on the relationship of the princes to the emperor see *WA Br.* 8, 367: Nam Principes Germaniae plus iuris habent contra Caesarem, quam illic populus contra Saul, vel Ahikam contra Joiakim, ut qui communi consilio gubernent imperium cum Caesare, et Caesar non sit monarcha nec posset deiectis Electoribus mutare formam imperii, nec esset ferendum, si tentaret.

105 *WA* 39, 2, 39–44. Luther's theses are discussed in detail in Rudolph Hermann, 'Luthers Zirkulardisputation über Mt 19, 21' in *Gesammelte Studien zur Theologie Luthers und der Reformation*, Göttingen 1960, 206–50. See also Müller, op. cit., 73–5; Dörries, 3, 241–6.

106 *WA* 39, 2, *Zirkulardisputation*, Introduction, 34–5.

107 Ibid., 40–1.

108 For Luther's concept of the three divine hierarchies, see Harald Diem, *Luthers Lehre von den zwei Reichen*, Evangelische Theologie, Beiheft 5, Munich 1938, 56–61; Gustaf Törnvall, *Geistliches und weltliches Regiment bei Luther*, Munich 1947, 38–40.

109 *WA* 39, 2, 42–3.

110 Printed in *WA* 39, 2, 52–89.

111 Ibid., 56–7.

112 Ibid., 60.

113 Ibid., 59 and *passim*.

114 Ibid., 60 and *passim*.

115 Ibid., 74.

116 Ibid., 58–9.

117 Ibid., 56–62, 64–5, 74–6.

118 Ibid., 56 f., 65, 74 f.

119 Ibid., 77.

120 Ibid., 78. The phraseology attributed to Luther here, especially in report A, is very similar to that of the *Table Talk* of 7 February 1539, *WA TR* 4, no. 4342, pp. 236–7, where the argument that the emperor shares his authority with the electors is developed at greater length. See also *Table Talk*, 8 and 9 May 1539, ibid., no. 4582, p. 388.

121 *WA* 39, 2, 78.

122 See ibid., Introduction, 35–8. For the posthumous use made of Luther's writings during the Schmalkaldic war, see Dörries, 3, 261–4.

123 Cf. his preface to the German translation of *Consilium delectorum cardinalium et aliorum prelatorum de emendanda ecclesia* (1538), *WA* 50, 288–91.

124 A fourth line of argument which appears in several of the collective opinions presented by the Wittenberg theologians at this period, especially those written by Melanchthon, is the claim that resistance to the emperor is justified on the basis of the natural law principle of self-defence (see above, 31 n. 92)—a claim which again involves a reversal of Luther's earlier views. But although Luther signed the

joint *Gutachten* of 1536, 1538 and 1539, he did not make use of the natural law argument in any of his own writings and, in my view, it must be considered doubtful whether he ever fully accepted it in his own mind.

125 For Beza's early views, see Robert M. Kingdon, 'The First Expression of Theodore Beza's Political Ideas', *ARG*, 46, Gütersloh 1955, 88–99.

126 For an analysis of the arguments of the Magdeburg *Bekenntnis*, see J. W. Allen, *A History of Political Thought in the Sixteenth Century*, London 1928, 103–6. Allen, however, tends to exaggerate the revolutionary significance of the arguments of the Magdeburg *Bekenntnis*, largely because he virtually ignores the previous development of resistance theory among the German Lutherans. He also suggests that there is no causal connexion between German resistance theory and the later ideas of the English Marian exiles and the French Huguenots (104, 106). But, as Kingdon points out (92–4), Beza in his *De haereticis a civili magistratu puniendis* (1554) refers specifically to the example of Magdeburg; and there can be little doubt that Calvin, Beza and the English Marian exiles were drawing on a well-established Lutheran tradition when they propounded the theory of the right of inferior magistrates to resist their superiors.

127 Heckel, *Lex Charitatis*, App. 1, 295–306.

128 Dörries, 3, 265–6. See also, 245f.

PROBLEMS OF LUTHER'S 'ZWEI-REICHE-LEHRE'

1 Among the more important books and articles relating to the *Zwei-Reiche-Lehre* which have appeared since 1930 are: F. Lau, „Äusserliche Ordnung" und „Weltlich Ding" in *Luthers Theologie*, Göttingen 1933; Harald Diem, *Luthers Lehre von den zwei Reichen*, Evangelische Theologie, Beiheft 5, 1938; G. Törnvall, *Geistliches und weltliches Regiment bei Luther*, Munich 1947; original Swedish edition, 1940; Hermann Diem, *Luthers Predigt in den zwei Reichen* (Theologische Existenz Heute, N.F. 6, 1947); A. Nygren, 'Luthers Lehre von den zwei Reichen' in *Theologische Literaturzeitung*, 1949, cols. 1–8; F. Lau, *Luthers Lehre von den beiden Reichen* (Luthertum, Heft 8, Berlin 1952); J. Heckel, *Lex charitatis* (Abhandlungen der Bayerischen Akademie der Wissenschaften, Phil.-hist. Kl., N.F. 36, Munich 1953); G. Hillerdal, *Gehorsam gegen Gott und Menschen*, Göttingen 1955; P. Althaus, 'Die beiden Regimente bei Luther' in *Theologische Literaturzeitung*, 1956, cols. 129–36; H. P. Gerstenkorn, *Weltlich Regiment zwischen Gottesreich und Teufelsmacht*, Bonn, 1956; P. Althaus, 'Luthers Lehre von den beiden Reichen im Feuer der Kritik' in *Luther-Jahrbuch 1957*, 40–68; J. Heckel, *Im Irrgarten der Zwei-Reiche-Lehre* (Theologische Existenz Heute, N.F. 55, 1957); G. Wingren, *Luther on Vocation*, Philadelphia, 1957; English edition

under title *The Christian's Calling*, London 1958; original Swedish edition, 1942; H. Bornkamm, *Luthers Lehre von den zwei Reichen im Zusammenhang seiner Theologie*, Gütersloh, 1958; E. Wolf, 'Königsherrschaft Christi und lutherische Zwei-Reiche-Lehre' in *Peregrinatio*, Band ii, Munich 1965; P. Althaus, *Die Ethik Martin Luthers*, Gütersloh 1965, esp. 49–87.

For a more detailed bibliography to 1955, see Althaus, *Luther-Jahrbuch 1957*, 40 n. 3; for more recent works, see the annual bibliographies of Luther studies published in *Luther-Jahrbuch*. An excellent brief survey of the development of research into the problem of the *Zwei-Reiche-Lehre* will be found in E. Wolf, 'Die „lutherische Lehre" von den zwei Reichen in der gegenwärtigen Forschung', *Zeitschrift für evangelisches Kirchenrecht*, 1957/8, 255–73.

2 Cf. Bornkamm, *Luthers Lehre von den zwei Reichen im Zusammenhang seiner Theologie*, 15; Heckel, *Im Irrgarten der Zwei-Reiche-Lehre*, 6 ff.

3 Cf. Martin Luther, *Werke* (Kritische Gesamtausgabe, Weimar, 1883–, cited hereafter as *WA*), 10, pt. iii, 371: 'Wer ist aber das reich gottes? Das ist das Cristlich glaubig volck Cristi'. *WA*. 18, 659: 'Quid enim est universum genus humanum, extra spiritum nisi regnum Diaboli (ut dixi) confusum cahos tenebrarum?'

4 *WA*. 24, 6: 'Das sind nu zwey reich: Weltlich, das mit dem schwerd regirt und eusserlich gesehen wird, Das geistlich regirt allein mit gnaden und vergebung der sunden, und dasselbige reich sihet man nicht mit leiblichen augen, sondern wird allein mit dem glauben gefasse'. *WA*. 10. iii, 371: 'Das weltlich reich hat Cristus in den kindern von Israel von Mosi an biss auff Jesum gebraucht, da er in die gesecz gab, als in cleydung, essen, trincken, cerimonien und andern dingen. Aber do Cristus ist mensch worden, hat er das geistlich angenommen und das weltlich lassen fallen'.

5 *WA*. 36, 385: 'So lautet lex. Ist wol auch unsers herr Gotts reich, sed ist ein zeitlich gesetze und regiment'. Cf. *WA*. 28, 281 ('Wochenpredigten über Joh. 16–18', 2nd edition, ed. Poach): 'Wir aber, wie ir offt gehört habt, leren also. Es ist zweyerley Reich, Gottes Reich und der Welt Reich, Oder wie mans sonst pfleget zu nennen, Geistlich Regiment und Weltlich Regiment'.

6 *WA*. 16, 261: 'Ich hab offt davon gesagt und wolts ja mechtig gerne, das wir von einander scheideten diese zwey Reiche, denn die Vernunfft, wie schön und herrlich sie auch ist, so gehört sie doch in das Weltreich alleine, da hat sie ire herrschafft und gebiete. Aber im Reich Christi, da hat alleine Gottes Wort die oberhand'. *WA*. 32, 473: 'Das gehoret inns weltliche regiment, welchs uns nicht angehet . . . Hie aber reden wir von einem andern Reich, das doch jenes nicht schwechet noch auffhebt, nemlich geistlich leben und wesen unter den Christen'.

7 For a well-known example of sixteenth-century English usage, see the

title of John Knox's famous pamphlet, *The First Blast of the Trumpet against the Monstrous Regiment of Women* (1558).

8 Cf. *WA.* 19, 629: 'Denn er [Gott] hat zweyerley regiment unter den menschen auff gericht. Eins geistlich, durchs wort und on schwerd, da durch die menschen sollen frum und gerecht werden, also das sie mit der selbigen gerechtickeit das ewige leben erlangen. Und solche gerechtickeit handhabet er durchs wort, wilchs er den predigern befolhen hat. Das ander ist ein weltlich regiment durchs schwerd, auff das die ienigen, so durchs wort nicht wollen frum und gerecht werden zum ewigen leben, dennoch durch solch weltlich regiment gedrungen werden, frum und gerecht zu sein für der welt. Und solche gerechtickeit handhabet er durchs schwerd'.

9 For the use of *weltliches Regiment* in the sense of 'temporal government', as contrasted with the ministry of the Word, cf. *WA.* 30. ii, 555: 'Darumb, gleich wie des predigampts werck und ehre ist das es aus sundern eitel heiligen, aus todten lebendige, aus verdampten seligen, aus teuffels diener, Gottes kinder macht. Also ist des weltlichen regiments werck und ehre, das es aus wilden thieren, menschen macht und menschen erhellt, das sie nicht wilde thiere werden'. For an example of the use of the term in the wider sense of the temporal order of man's earthly life, cf. *WA.* 32, 382: 'Wir haben aber genug gehoret, das Christus hie gar nichts wil reden inn das weltlich regiment und ordnung ...'.

10 See Althaus, *Die Ethik Martin Luthers,* 55–6.

11 Cf. *WA.* 30. ii, 131: 'Es gehört ynn leibliche, weltliche sachen'; 562, 'Aber ynn weltlichem reich, müs man aus der vernunfft ... handeln Denn Gott hat der vernunfft unterworffen solch zeitlich regiment und leiblich wesen.'

12 Cf. *WA.* 15, 302: '... denn die welt will und mus böse seyn'; 306; 'So habe ich nu offtmals geleret, das man die wellt nach dem Euangelio und Christlicher liebe nicht soll noch mag regieren, sondern nach strengen gesetzen mit schwerd und gewallt, darumb das die wellt böse ist und widder Euangelion noch liebe annympt, sondern nach yhrem mutwillen thut und lebt, wo sie nicht mit gewalt gezwungen wird.'

13 *WA.* 18, 658: '... mundum esse regnum Satanae, ubi praeter naturalem caecitatem agnatam ex carne etiam nequissimis spiritibus regnantibus super nos in ipsa caecitate induramur et daemoniacis nec iam humanis tenebris tenemur.' Cf. *WA.* 11, 267: 'Die wellt aber ist Gottis feyndt'; *WA. Br.* 5, 115: 'Memento, quod mundus est mundus, i.e. hostis verbi Dei et inimicus Dei.'

14 *WA.* 11, 251: 'Zum reych der wellt oder unter das gesetz gehören alle, die nicht Christen sind.' *WA.* 44, 647: 'Sed regnum mundi manet regnum Sathanae.'

15 Cf. above, 44 n. 4 and 44 n. 6.

16 The term is used in this sense by such scholars as Lau, Althaus, Harald and Hermann Diem, Wingren, and Bornkamm (see above, 42 n. 1).

17 The leading exponent of this usage is Johannes Heckel; cf. also Gerstenkorn, *Weltlich Regiment zwischen Gottesreich und Teufelsmacht*. For an example of the way in which the two usages can sometimes be confused, see Anders Nygren 'Luthers Lehre von den zwei Reichen' in *TLZ*, 1949, cols. 1–8, where the term appears to be employed in both senses without any attempt to distinguish clearly between the two concepts.

18 Cf. *WA*. 19, 629, *WA*. 24, 6, quoted above 44 n. 3 and 43 n. 2.

19 Cf. especially *WA*. 1, 692, *WA*. 36, 385, 387. For a discussion of the significance of Luther's concept of *das Reich Gottes zur Rechten und Linken* or *mit der rechten und linken Hand*, see Heckel, *Lex charitatis*, 41 ff., *Im Irrgarten der Zwei-Reiche-Lehre*, 33–5, and Althaus, 'Die beiden Regimente bei Luther' in *TLZ*, 1956, col. 133.

20 *WA*. 1, 692: 'Zum andern, durch die rechten gotes wirt verstanden, das des herrn Christi künigreich ain gaistlich verborgen reich sey'. *WA*. 15, 724: 'Ist nit weltlich oder zeytlich, sondern geystlich, stehet auch nit in essen oder trincken, nach keinem eusserlichen dinge, sondern nur in gerechtfertigunge, befridunge und tröstunge des menschen hertzen und gewissen.'

21 *WA*. 11, 251: 'Darumb hatt Gott die zwey regiment verordnet, das geystliche, wilchs Christen unnd frum leutt macht durch den heyligen geyst unter Christo'. *WA*. 15, 725: 'Got regniret in den hertzen, in dem das er fryde, ruhe, trost etc. darinnen machet durch sein wort, gleych als die sunde das widerspil'.

22 *WA*. 51, 11: 'Und ist Christi Reich ein hör Reich, nicht ein sehe Reich'. Ibid., 13: '...so stehet doch das euserlich und weltlich Reich allein im thun und nachdruck, da sehen und feust zugehören. Aber das Reich Christi stehe allein im gehöre, also das ich das wort höre, nem es an und gleube es'.

23 *WA*. 10. iii, 175: '...aber das hertz khan es [das weltliche Schwerd] nicht zwingen und zum glauben bringen...hye muss man zur thur hynein geen und das wort predigen...so bringt manss zum glauben, sunst mit nichte'.

24 *WA*. 36, 385: 'Ist wol auch unsers herr Gotts reich, sed ist ein zeitlich gesetze und regiment, aber er wil gleichwol haben, das man es hallt, und ist das Reich mit der lincken hand'.

25 *WA*. 11, 251: '...unnd das welltliche, wilchs den unchristen und bössen weret, dass sie eusserlich müssen frid hallten und still seyn on yhren danck'. *WA*. 51, 69: '...und solch Regiment dienet hie auff erden, damit dis leben erhaltten werde'.

26 *WA*. 32, 421: 'Richten odder regiren und oberhand habend sol niemand denn Gott allein odder denen ers befilet, durch welche er das regiment aus richtet als seine diener...Denn wer da straffet der thuts als an Gottes stat und gehet alles aus seiner krafft, das man recht handhabt, schutzet und erhelt'.

27 *WA*. 11, 262: 'Das welltlich regiment hatt gesetz, die sich nicht

weytter strecken denn uber leyb und gütt und was eusserlich ist auff erden. Denn uber die seele kan und will Gott niemant lassen regirn denn sich selbs alleyne'. Cf. *WA*. 51, 13, quoted above, n. 22.

28 *WA*. 47, 284: 'Wir sollen aber lernen das Geistlich und Weltlich regiment so weith von einander scheiden als himel und Erden'. *WA*. 49, 224: 'Ich habs die 20 jahr offt geschrieben, ut bene distinguatur weltlich und geistlich regiment'.

29 *WA*. 11, 252: 'Darumb muss man dise beyde regiment mit vleyss scheyden und beydes bleyben lassen: Eyns das frum macht, Das ander das eusserlich frid schaffe und bösen wercken weret. Keyns ist on das ander gnüg ynn der wellt'.

30 *WA*. 11, 249: 'Hie müssen wyr Adams kynder und alle menschen teylen ynn zwey teyll: die ersten zum reych Gottis, die andern zum reych der welt. Die zum reych Gottis gehören, das sind alle recht glewbigen ynn Christo unnd unter Christo. Denn Christus ist der könig unnd herr ym reych Gottis'; 251, 'Zum reych der wellt oder unter das gesetz gehören alle, die nicht Christen sind'. Cf. *WA*. 18, 782.

31 Cf. Luther's exposition of the parable of the tares in *Fastenpostille* (1525), *WA*. 17. ii, 124–6.

32 *WA*. 18, 782: 'Sciunt (inquam) duo esse regna in mundo mutuo pugnantissima, in altero Satanam regnare, qui... cunctos tenet captivos ad voluntatem suam, qui non sunt Christi spiritu ab eo rapti ...nec sinit eos sibi rapi ullis viribus nisi spiritu Dei.... In altero regnat Christus, quod assidue resistit et pugnat cum Satanae regno, in quod transferimur non nostra vi, sed gratia Dei, qua liberamur a praesenti soeculo nequam et eripimur a potestate tenebrarum'.

33 *WA*. 36, 570: '...bis so lange das stündlin kompt, da Christus wird des ein ende machen und sich offentlich dar stellen inn seiner maiestet und herrschafft, da du wirst sehen und fülen, was du itzt gleubest, die sund aus getilget und erseufft, den tod auffgehaben und aus den augen genomen, den Teuffel und welt dir zun fussen ligen'.

34 Cf. Törnvall, *Geistliches und weltliches Regiment bei Luther*, 185 ff.; Hillerdal, *Gehorsam gegen Gott und Menschen*, 25 ff.; Gerstenkorn, *Weltlich Regiment zwischen Gottesreich und Teufelsmacht*, especially 50 ff.

35 *WA*. 15, 725: 'Also gibt Gotis Reich solliche dingk geystlich and zerbricht der sunden reych und ist nit anderst dann ein vertilgunge und vergebung der sünden'. *WA*. 12, 329: 'Denn weyl wyr nicht alle gleuben, sondern der meyst hauff unglewbig ist, Hatt ers also geschaffen und verordnet, auff das die wellt eynander nicht fresse, das die ubirkeyt das schwerdt füre und den bösen were, wenn sie nicht wollen frid haben, das sie as müssen thun'.

36 *WA*. 23, 514: 'Widden solche Gotts regimente tobet nu der Satan, des ampt nichts anders ist denn alles zubrechen und zurstören, was Gott durch diese regimente schafft und thut'.

37 *WA*. 23, 515: 'Widder das geistliche regiment hat er [Satan] die

ketzer, falsche lerer, heuchler, falsche brüder, da feyret er auch nicht, bis ers zu nichte mache, Widder das weltliche hat er auffrürissche ungehorsame buben, böse gifftige rethe an fursten höfen, schmeychler, verrether, kundschaffer, tyrannen, wütrichen und alles was da dienet zu krieg, unfriede und verterben der land und leute'. Cf. *WA*. 42, 526: 'Vult Deus esse imperia, vult damnari nocentes, et defendi pios. Sed Sathan corrumpit animos, ut Magistratus degenerent in Tyrannos'.

38 Cf. Törnvall, *Geistliches und weltliches Regiment bei Luther*, 185 ff.; Hillerdal, *Gehorsam gegen Gott und Menschen*, 25 ff.

39 Heckel's views were first put forward in *Lex charitatis* (1953), see especially *Zweiter Teil, Erster Abschnitt* 'Luthers Lehre von den beiden Reichen als Grundlage seiner Rechtslehre', 31–46. Subsequently he developed his criticisms of the conventional approach to the *Zwei-Reiche-Lehre* in a number of articles and reviews. The clearest statement of his position is to be found in his pamphlet, *Im Irrgarten der Zwei-Reiche-Lehre* (Theologische Existenz Heute, N.F. 55, 1957) where he seeks to defend his position against the arguments of his critics, and in particular those of Paul Althaus in *Theologische Literaturzeitung*, 1956, and *Luther-Jahrbuch 1957* (see above, 42 n. 1).

40 Heckel, *Lex charitatis*, 31, 41–3; *Im Irrgarten*, 5–7, cf. his criticism of Althaus (25).

41 Heckel, *Lex charitatis*, 31 ff.; *Im Irrgarten*, 6–7.

42 Heckel, *Lex charitatis*, 34–6, 37–8; *Im Irrgarten*, 6.

43 Heckel, *Lex charitatis*, 35 ff.; *Im Irrgarten*, 6–7.

44 Heckel, *Im Irrgarten*, 6, 10.

45 Heckel, *Im Irrgarten*, 8 ff., especially 12. Cf. *Lex charitatis*, 41 ff.

46 Cf. Althaus, *TLZ*, 1956, cols. 130 ff., *Luther-Jahrbuch 1957*, 42 ff.; Lau, *Luthers Lehre von den beiden Reichen*, 30; Törnvall, *Geistliches und weltliches Regiment bei Luther*, especially ch. v, 'Die Regimente und der einzelne Mensch', 166 ff.

47 Törnvall, *Geistliches und weltliches Regiment bei Luther*, 166 ff.; Lau, *Luthers Lehre von den beiden Reichen*, 30–1.

48 Cf. Lau, *Luthers Lehre von den beiden Reichen*, 34; Althaus, *TLZ*, 1956, cols. 134–5; Törnvall, *Geistliches und weltliches Regiment bei Luther*, 173.

49 Cf. Lau, *Luthers Lehre von den beiden Reichen*, 37; Törnvall, *Geistliches und weltliches Regiment bei Luther*, 19–20, 118 ff.

50 Heckel, *Lex charitatis*, 42–3; *Im Irrgarten*, especially 10–12.

51 Heckel, *Im Irrgarten*, 12, 15–16, 27 ff.; cf. *Lex charitatis*, 41 ff.

52 Heckel, *Lex charitatis*, 36, 38–9; *Im Irrgarten*, 12 ff.

53 Heckel, *Im Irrgarten*, 15–16, 28; cf. *Lex charitatis*, 133–5, 147.

54 Heckel, *Lex charitatis*, 148 ff.; *Im Irrgarten*, 17–18, 28.

55 Heckel, *Lex charitatis*, 43, 134; *Im Irrgarten*, 25 ff.

56 Heckel, *Im Irrgarten*, 26 ff.

57 Heckel, *Lex charitatis*, 134 n. 1093, 147; cf. *Im Irrgarten*, 28–9.

58 *WA.* 11, 251.

59 *WA.* 12, 330.

60 Heckel, *Im Irrgarten*, 29.

61 *WA.* 32, 390.

62 *WA.* 10. iii, 379: 'Aber iczundt hat der teuffel den meisten hauffen gesammelt unnd under seinem regiment, Darümb mus ein ander regiment sein, da kümpt das weltlich schwertt, da muss man fürsten und amptleutt haben die sein uns von nöten'. *WA.* 42, 79: 'Politia autem ante peccatum nulla fuit, neque enim ea opus fuit. Est enim Politia remedium necessarium naturae corruptae. Oportet enim cupiditatem constringi vinculis legum et poenis, ne libere vagetur'.

63 *WA.* 12, 330: 'Die Christen lassen sich das wort Gottis regiren, durffen des welltlichen regyments gar nichts fur sich selbs'.

64 *WA.* 23, 514: 'Durchs schwerd aber verstehe ich alles was zum weltlichen regiment gehört, als weltliche rechte und gesetze, sitten und gewonheite, geberden, stende, unterscheidene empter, person, kleider, etc.'. *WA.* 32, 307: 'Zum weltlichen regiment gehoret, das man gelt, gut, ehre, gewalt, land und leute habe und kan on dis nicht bestehen'. Cf. Althaus, *TLZ*, 1956, col. 131, *Luther-Jahrbuch 1957*, 43.

65 Cf. *WA.* 42, 79, cited above, 54 n. 62: 'Politia autem ante peccatum nulla fuit', etc.; 582: 'Tam fera et corrupta est humana natura. Opus habet coniugio ceu remedio libidinis.'

66 Cf. *WA.* 32, 390, quoted above, 53 n. 61.

67 *WA.* 7, 50: 'Homo enim duplici constat natura, spirituali et corporali: iuxta spiritualem, quam dicunt animam, vocatur spiritualis, interior, novus homo, iuxta corporalem, quam carnem dicunt, vocatur carnalis, exterior, vetus homo.... Haec diversitas facit, ut in scripturis pugnantia de eodem homine dicantur, cum et ipsi duo homines in eodem homine sibi pugnent, dum caro concupiscit adversus spiritum et spiritus adversus carnem, Gal. 5'.

68 *WA.* 7, 59.

69 *WA.* 32, 391.

70 *WA.* 32, 390: 'Sihe so reden wir itzt von einem Christen in relatione, nicht als von einem Christen, sondern gebunden inn diesem leben an ein ander person'.

71 *WA.* 34. ii, 300: 'Nos habemus 2^{cem} beruff, spiritualem et externam. Spiritualis est, quod omnes sumus per Euangelium vocati ad baptismum et Christianam fidem, ut per verbum et baptismum simus incorporati Christo, et per hoc vocamur fratres, etc.'; 306: 'Altera vocatio, externa scilicet, macht ein unterscheid, Est yrdisch, quanquam etiam divina. Ibi furst non rusticus, scholasticus non Magister, servus non dominus, pater non filius, vir non mulier'. Cf. *WA.* 32, 316.

72 *WA.* 32, 390: 'Darumb ists nicht wol muglich, ein Christ mus ja irgend eine welt person sein, weil er ja zum wenigsten mit leib und gut unter dem Keiser ist, Aber fur seine eigen person nach dem

Christlichen leben ist er gar allein unter Christo und nicht des Keisers noch einiges menschen'.

73 *WA.* 30. ii, 136: 'Es wird das Euangelion aller welt gepredigt und gleuben doch gar wenig, Noch gleubt und bleibt gleichwol die Christenheit'.

74 *WA.* 11, 250: 'Nu aber keyn mensch von natur Christen odder frum ist, sondern altzumal sunder und böse sind, weret yhnen Gott allen durchs gesetz, das sie eusserlich yhr bossheyt mitt wercken nicht thüren nach yhrem muttwillen uben'.

75 Heckel, *Im Irrgarten,* 12–15, 34; cf. *Lex charitatis,* 42, 44 f.

76 *WA.* 31. i, 77–8: 'Da gehet an das danckopfer inn sonderheit fur das weltliche regiment und fur den lieben friede, welchs gar ein grosse gabe Gottes ist und freilich unter den zeitlichen gaben, die aller grösseste, Denn wo kein regiment odder friede were, so kündten wir gar nicht bleiben'. Cf. *WA.* 30. ii, 554–5.

77 Cf. 'Das schöne Confitemini' (1530): *WA.* 31. i, 68 ff.

78 *WA.* 42, 100: 'An non enim magnum est, quod etiam in innocentiae statu Deus coniugium ordinavit et instituit?' Cf. ibid., 87, for the institution of 'oeconomia', i.e. the household or family. See also Lau, „Äusserliche Ordnung" und „Weltlich Ding" in Luthers Theologie, 108–9, and *Luthers Lehre von den beiden Reichen,* 49; Althaus, *TLZ,* 1956, 132, *Luther-Jahrbuch 1957,* 43–4, and *Die Ethik Martin Luthers,* 90.

79 *WA.* 42, 58–9, 152.

80 *WA.* 21, 521. Cf. *WA.* 42, 57: 'Et tamen operatur Deus adhuc, si quidem semel conditam naturam non deseruit, sed gubernat et conservat virtute verbi sui'.

81 *WA.* 31. i, 217: 'Denn wir nu offt gesagt, das Gottes wort heiliget und vergöttet alle ding, dazu es gesetzt wird. Darumb heissen solche stende so mit Gottes wort gestifftet sind, alles heilige Göttliche stende, ob gleich die personen nicht heilig sind'. *WA.* 31. i, 234: 'Damit bestettigt er zu gleich auch alle handwerg, stende und hendel, so ynn solchen weltlichen herrschafften sind ... Ja es sind alles stende, von Gott eingesetzt, das sie yhm dienen sollen durch das wort Gene. 3'.

82 *WA.* 31. i, 193.

83 For Luther's concept of God's continuous activity in his creation, see especially P. Althaus, *Der Schöpfungsgedanke bei Luther* (Bayerische Akademie der Wissenschaften, Phil.-hist. Klasse, Sitzungsberichte, 1959, Heft 7).

84 *WA.* 46, 558: 'S. Johannes zeiget hiemit an, das ... Gott hab die Welt und alle Creaturn durch das Wort, seinen eingebornen Son und Göttliche weisheit, nicht alleine geschaffen, sondern durch dasselbe auch fur und fur regirt und erhalten bis an der welt ende'. Cf. ibid., 559–60 for a description of the way in which God not only maintains his creation in being but is continually engaged in replenishing it with new creatures.

85 Cf. *WA*. 17. ii, 192: 'Und summa, Alle creaturen sind Gottes larven und mumereyen, die er will lassen mit yhm wircken und helffen allerley schaffen'; *WA*. 31. i, 436: 'Es sind unsers herrn Gotts larven, darunter wil er verbogen sein und alles thun'. For Luther's concept of creatures as God's 'masks', see F. Blanke, *Der verborgene Gott bei Luther* (Stimmen aus der deutschen christlichen Studentenbewegung, Heft 60, Berlin 1928), 5 ff.; Harald Diem, *Luthers Lehre von den Zwei Reichen*, 150–1; G. Wingren, *Luther on Vocation*, 137 ff.; P. Althaus, *Der Schöpfungsgedanke bei Luther*, 5 ff.

86 *WA*. 42, 12: 'Necesse enim est, ut Deus, cum se nobis revelat, id faciat per velamen et involucrum quoddam et dicat: Ecce sub hoc involucro me certo apprehendes'; 316: 'Tamen, sicut Augustinus erudite dicit, Deus res conditas sic administrat, ut eas propriis motibus agere sinat, hoc est ... Deus utitur mediis certis, et sua miracula sic temperat, ut tamen ministerio naturae et mediis naturalibus utatur'. Cf. *WA*. 31. i, 436: 'Er kunde wol kinder schaffen on man und weib. Aber er wills nicht thun, sondern gibt man und weib zu samen, auff das scheine, als thu es man und weib, und er thuts doch unter solcher larven verborgen'.

87 *WA*. 30. i, 136.

LUTHER'S 'TOWER EXPERIENCE'

1 The best modern introduction to the study of the problem is *Der Durchbruch der reformatorischen Erkenntnis bei Luther*, ed. B. Lohse, *Wege der Forschung* 123 (Darmstadt 1968), which contains a selection of extracts from many of the most important books and articles relating to the controversy, published between 1904 and 1966. Several of the items printed in Lohse include historiographical surveys of the development of the debate: see especially Lohse's introduction (ix–xxiii) and the articles by G. Pfeiffer (163–202), H. Bornkamm (289–383) and, for the later period, O. H. Pesch (445–505). Useful surveys in English of the earlier phases of the controversy will be found in J. Mackinnon, *Luther and the Reformation*, 4 vols. (London 1925–30) i, 147–56, and G. Rupp, *The Righteousness of God: Luther Studies* (London 1953), chap. 6, 121–37. O. Scheel, *Dokumente zu Luthers Entwicklung (bis 1519)*, 2nd revised ed. Göttingen 1929, contains a comprehensive collection of primary texts relating to Luther's early development.

2 *WA TR*. 3, no. 3232c (Lauterbach), 228; Scheel, *Dokumente*, no. 235, 91. Other reports of the same conversation are to be found in *WA TR*. 2, no. 1681, 177 (Scheel, *Dokumente*, no. 238, 94) and *WA TR*. 3, no. 3232a and b, 228 (Scheel, *Dokumente*, no. 235, 91). In all these versions the phraseology in which the discovery is described is very similar, so that we may be sure that the gist of Luther's remarks is accurately recorded. The most important difference between the

reports, which has given rise to considerable controversy, lies in the words used to describe the place where the discovery is alleged to have taken place. Lauterbach, quoted in the text, has *in hac turri et hypocausto* (generally interpreted as the heated room where Luther had his study) and *in diesem thurn*; Cordatus's very similar account has *in hac turri* (*in quo secretus locus erat monachorum*) and *auff diesem thurm* (*WA TR*. 3, no. 3232a, 228); Schlaginhaufen has *Dise kunst hatt mir der S S* [*Spiritus Sanctus*] *auf diss Cl eingeben* (*WA TR*. 2, no. 1681, 177), subsequently expanded in Rörer's version to *auf dieser cloaca*, with the words *in horto* inserted above in the MS (ibid., n. 1); Aurifaber's later printed version omits the reference to the place altogether (ibid., 177). On the strength of the readings *Cl* and *cloaca* and Cordatus's phrase *in qua secretus locus erat monachorum*, Grisar argued that Luther's 'tower-experience' must have taken place in the privy: see H. Grisar, *Luther*, trans. E. M. Lamond, London 1913–17, i, 392, 396–7. Not surprisingly this view has been hotly contested by protestant scholars, chiefly on the ground that Schlaginhaufen's cryptic *auf diss Cl* is neuter and so cannot legitimately be expanded to *cloaca* which is feminine. This also rules out the suggestion of some scholars that *Cl* is an abbreviation for *cella*. For a discussion of this point, see the extract from E. Stracke, *Luthers grosses Selbstzeugnis* [*1545 über seine Entwicklung zum Reformator*], *SVRG* 140 (1926), in Lohse, op. cit., 111, n. 9. Stracke argued that *Cl* is the standard abbreviation for *clarissimum* and that it refers not to the place where Luther's experience took place but either to the text in Paul or to the concept of *iustitia Dei*. However, this seems improbable. Perhaps the most plausible suggestion is that *Cl* is an abbreviation for *claustrum*: see U. Saarnivaara, *Luther Discovers the Gospel: New Light upon Luther's Way from Medieval Catholicism to Evangelical Faith*, Saint Louis 1951, 48, n. 104.

3 *WA TR*. 4, no. 4007, 72–3; Scheel, *Dokumente*, no. 404, 148.

4 *Da reumet ich das abstractum und concretum zusamen*: Luther means that he reconciled the abstract concept *iustitia Dei* with the concrete state of being righteous (*iustus*); in other words he perceived that 'the righteousness of God' is that by which men are made righteous (compare the two previous descriptions).

5 *WA TR*. 5, no. 5518, 210; Scheel, *Dokumente*, no. 474, 172.

6 For example, *WA TR*. 5, no. 5247, 26, September 1540 (Scheel, *Dokumente*, no. 449, 162); *WA TR*. 5, no. 5553, 234–5, winter 1542/3 (Scheel, *Dokumente*, no. 476, 173); Lectures on Genesis, *WA* 43, 537 (Scheel, *Dokumente*, no. 460, 166–7). The fullest description is to be found in the Preface to the 1545 edition of Luther's Latin writings, *WA* 54, 185–6 (Scheel, *Dokumente*, no. 511, 191–2), quoted below, 71–3.

7 Grisar is generally credited with having coined the term *Turmerlebnis*: see Grisar, *Luther*, i, 377.

8 P. J. Reiter, *Martin Luthers Umwelt, Charakter und Psychose sowie die Bedeutung dieser Faktoren für seine Entwicklung und Lehre. Eine historisch-psychiatrische Studie*, Copenhagen 1937–41, ii, 320–2; E. H. Erikson, *Young Man Luther: A Study in Psychoanalysis and History*, London 1959, 198–200; N. O. Brown, *Life against Death: the Psychoanalytical Meaning of History*, London 1959, chap. 14, esp. 202–6. For a discussion of the problem, see above, 61, n. 2.

9 See, in particular, the account in the 1545 preface, *WA* 54, 185–6, quoted below, 71–3.

10 *WA* 54, 185–6: see below, 71–3.

11 The *Dictata super Psalterium* was published by G. Kawerau in *WA* 3–4 (1885–6); the lectures on Romans by J. Ficker in *Anfänge reformatorischer Bibelauslegung*, 1, *Luthers Vorlesung über den Römerbrief 1515/16*, Leipzig 1908. Earlier German historians had tended to place Luther's discovery very early in his career, during his Erfurt period. His most famous nineteenth-century biographer, Julius Köstlin, for example, dated it to the third and last year of his monastic life at Erfurt before his first call to Wittenberg, in other words to 1508: see J. Köstlin, *Life of Luther*, Eng. trans., London 1883, 54–5.

12 H. Denifle, *Luther und Luthertum in der ersten Entwickelung quellenmässig dargestelt*, Mainz 1904–9, i, 404–15, 392–5, reprinted in Lohse, op. cit., 1–18.

13 R. Seeberg, *Lehrbuch der Dogmengeschichte*, Leipzig 1908–17, 4, *Die Lehre Luthers*, 68–9; O. Ritschl, *Dogmengeschichte des Protestantismus*, Leipzig/Göttingen 1908–27, ii, 11. See also H. Boehmer, *Luther im Lichte der neueren Forschung: Ein kritischer Bericht* first ed. Leipzig 1906, 32–3. This view has generally been held to be incompatible with Luther's statement in a sermon of 21 May 1537 that at the time he became a doctor [that is, October 1512] he was ignorant of the light—'Iterum acquisivimus lucem. Sed ego, cum doctor fierem, nescivi': *WA* 45, 86; Scheel, *Dokumente*, no. 364, 135–6.

14 K. Holl, 'Der Neubau der Sittlichkeit' in *Gesammelte Aufsätze zur Kirchengeschichte*, i, *Luther*, 6th ed. Tübingen 1932, 193–7.

15 O. Scheel, *Martin Luther. Vom Katholizismus zur Reformation*, 2nd ed. Tübingen 1917, ii, 321; H. Strohl, *L'Évolution Religieuse de Luther jusqu'en 1515, Études d'Histoire et de Philosophie Religieuses publiées par la Faculté de Théologie Protestante de l'Université de Strasbourg* i, Strasbourg/Paris 1922, 143–6; Mackinnon, *Luther and the Reformation*, i, 150–1.

16 H. Boehmer, *Der junge Luther*, Gotha 1924, 110. This represents Boehmer's final position. In the first edition of his *Luther im Lichte der neueren Forschung* (1906) he argued against Denifle that it took place in the winter of 1508–9 during Luther's first period at Wittenberg (see above, n. 13). Subsequently he modified this. In the fifth edition of *Luther im Lichte der neueren Forschung* (1918) he placed it at the end of 1512 or the beginning of 1513, in the period between

Luther's advancement to the professoriate at Wittenberg and the commencement of the first lectures on the Psalms: see H. Boehmer, *Luther and the Reformation in the Light of Modern Research*, trans. E. S. G. Potter from the 5th German ed., London 1930, 60. Finally in his monograph *Luthers erste Vorlesung, Berichte über die Verhandlungen der sächsischen Akademie der Wissenschaften*, PhK 75 (1923) pt. 1, Leipzig 1924, and in his popular biography *Der junge Luther*, he narrowed the date down still further to April/May 1513.

17 E. Hirsch, 'Initium theologiae Lutheri' in *Festgabe für D. Dr. Julius Kaftan*, Tübingen 1920, 150–69, reprinted in Lohse, op. cit., 64–95.

18 E. Vogelsang, *Die Anfänge von Luthers Christologie nach der ersten Psalmenvorlesung, Arbeiten zu Kirchengeschichte* 15, Berlin/Leipzig 1929, esp. 57–9.

19 H. Bornkamm, 'Luthers Bericht über seine Entdeckung der iustitia dei', *ARG* 37 (1940), 117–28; 'Iustitia dei in der Scholastik und bei Luther', *ARG* 39 (1942), 1–46; 'Die Frage der iustitia dei beim jungen Luther', *ARG* 52 (1961), 15–29, 53 (1962), 1–59, reprinted together in Lohse, op. cit., 289–383. Bornkamm's views have changed slightly during the course of his career. In his 1940 article he originally argued for a date in the spring of 1515 at the time when Luther was preparing the lectures on Romans. In his 1942 article he revised his opinion and came out in favour of Vogelsang's theory. In his third article, written twenty years later, while somewhat modifying his earlier agreement with Vogelsang's arguments, he reaffirmed his belief that Luther's new understanding of Romans i. 17 dates back to his first lectures on the Psalms (see Lohse, op. cit., esp. 299, 381).

20 A. V. Müller, *Luthers Werdegang bis zum Turmerlebnis*, Gotha 1920, chap. 6, esp. 128–30.

21 Stracke, *Luthers grosses Selbstzeugnis* in Lohse, 114.

22 Cf. E. G. Rupp, *Righteousness of God*, 137: 'We conclude, therefore, that, as Vogelsang suggests, the new orientation of thought seems likely to have occurred in the course of the lectures on the Psalms, 1514. It is hardly likely that any closer date will be arrived at'.

23 Grisar, *Luther*, i, chap. 10, 374–404. In many respects Grisar's arguments foreshadow those of Saarnivaara and Bizer. Thus he maintains that Luther had not yet arrived at his mature doctrine of justification in the lectures on Romans; that this only occurred in 1518 or at the beginning of 1519; and that the evidence of the 1545 preface is correct in dating the 'tower-experience' to the time when he was beginning the second lectures on the Psalms.

24 Saarnivaara, *Luther Discovers the Gospel*, esp. 74–87.

25 Ibid., 92–120. 'Our conclusion is that Luther's tower experience took place during the time he was preparing his second course of lectures on the Psalms, probably in the autumn or early winter of 1518' (108). Cf. 103: 'The only possible conclusion is that his dating of this discovery is his *Preface* of 1545 is correct.'

26 See, for example, F. E. Cranz, *An Essay on the Development of Luther's Thought on Justice, Law, and Society*, Harvard Theological Studies 19, Cambridge Mass., 1959, esp. 41, n. 1; A. G. Dickens, *Martin Luther and the Reformation*, London 1967, 25–31.

27 E. Bizer, *Fides ex auditu: Eine Untersuchung über die Entdeckung der Gerechtigkeit Gottes durch Martin Luther*, Neukirchen 1958, 2nd revised ed. 1961, 3rd ed. with new postcript 1966. References in this article are to the third edition, the text of which is identical with that of the second edition except for the addition of the postscript, 179–204. Excerpts from the third edition will be found in Lohse, op. cit., 115–62. For a full discussion in English of Bizer's views, see the review article by E. G. Rupp, *ZKG* 71 (1960), 351–5.

28 He does not cite Saarnivaara in the first two editions and only refers to him briefly in the postscript to the third edition, 187.

29 Bizer, *Fides ex auditu*, see esp. the section 'Das Selbstzeugnis von 1545 und die Operationes in Psalmos', 165–71.

30 See esp. his discussions of the first lectures on the Psalms, ibid., 15–22, and the lectures on Romans, 23–52.

31 Ibid., 166–7: 'Was Luther entdeckt hat, ist zunächst die Theologie des Wortes und *im Zusammenhang* damit die Bedeutung des Glaubens. Das Wort zeigt nicht einfach den Weg zur Gerechtigkeit und beschreibt diesen nicht nur, sondern es ist das Mittel, wodurch Gott den Menschen rechtfertigt, weil es den Glauben weckt' (167). Compare the postscript to the third edition (1966), 180: 'Meine These ist nun, dass Luther in der Vorrede davon berichte, wie er "das Wort als Gnadenmittel" entdeckt habe'.

32 Cf. Bizer, *Fides ex auditu*, 94.

33 For a very full account of the development of the controversy following the publication of *Fides ex auditu*, see O. H. Pesch, 'Zur Frage nach Luthers reformatorischer Wende', *Catholica* 20 (Münster 1966), 216–43 and 264–80, reprinted in Lohse, op. cit., 445–505.

34 See, in particular, R. Prenter, *Der barmherzige Richter. Iustitia dei passiva in Luthers Dictata super Psalterium 1513–15*, Acta Jutlandica 33, 2, Aarhus/Copenhagen 1961, extract in Lohse, 203–42, and the extended critique of Bizer by H. Bornkamm, 'Zur Frage der iustitia dei beim jungen Luther', *ARG* 52 (1961) and 53 (1962) in Lohse, 289–383. For Bizer's reply to their criticisms, see *Fides ex auditu*, postscript (1966), 179–204.

35 See A. Peters, 'Luther's Turmerlebnis', *Neue Zeitschrift für Systematische Theologie* 3, Berlin 1961, 203–36, in Lohse, 243–88; K. Aland, *Der Weg zu Reformation, Zeitpunkt und Charakter des reformatorischen Erlebnisses Martin Luthers*, Theologische Existenz Heute, N.F. 123, Muniche 1965, extracts in Lohse, 384–412. Other notable converts to the idea of a late date include H. Jedin and E. Wolf, see Pesch in Lohse, 455–6. See also the important recent article by Martin Brecht, 'Iustitia Christi: Die Entdeckung Martin

Luthers', *Zeitschrift für Theologie und Kirche* 74, Tübingen 1977, 179–223, which appeared too late for consideration in this paper but which argues that 'Luther made the decisive discovery of his theology in the spring of 1518' (222). I am grateful to Professor Brecht for kindly sending me a copy of his article through the good offices of Dr. E. Langstadt.

36 For the difficulty and importance of defining the terms 'reformation' and 'pre-reformation' in relation to Luther's early thought, see Bornkamm in Lohse, op. cit., 376–7; L. Grane, *Modus loquendi theologicus: Luthers Kampf um die Erneuerung der Theologie (1515–1518)*, *Acta Theologica Danica* 12, Leiden 1975, 11–12.

37 Cf. Bornkamm in Lohse, esp. 376, 381–2.

38 See Grane, *Modus loquendi theologicus*, 11. For a more detailed survey of the literature to 1966, see Pesch in Lohse, 445–505.

39 Cf. Bornkamm's criticisms of Bizer, Lohse, 334.

40 Cf., for example, the many passages in which Luther appears to treat justification in Augustine's sense as a life-long process of renewal which will not be completed until the next world, for example, *WA* 56, 272–3.

41 Cf. Cranz, *Development of Luther's Thought*, chap. 2, 41–71; Peters in Lohse, 242–88.

42 *WA TR*. 1, no. 352, 146.

43 *WA* 54, 186; Scheel, *Dokumente*, no. 511, 192.

44 *Connexionem verborum*: Luther means the connexion between the first phrase 'the righteousness of God is revealed in it the gospel' and the second 'the just shall live by faith'. Compare his accounts in the *Table Talk*, quoted above, 60–1.

45 *WA* 54, 185–6; Scheel, *Dokumente*, no. 511, 191–2.

46 'Interim eo anno iam redieram ad psalterium denuo interpretandum', etc. (*WA* 54, 185; Scheel, *Dokumente*, 191).

47 E. Hirsch pointed out that the use of the term 'passive' in relation to *iustitia Dei* first occurs in Luther's writings in *De servo arbitrio* (1525) and it did not become a regular part of his theological vocabulary until the 1530s, so that the language in which he describes his discovery in the 1545 preface is that of his old age ('Initium theologiae Lutheri', Lohse, 71–5).

48 See above, 61.

49 Cf. the statement in *WA TR*. 4, no. 4007, 73: 'Sed postea cum consequentia viderem ... et insuper August [inum] consulerem, da wardt ich frolich' (see above, 61).

50 *WA* 56, 158.

51 Ibid., 171–2.

52 Ibid., 172.

53 For Luther's use of Augustine's *De spiritu et littera* in the lectures on Romans, see B. Lohse, 'Die Bedeutung Augustins für den jungen

Luther', *Kerygma und Dogma* 11, Göttingen 1965, 116–36; Grane, *Modus loquendi theologicus*, esp. chap. 1, 23–62.

54 Stracke, *Luthers grosses Selbstzeugnis*, Lohse, 112–13. Cf. E. G. Rupp, *The Righteousness of God*, 123.

55 Hirsch, 'Initium theologiae Lutheri', Lohse, 86 n. 62; Mackinnon, *Luther and the Reformation*, i, 150.

56 F. Loofs, *Leitfaden zum Studium der Dogmengeschichte*, 4th revised ed. Halle 1906, 689; O. Scheel, *Die Entwicklung Luthers bis zum Abschluss der Vorlesung über den Römerbrief*, *SVRG* 100 (1910), 117.

57 Boehmer, *Luther in the Light of Modern Research*, 45.

58 Cf. E. G. Rupp, *Righteousness of God*, 123; Rupp, however, followed Stracke in holding that the passage should be regarded as a digression (see above, n. 54).

59 Bizer, *Fides ex auditu*, 10, 127–30, 165–71. Cf. Saarnivaara, *Luther Discovers the Gospel*, 97–9.

60 Bizer, *Fides ex auditu*, 165–7, 180, see above, 66 n. 31. Other supporters of the revisionist theory tend to interpret Luther's discovery in the tower rather differently. Saarnivaara equates it with Luther's 'discovery of the full Reformation insight into justification, that God justifies the sinner by graciously imputing, or reckoning, the merits of Christ to him as his righteousness', though he also writes that 'from another point of view, the content of the discovery was the "Lutheran" distinction between the Law and the Gospel' (*Luther Discovers the Gospel*, 46). Aland adheres to the traditional view that the 'tower-experience' involved the realisation that *iustitia Dei* is the passive righteousness by which God justifies man through faith and that this righteousness is revealed in the Gospel (Lohse, 406); but he places this discovery in 1518 (409).

61 See Rupp, *ZKG* 71 (1960), 354; Bornkamm in Lohse, 353–6.

62 Bizer, *Fides ex auditu*, 184; Saarnivaara, *Luther Discovers the Gospel*, 109–11; Aland in Lohse, 399–401.

63 In his article ' "Iustitia Christi" and "Iustitia Dei": Luther and the Scholastic Doctrines of Justification', *HTR* 59 (1966), 1–26, H. A. Oberman appears to cast doubt on the historicity of Luther's 'tower-experience' by pointing out that it belongs to a well-established literary tradition of conversion experiences, including those of Augustine and Calvin. 'This state of affairs,' he writes, 'allows us to conclude that there is a "Turmerlebnis" tradition which provides for a conceptual framework and an established language, in which and through which one can formulate one's own important discoveries' (9). Although Oberman does not explicitly deny that Luther's 'tower-experience' took place, the implication of his remarks is clearly that Luther's accounts of the 'tower-experience' should be treated as essentially a literary or metaphorical way of expressing his religious discovery. I find this attempt to rationalise the 'tower-experience'

unconvincing. While Oberman is undoubtedly right to draw attention to the precedents in Christian literature for Luther's 'tower-experience', it does not follow from this that Luther's accounts do not relate to a genuine personal experience of his own. In view of his repeated and unequivocal statements about his discovery, I see no reason to doubt that he did experience a moment of illumination at Wittenberg, even if perhaps he afterwards magnified its importance.

64 Although there are few overtly autobiographical passages in the lectures on Romans referring to Luther's personal religious experiences, such as occur in some of his other lectures, the general tenor of the lectures on Romans suggests a confident assurance that men are justified through God's grace, and not through their own righteousness, which would appear to indicate that he had now found the answer to the spiritual crisis of his early years in the monastery.

65 See Rupp, *Righteousness of God*, 154–5, 195–6, 205; Bizer, *Fides ex auditu*, 148–64.

66 This is admitted by some exponents of the revisionist theory. Cf. Saarnivaara, *Luther Discovers the Gospel*, 46: 'the "tower experience" of Luther was not the beginning, but the relative end of his development'; ibid.: 'Luther's experience in the tower was not his conversion. It was the final exegetico-religious discovery of the evangelical way of salvation.' See also Peters in Lohse, 255: 'In dem "Turmerlebnis" beschreibt Luther das geistige Ringen, in welchem seine systematische wie exegetische Erwägungen zu einem geschlossenen Ganzen zusammenschiessen'.

WHO WROTE 'THE SUPPER OF THE LORD'?

1 The full title of the original edition is 'The Souper/of the Lorde./ wher unto, that thou mayst be the better pre-/pared and suerlyer instructed: have here/firste the declaracion of the later par-/te of the 6 ca. of S. Johā, beginnin-/ge at the letter C the fowerth ly-/ne before the crosse, at these wor-/dis: Verely, vere. &c wheryn/incidently M. Moris let-/ter agenst Johan Fry-/the is confu-/ted'. The colophon reads 'Imprinted at Nornburg, by Niclas twonson, 5 April. An.1533'. However, no printer of this name is known and it clearly belongs to the category of English protestant books which were printed in the Low Countries with fictitious imprints. Miss Kronenberg suggests that the real printer was Symon Cock of Antwerp, who published several other works for English reformers, also without giving his name: M. E. Kronenberg, 'Forged Addresses in Low Country Books in the Period of the Reformation', *The Library*, Fifth Series, ii, Oxford 1948, 89.

2 C. Anderson, *The Annals of the English Bible*, London 1845, i, 349–350, 354–356.

3 *The Works of the English Reformers—William Tyndale and John Frith*, ed. Thomas Russell, London 1831, iii, 17–69.
4 *The Works of William Tyndale*, ed. Henry Walter, Parker Society, Cambridge 1848–50, iii, 217–68.
5 Tyndale, *Doctrinal Treatises*, Parker Society, Cambridge 1848, 'Biographical Notice of William Tyndale', lvii.
6 Tyndale, *An Answer to Sir Thomas More's Dialogue, &c.*, Parker Society, Cambridge 1850, 218–21.
7 'I do not wish, however, to be considered as positively affirming the treatise to be Tyndale's.... But still there are objections of such force, that I must confess myself rather inclined to attribute the treatise to Joye's pen, if I could but be satisfied that he was capable of writing so correctly, and of keeping so clear of vulgarity in a controversy with a popish persecutor': *Notes and Queries*, First Series, No. 23, 6 April 1850, 363.
8 R. Demaus, *William Tyndale*, London 1872, 367 and n.
9 'Thomas More also leaves the matter open. But he evidently suspects that he is dealing with Tyndale, and he was almost certainly right': J. F. Mozley, *William Tyndale*, London 1937, 253. Mozley also discussed the matter in an article, entitled 'Tyndale's Supper of the Lord' in *Notes and Queries*, clxxxiii, 21 November 1942, 205–6. Here he argues very strongly that 'The Supper of the Lord' was the work of Tyndale, but he offers no new external evidence.
10 'Tyndale now joined in the fray, for on 5th. April, there was published an anonymous work *The Supper of the Lord*, which may with great probability be ascribed to him': *The Work of William Tyndale*, ed. S. L. Greenslade, London 1938, Introduction, 15. However, when discussing the work later on, he is careful to state that Tyndale's authorship is not absolutely certain, see 45.
11 Tyndale, *Answer to More, &c.*, 267. In all sixteenth century editions after the first, 'M. Mocke' was changed to 'M. More'. In the Parker Society text of Tyndale's works the spelling has been modernised, and for the sake of uniformity I have followed this practice in all passages quoted in this article, even when sixteenth century editions have been used.
12 Sir Thomas More, 'The Answer to the First Part of a Poisoned Book which a Nameless Heretic hath Named The Supper of the Lord', printed in *The Works of Sir Thomas More*, London 1557, 1036–7.
13 John Bale, *Illustrium Maioris Britanniae Scriptorum Summarium*, Ipswich 1548, 240: John Bale, *Scriptorum Illustrium Maioris Britanniae Catalogus*, Basle 1557, 721.
14 Gilbert Burnet, *History of the Reformation*, ed. Nicholas Pocock, Oxford 1865, iv, 518.
15 *The Whole Works of Tyndale, Frith and Barnes*, London 1573, 'Tyndale's Works', 457.
16 Ibid., 456.

17 Ibid., 456.

18 'Amongst his other books which he compiled, one work he made also for the declaration of the sacrament (as it was then called) of the altar; which he kept by him, considering how the people were not as yet fully persuaded in other matters tending to superstitious ceremonies and gross idolatry.... Wherefore Master Tyndale, being a man both prudent in his doings, and no less zealous in the setting forth of God's holy truth after such sort as it might take most effect with the people, did forbear the putting forth of that work, not doubting but, by God's merciful grace, a time should come to have that abomination openly declared as it is at this present day: the Lord Almighty be always praised therefore, Amen!': John Foxe, *Acts and Monuments*, ed. S. R. Catley, London 1837–41, v, 119.

19 In Foxe's edition of *The Whole Works of Tyndale, Frith and Barnes*, the title is given as 'A Fruitful and Godly Treatise expressing the right institution and usage of the Sacrament of Baptism and the Sacrament of the Body and Blood of Our Saviour Jesu Christ'. But the earliest edition to survive (printed by R. Stoughton, c. 1548) was published under the title of 'A Brief Declaration of the Sacraments; expressing the first original, how they came up and were institute, with the true and most sincere meaning and understanding of the same, very necessary for all men that will not err in the true use and meaning thereof, compiled by the godly learned man, William Tyndale'. This edition is undated, but cannot have appeared before 1548, when Stoughton started printing. In consequence, it has usually been conjectured that an earlier edition, of which no copies have survived, was published during Tyndale's life-time: for Foxe prints the tract along with the rest of Tyndale's works 'newly imprinted according to his first copies, which he himself set forth'. (See Henry Walter's 'Introductory Notice' to 'A Fruitful and Godly Treatise', in Tyndale, *Doctrinal Treatises*, 346: the S.T.C. even lists a hypothetical edition with the title of 'A Fruitful and Godly Treatise expressing the right institution and usage of the Sacraments', for which it suggests the date 1533.) However, in view of Foxe's report that Tyndale deliberately refrained from publishing a work on the sacraments which he had written, it is possible that 'A Fruitful and Godly Treatise' was not published during his life-time, and that Stoughton's edition was, in fact, the first to appear.

20 More, *Works*, 1036–7.

21 Ibid., 1037.

22 Tyndale, *Answer to More, &c.*, 218.

23 More, *Works*, 1039.

24 Mozley suggests that Bale's attribution may have been based on the same protestant conjectures which More reported in his 'Answer to the First Part of a Poisoned Book' (*Notes and Queries*, clxxxiii, 305). But this is merely an hypothesis for which Mozley advances no evi-

dence, while he completely ignores the testimony of the proclamation of 1542. The only other direct contemporary evidence also seems to support the view that 'The Supper of the Lord' should not be ascribed to Tyndale, though it is too vague to be of much value. About 1548 'The Supper of the Lord' was reissued by Robert Crowley, who added a 'Preface to the Christian Reader'. Unfortunately Crowley does not give any information about the origin of the work or the identity of its author. In his only reference to him he says 'the author of this little book . . . is detested as a heretic, wherefore we may well say with Christ, "The Light is come into the world, and men have loved darkness more than light" '. (*The Supper of the Lord*, London 1548?, 'Preface to the Christian Reader'.) But as Walter pointed out (Tyndale, *Answer to More. &c.*, 220–1), Crowley does not suggest that the author of 'The Supper of the Lord' had been martyred for the faith, as he might have been expected to do had he supposed it to be the work of Tyndale. Instead the passage may imply that the author was still alive at that time, and Joye, it may be noted, did not die until 1533. But tantalising as it is, the passage is too obscure to allow any deductions to be drawn from it.

25 *Works of Tyndale, Frith and Barnes*, 455–6. The letter is reprinted by Walter in his Biographical Notice, Tyndale, *Doctrinal Works*, liii–lvi; Demaus, op. cit., 359–63; Mozley, op. cit., 248–51.

26 *Works of Tyndale, Frith and Barnes*, 'Tyndale's Works', 455.

27 More, *Works*, 1037.

28 Tyndale, *Answer to More, &c.*, 220.

29 'Whilst by writing anonymously he might intend to avoid giving Frith's judges any legal ground for convicting him of being engaged in the same conspiracy against their church with one whose works had been authoritatively described as heretical', wrote Walter in his introduction to 'The Supper of the Lord', in Tyndale, *Answer to More, &c.*, 220. Mozley takes the same view in *William Tyndale*, 253.

30 'But of this I challenge George Joye that he did not put his own name thereto and call it rather his own translation: and that he playeth boo peep and in some of his books putteth in his name and title and in some keepeth it out', William Tyndale, yet once more to the Christian Reader, reprinted in 'An Apology made by George Joye to satisfy, if it may be, W. Tyndale', ed. Edward Arber (English Scholar's Library, London 1895), x.

31 Joye, *An Apology to W. Tyndale*, 28.

32 See above, 85–7.

33 *Letters and Papers—Foreign and Domestic—of the Reign of Henry VIII*, ed. J. S. Brewer and James Gairdner, London 1862–1910, viii, 1535. No. 823: Edward Foxe to Cromwell, 4 June 1535.

34 Mozley argues from this letter that Joye could not have been a Zwinglian, or at least not a very convinced one, since he was ready to conform in 1535, and that he could not, therefore, have written 'The

Supper of the Lord': *Notes and Queries*, clxxxiii, 305. But this argument misses the point of Foxe's letter: for if bishop Foxe considered it worthwhile to report to the government that Joye had undertaken never to attack transubstantiation again, Joye must previously have been known for his heretical views on the sacrament.

35 It should, however, be pointed out that Bale mentions two other treatises on the eucharist in his list of Joye's works—*De Baptismo et Eucharistia* (Incipit, 'Quia constat homo ex duabus'), which is listed in both editions of his Catalogue (1548 edition, 240; 1557 edition, 721); and *De Eucharistia* (Incipit, 'Haud mirandum, chari fratres') which is only mentioned in the 1557 edition (721). These works are not recorded in the *Short-Title Catalogue* and appear to be otherwise unknown. However, Mozley suggests that the treatise mentioned in Tyndale's letter to Frith should be identified with one of these, rather than with 'The Supper of the Lord': *Notes and Queries*, clxxxiii, 305.

36 To appreciate the similarity of their eucharistic doctrine both treatises should be read in their entirety. Nevertheless, one may compare the following passages especially: 'The Supper of the Lord' in Tyndale, *Answer to More, &c.*, 237 f., 242–3, 251: 'A Fruitful and Godly Treatise', in Tyndale, *Doctrinal Treatises*, 357–9, 365 f.

37 Tyndale, *Doctrinal Treatises*, 357–8.

38 'Neither our salvation so greatly standeth in that or in any other sacrament, that we would not be saved without them, by preaching the word only': ibid., 359.

39 Tyndale, *Answer to More, &c.*, 250–1.

40 Ibid., 246.

41 Ibid., 246.

42 Ibid., 265.

43 The most complete statement of Luther's position is to be found in *Von Weltlicher Obrigkeit* (1523).

44 Preface to Melanchthon's *Instructions for the Visitors of the Saxon Church* (1527); Martin Luther, *WA*, 26, 197.

45 It is always possible that Tyndale had changed his mind on this point by 1533, as *The Obedience of a Christian Man* was written in 1528. Nevertheless, even in the political sections of the 'Exposition of Matthew v, vi and vii', which appeared in 1532 (Tyndale, *Expositions of Scripture*, Parker Society, Cambridge 1849, especially 58–70), there is no suggestion that the Christian magistrate is *ex-officio* head of the Church.

46 Tyndale, *Answer to More, &c.*, 220. Mozley, however, questions the force of this argument: *Notes and Queries*, clxxxiii, 306.

47 Tyndale, *Doctrinal Treatises*, 347.

48 Ibid., especially 347–54, 375–8.

49 Tyndale, *Answer to More, &c.*, 177.

50 Cf. especially *Doctrinal Treatises*, 371; *Answer to More, &c.*, 177.

SIR FRANCIS KNOLLYS'S CAMPAIGN

1 Samuel Johnson, *A Dictionary of the English Language,* 3rd ed., London: W. Strahan, 1765, i, sig. 7F.

2 For a classic statement of this view, see 'An Answere unto a Letter of Master Harrisons by Master Cartwright being at Middleborough' (1584) in *Cartwrightiana,* ed. Albert Peel and Leland H. Carlson, Elizabethan Nonconformist Texts, i, London 1951, 49–58.

3 Peel and Carlson, *Cartwrightiana,* 50.

4 Cf. Patrick Collinson, *The Elizabethan Puritan Movement,* London 1967, 13.

5 There is no biography of Knollys. The fullest account of his career is still that written by Sir Sidney Lee for the *DNB,* although it is inaccurate on many points of detail. For his early life down to 1559, see Christina Hallowell Garrett, *The Marian Exiles,* Cambridge 1938; repr. 1966, 210–13.

6 Thomas Fuller, *The Church-History of Britain, From the Birth of Jesus Christ until the Year M.DC.XLVIII,* London 1655, Book IX, 152, quoted above, 94. Miss Garrett suggests that Knollys visited Geneva briefly, along with his son Henry, in November 1553, as an envoy sent by Cecil to Calvin 'with the object of obtaining permission for the establishment of a colony of English religious emigrants within their borders', and she identifies the two Knollyses with the unnamed English gentleman and his son who were referred to by Calvin in a letter to Viret dated 20 November 1553 (*Marian Exiles,* 211–12). However, this theory, like Miss Garrett's general hypothesis regarding Cecil's role in organising the emigration of English protestants at Mary's accession with which it is closely linked, must be regarded as purely speculative and there is no concrete evidence that Knollys left England before 1555. All that is known with certainty of Knollys's period of exile is that he was in Basle in the winter of 1556–7, when his name appears in the Matriculation Register of the university, and that he subsequently moved to Frankfurt, where he was one of those who attempted to mediate between the two rival factions in the contentions of 1557, although he eventually subscribed the new Discipline in December 1557; he also appears to have visited Strassburg as a delegate from the Frankfurt congregation (*Marian Exiles,* 212). Miss Garrett is almost certainly correct in arguing against the *DNB* that he did not return to England until after Elizabeth's accession (*Marian Exiles,* 212).

7 Knollys's wife was Catharine Carey, daughter of Anne Boleyn's elder sister, Mary, and sister of Henry Carey, Lord Hunsdon. For the importance of the Boleyn connexion in Elizabeth's Privy Council, see Michael Barraclough Pulman, *The Elizabethan Privy Council in the Fifteen-seventies,* Berkeley, Los Angeles, London 1971, esp. 37, 39–42.

8 J. E. Neale, *Elizabeth I and her Parliaments 1559–1581,* London 1953, 57ff.

9 See the letter from Edwin Sandys, bishop of London, Knollys, Sir
Thomas Smith and Sir Walter Mildmay to John Parkhurst, bishop of
Norwich, 6 May 1574, printed in George Cornelius Gorham, *Gleanings
of a Few Scattered Ears during the Period of the Reformation in
England*, London 1857, 487–8, and the letter from Knollys to Sir
Thomas Wilson, 4 January 1577/8, B. L. Harleian MS. 6992, no. 44,
cited in John Strype, *The History of the Life and Acts of the Most
Reverend Father in God, Edmund Grindal*, Oxford 1821, 354.

10 Cf. the paper entitled 'Mr Tresorer of the howshold his opynyon
towchyng hir majesties safetye 6th. Julii. 1586': B. L. Lansdowne MS.
51, no. 12, printed in John Strype, *The Life and Acts of John
Whitgift, D.D.*, Oxford 1822, iii, 199–200.

11 In general, most modern historians have tended to apply the label
'Puritan' to Knollys automatically, e.g., Neale, *Elizabeth I and her
Parliaments 1559–1581*, 57: 'Sir Francis Knollys . . . who throughout
his career—as we shall have occasion to note—proved a godly, out-
spoken Puritan'; Conyers Read, *Lord Burghley and Queen Elizabeth*,
London 1960, 465: 'As for Knollys, he was first, last and all the time
a belligerent Puritan'; A. G. Dickens, *The English Reformation*,
London 1964, 299: 'Knollys in particular was to figure for many
years among the most ardent Puritan laymen of the reign'; G. R.
Elton, *England under the Tudors*, London 1955, 293: 'that staunch
puritan, Sir Francis Knollys'. A significant exception is Patrick
Collinson, who for the most part avoids the use of the term 'Puritan'
in his frequent references to Knollys and instead prefers to describe
him (I think, correctly) as 'an old-fashioned protestant': *Elizabethan
Puritan Movement*, 386.

12 See Fuller, *Church-History of Britain*, Boox IX, 152, cited above, 94.
Neale suggests that Knollys, along with at least four of his colleagues
on the Privy Council (Bedford, Mildmay, Warwick and Walsingham)
'would all perhaps have welcomed some form of Presbyterian experi-
ment' (*Elizabeth I and her Parliaments 1559–1581*, 292), but I can
find no evidence that this is true of Knollys and it is questionable how
far it is true of any of the others.

13 On at least one occasion, in 1572, he rebuked Elizabeth for permitting
the Prayer Book order of service to be 'daily broken as well in her
own chapel as in her closet', see Neale, *Elizabeth I and her Parliaments 1559–1581*, 303.

14 Cf. Neale, *Elizabeth I and her Parliaments 1559–1581*, 198–9, 201–2;
J. E. Neale, *Elizabeth I and her Parliaments 1584–1601*, London 1957,
62.

15 See his letter to Lord Burghley, 29 April 1593, reporting his speech in
parliament in February 1593: B. L. Lansdowne MS. 75, no. 37, summarised in Strype, *Whitgift*, ii, 124–7 (discussed later, 127–30). The
DNB states that Knollys entered parliament for the first time in
1542 as member for Horsham. But it is clear from this letter that he

was already a member in 1534. The editors of the *History of Parliament*, to whom I am indebted for information regarding Knollys's parliamentary career, think that he probably entered parliament at a by-election in 1533, as he would have been too young to have been elected in 1529, although this cannot be confirmed since no by-election returns survive for this parliament.

16 See the letter from Knollys to archbishop Whitgift, 20 June 1584, summarised in Historical Manuscripts Commission, *Calendar of the Manuscripts of the Most. Hon. The Marquis of Salisbury, K.G., &c., preserved at Hatfield House, Hertfordshire*, London 1883–, iii, 35–6, and the related letter from Knollys to Lord Burghley, 13 June 1584: P.R.O. State Papers Domestic, Elizabeth, vol. 171, no. 23, summarised briefly in *Calendar of State Papers, Domestic Series, of the Reigns of Edward VI, Mary, Elizabeth*, ed. R. Lemon and M. A. E. Green, London, 1856–72, ii (1581–90), 181. As Fuller observed, it is curious that Knollys was not one of the privy councillors who signed the joint letter from the Council to Whitgift of 20 September 1584, protesting against his treatment of the Essex ministers (Fuller, *Church-History of Britain*, Book IX, 152); but the probable explanation for this is that he was absent from court at the time. Knollys was still actively attacking Whitgift in January 1585, when he drew up a libellous syllogism accusing the archbishop of Canterbury of practising 'poopyshe tyrannye to the indangeryng of hir majesties safetye': B. L. Lansdowne MS. 97, no. 15. Part of Whitgift's reply to this syllogism was printed by Strype in *Whitgift*, i, 563–5, under the year 1589, as if it was connected with the later controversy over the *jure divino* theory of episcopacy. But this is clearly a mistake, since the original manuscript of Knollys's paper, which is written in Knollys's own hand, bears the endorsement 'the. 30. of Januarye. 1584 [i.e. 1585]'. Strype also states incorrectly that the conclusion of Whitgift's reply is lost: in fact, the whole of his answer is to be found in B. L. Lansdowne MS. 396, fols. 51–6.

17 See the letter from Knollys to Lord Burghley, 4 August 1589: B. L. Lansdowne MS. 61, no. 54, cited later, 101–2.

18 Strype, *Whitgift*, i, 558–65, 597–601, 614; ii, 32–4, 50–5, 71–3, 121–7; iii, 220–8; John Strype, *Annals of the Reformation and Establishment of Religion . . . during Queen Elizabeth's Happy Reign*, Oxford 1824, iii, ii, 97–102, 601–2; iv, 6–9.

19 One of the few historians to recognise that Strype's account of the controversy was unsatisfactory was Roland G. Usher in a little known article, 'The Supposed Origin of the Doctrine of the Divine Right of Bishops' in *Mélanges d'Histoire Offerts à M. Charles Bémont par ses Amis et ses Élèves*, Paris 1913, 539–47, subsequently reprinted under the title 'Bancroft and the Divine Right of Bishops' in *Theology*, l (1920), 28–34. However, though critical of Strype (see esp. *Mélanges*, 546, n.1), Usher was unable to shake off Strype's influence and his

own account of the controversy is misleading. I am indebted to Dr. W. J. Baker of the University of Maine for drawing my attention to this article.

20 See esp. Strype, *Whitgift*, i, 558–63.

21 Strype, *Whitgift*, ii, 50–2. Although Strype purports to be quoting here from a letter of Knollys to Burghley, dated 31 March 1590 (B. L. Lansdowne MS. 64, no. 32), the first part of the letter as quoted on 50 is, in fact, taken from Knollys's letter to Burghley of 4 August 1589 (B. L. Lansdowne MS. 61, no. 54).

22 Strype, *Whitgift*, i, 597–8, 603–5. Both these extracts come from the same letter from Knollys to Burghley, dated 5 July 1589 (B. L. Lansdowne MS. 61, no. 47).

23 These papers formed part of a group of MSS. relating to puritan activities in the years 1588–90, which Thomas Brett sent to Strype in June 1711, and which Strype quoted extensively in his *Whitgift*. In a letter to Strype, dated 25 June 1711, Brett stated that these papers 'are descended to me from *Sir John Boys* who was Brother to my Mothers Great-Grandfather. He was a Lawyer with whom Archbishop *Whitgift* advised in matters of common Law, being ye Steward both of his Court at *Canterbury*, & that of ye Dean & Chapter. And I suppose these Papers were put into his Hands that he might give his Grace Advice how to deal with ye Puritans according to our Laws': Cambridge Univ. Library Baumgartner MSS., Strype Papers, 6, no. 429. In this letter Brett asked Strype to return the papers when he had finished with them and Strype seems to have complied with this request, but they have since disappeared. They are not among Brett's correspondence in the Bodleian nor among the Brett family papers now in the Kent County Record Office at Maidstone, although it is possible that they may still survive elsewhere. In his letter of 25 June 1711, Brett enumerated the nine items that he was sending to Strype in some detail. The papers which relate to the controversy over the *jure divino* theory of episcopacy can be identified as Item 3, which Brett described as follows: '3. Is stitched in Paper, & contains a Controversy about ye Superiority of Bishops whether it be *Iure divino* or *humano*, occasioned by a Sermon preached at Court Jan. 12. 1588. The Title on ye outside Leaf is, *Touching Superiority of Bishops, with a Syllogism, & an Answer to ye Same, & a Reply thereunto*'.

24 These papers were at one time in Strype's own possession, having been lent to him by Sir William Hickes of Ruckholt, the grandson of Burghley's secretary, Sir Michael Hickes. After Sir William's death in 1703, they remained in Strype's custody until his own death in 1737, when they were sold by his representatives to the antiquary, James West, after whose death in 1772 they were purchased by Lord Shelburne, later first Marquess of Lansdowne (see *DNB*, sub Strype). Strype does not appear to have made any use of the Burghley papers at Hatfield.

25 Strype, *Whitgift*, i, 558-9.
26 I have discussed the development of the theory of episcopacy in the Elizabethan period more fully in an earlier essay, 'Anthony Marten and the Elizabethan Debate on Episcopacy' in *Essays in Modern English Church History in Memory of Norman Sykes*, ed. G. V. Bennett and J. D. Walsh, London 1966, 47-60.
27 *The Works of John Whitgift, D.D.*, ed. John Ayre, Parker Society, Cambridge 1851-3, ii, 378.
28 Cf. Whitgift, *Works*, i, 6.
29 Whitgift, *Works*, ii, 265.
30 Letter of Sir Francis Knollys to Lord Burghley, 4 August 1589: B. L. Lansdowne MS. 61, no. 54, printed in Strype, *Annals*, iv, Appendix IV, 6-9. Unfortunately Knollys does not state when his interview with Elizabeth took place. But it presumably occurred between July 1586, when he wrote the memorandum entitled 'Mr Tresorer of the howshold his opynyon towchyng hir majesties safetye 6th. Julii. 1586' (see above, 233, n. 10), which includes a proposal that the bishops should be restrained from condemning 'knone, zealous preachers agaynst the poopes supremacye, for refusing to subscrybe to unlawfull artykles', and the autumn of 1588.
31 Knollys had touched on the question of the bishops' authority in his letter to Burghley of 13 June 1584, in which he complained of 'the absolute authoritie of Bisshoppes (specially over theyre brethern) that hathe no fowndation in the worde of god, nor otherwyse but by lawe posityve, specially in yngland' and accused the bishops of seeking to draw their authority 'upp to a hyre fowndation withowt controlment of prynce or cownsayle': P.R.O., S.P. Dom., Eliz. 171, no. 23. But at that stage he was primarily concerned with establishing the illegality of Whitgift's attempts to enforce subscription to his articles and it was not until 1588 that he began to make the *jure divino* theory of episcopacy his main target of attack.
32 It is printed in full in H.M.C., *Calendar of Salisbury MSS.*, iii, 367-70, where it is wrongly calendared as 'Dr. Hammond to Lord Burghley'. The confusion is due to the fact that the original paper is endorsed 'Mr Doctor Hammon to Mr Tresorer'—i.e. Knollys, who was Treasurer of the Household, not Burghley, who was Lord Treasurer.
33 Strype, *Whitgift*, iii, 220-4. See also Strype, *Whitgift*, i, 600-1.
34 Strype, *Whitgift*, i, 601.
35 For Hammond, see *DNB*, John Venn and J. A. Venn, *Alumni Cantabrigienses*, Part I (to 1751), Cambridge 1922-7, ii, 294. Hammond was appointed chancellor of the diocese of London by bishop Sandys in 1575 but was replaced by Edward Stanhope in 1577, when Aylmer succeeded Sandys as bishop of London (see Collinson, *Elizabethan Puritan Movement*, 202). Collinson implies that Hammond was removed because he was regarded by Aylmer as too moderate in his

attitude towards the puritans, but I have found no evidence to support this. At this period the chancellor of a diocese held office only during the tenure of the see by the bishop who had appointed him and it seems more likely that Aylmer was merely exercising the customary right of patronage of a new bishop when he appointed Stanhope, who had influential family connexions, as chancellor in place of Hammond.

36 Collinson, *Elizabethan Puritan Movement*, 257–8, 488 n.15.

37 See below, 111.

38 H.M.C., *Calendar of Salisbury MSS.*, iii, 367; Strype, *Whitgift*, iii, 220–1.

39 H.M.C., *Calendar of Salisbury MSS.*, iii, 367–9; Strype, *Whitgift*, iii, 221. Strype does not print Hammond's discussion of the scriptural texts which extends to over two pages in the *Calendar of Salisbury MSS.*

40 H.M.C., *Calendar of Salisbury MSS.*, iii, 369–70; Strype, *Whitgift*, iii, 221–2.

41 The first part of the 'Supply' is printed in Strype, *Whitgift*, iii, 222–4, but Strype omitted the concluding section of the paper which consisted of citations from Jerome and other writers on the subject of episcopacy. The subject matter of the 'Supply" suggests that it may have been composed a few weeks after Hammond's original letter, at the time of Knollys's attack on Bridges's sermon of 12 January 1589 (see below, 106 ff.).

42 Strype, *Whitgift*, iii, 222–3. At the end of his extract Strype states, 'Then the writer proceeds to alledge S. Hierom, and some modern writers, as Calvin, Musculus, Beza, Hemingius, Sanchy [i.e. Zanchius], and Sadelius, and Danaeus' (224).

43 This act, also known as the Act in Absolute Restraint of Annates, is printed in full in *Documents Illustrative of English Church History Compiled from Original Sources*, ed. Henry Gee and William John Hardy, London 1896, repr. 1910, 201–9.

44 B. L. Lansdowne MS. 59, no. 8. Printed in Strype, *Annals*, iii, ii, 601–2.

45 The full list is as follows: Jerome, Cyprian, Marsilius of Padua, Calvin, Musculus, Beza, Hemingius, Zanchius, Antonius Sadelius, Lambertus Danaeus.

46 Strype, *Whitgift*, iii, 224, cited above, n.42. Alternatively, it is possible that the Lansdowne document, which appears to be in the hand of Knollys's secretary, is not a new paper by Hammond but simply a selection of extracts from the 'Supply', which Knollys had copied out and forwarded to Lord Burghley.

47 See above, 235 n.23.

48 Strype, *Whitgift*, i, 560–3.

49 Strype, *Whitgift*, i, 563.

50 Strype formed this impression on first reading the MSS. In a letter to

Thomas Brett, written on 14 July 1711, to acknowledge the receipt of his papers, he commented, 'In ye 3d Paper, ye Preacher there mentioned, for ye Ius divinum of Bps, was (if I am not mistaken) Dr Bancroft & ye privy Counsellor I know to be Sr Fra. Knolles. For I have several original Letters of his about yt very Argument of ye Bps Superiority infringing ye Queens Supremacy. He was a mighty Patron of the Puritans': Correspondence of Thomas Brett, Bodleian MS. Eng. Theol. C. 24, fol. 414. It is typical of Strype that, having once formed the opinion, on the basis of what can only have been a hasty first reading of the documents, that Bancroft was the preacher referred to, he never subsequently revised his views.

51 R. G. Usher noticed this discrepancy, but he concluded that the date mentioned in Knollys's syllogism was an error for 9 February 1588/9, due to a careless blunder on Strype's part, and he accepted Strype's assumption that the syllogism was directed against Bancroft's Sermon: *Mélanges Offerts à M. Charles Bémont*, 546 n.1.

52 Bodleian Rawlinson MS. C. 167, fols. 43–4v. The fact that the phrase 'yor Honoures' is crossed out in the title and 'Sr ffr. Knowles' is inserted instead suggests that this must be either the original MS. of the reply which was sent to Knollys or a copy made directly from it.

53 Strype, *Whitgift*, i, 560. Bridges, in his answer, suggested that Knollys was not the author of the Syllogism—'the honour of the person that delivered it (but I think made it not) in all dutifulness always reserved' (562)—and Strype, presumably on the basis of this remark, stated that the reply to the preacher's answer was made 'by him that framed the syllogism' (563). However, it is clear from certain comments made on the syllogism in the first paragraph of the 'Short observations' that the author of the latter was not responsible for the syllogism and there is no reason to doubt that it was, in fact, the work of Knollys.

54 Strype, *Whitgift*, i, 560–3.

55 See also, 113–14, 116.

56 The authors cited in the 'Short observations' are: Jerome, Augustine, Marsilius of Padua, Calvin, the Magdeburg Centuriators, Musculus, Zanchius, Beza, Hemingius, Danaeus, Sadelius. On this occasion Hammond amplified the references in the Lansdowne paper of January 1588/9, by giving extensive quotations from most of the authors listed: Bodleian Rawlinson MS. C. 167, fols. 43v–44.

57 References to the folio nos. in Rawlinson MS. C. 167 are given at the end of this and the following paragraphs.

58 I.e., the Common Law, not the Civil Law.

59 Read, *Lord Burghley and Queen Elizabeth*, 448.

60 Thomas Cooper. For his views on episcopacy, see *An Admonition to the People of England. 1589.*, ed. Edward Arber, The English Scholars Library, No. 15, Birmingham 1882, esp. 36, 61ff.

61 P.R.O. State Papers Domestic, Elizabeth, vol. 223, no. 23. Summarised briefly in *Cal. S.P. Dom., Elizabeth*, ii (1581–90), 584.

62 Both these letters are printed in full in H.M.C., *Calendar of Salisbury MSS.*, iii, 412–13.

63 No attendances at the Privy Council are recorded for Knollys between 19 June and 28 November 1589: *Acts of the Privy Council of England*, New Series, ed. John Roche Dasent, London 1890–1907, xvii (1588–9), 299; xviii (1589–90), 241.

64 As an afterthought Knollys inserted the words 'and to Mr secretarye [i.e. Walsingham]' at this point, but without altering the wording of the rest of the sentence.

65 B. L. Lansdowne MS. 61, no. 47. Extracts from this letter are given in Strype, *Whitgift*, i, 597–8, 603–5.

66 B. L. Lansdowne MS. 61, no. 54. Printed in Strype, *Annals*, iv, 6–9. See also Strype, *Whitgift*, i, 598–600; ii, 55.

67 Knollys's wording is ambiguous. At the beginning of his letter he refers to the divine's 'answer to the beginninge of my booke'; later to 'his answer to the wrytinge of the grave, learned man, whiche I nomynated unto you, touchinge superiorite of byshopps'—a clear reference to Hammond. Although it is possible that the first reference may be to a separate paper by Knollys, it is more likely that only one work is intended, a paper by Hammond which Knollys had forwarded to Burghley. Whether this was a new paper by Hammond drawn up after his meeting with Burghley at the end of May or one of his earlier papers, there is no means of telling.

68 B. L. Lansdowne MS. 61, no. 57.

69 Strype, *Whitgift*, iii, 224–8. See also, *Whitgift*, i, 614. Strype's transcript of this letter, which he prints in full, was made from a contemporary copy in the Petyt MSS., now Inner Temple Petyt MS. 538, vol. 38, fols. 324–6.

70 B. L. Harleian MS. 6994, no. 106. At the end of the letter Knollys added a short postscript, written in his own hand: 'I do not marvayle, that their be so manye martanysts, synce ower bysshopps doe incroche uppon hir majesties supreme government, & alone wold have the expowndyng of the scriptures, by theyre unlawfull urged subscriptions'.

71 B. L. Lansdowne MS. 61, no. 66. Summarised in Strype, *Whitgift*, i, 600.

72 [Richard Bancroft], *A Survay of the Pretended Holy Discipline*, London 1593, esp. 104–6, 142.

73 Richard Bancroft, *A Sermon Preached at Paules Crosse the 9. of Februarie, being the first Sunday in the Parleament, Anno. 1588*, London, E. B. [Edward Bollifant] for Gregorie Seton, 1588, i.e. 1589, esp. 10ff., 69, 99. For a discussion of Bancroft's views, see W. D. J. Cargill Thompson, 'A Reconsideration of Richard Bancroft's Paul's Cross Sermon of 9 February 1588/9' in *JEH*, 20 (1969), 253–266.

74 In *Whitgift*, i, 559–60, Strype gives what appears to be a quotation from Knollys's letter to Reynolds. In fact, Knollys's letter does not

survive and the words Strype attributes to him in quotation marks are taken from Reynolds's reply. See Cargill Thompson, *JEH*, 20 (1969), 260 n. 1.

75 Reynolds's original letter, which Strype used, is in B. L. Lansdowne MS. 61, no. 27. It was printed twice in the seventeenth century, first, in 1608, the year after Reynolds's death, in *Informations, or a Protestation, and a Treatise from Scotland. Seconded with D. Reignoldes his letter to Sir Francis Knollis. And Sir Francis Knollis his speach in Parliament. All suggesting the usurpation of Papal Bishops*, 73–87, and again in 1641 when it was issued separately under the title of *The Iudgement of Doctor Reignolds concerning Episcopacy whether it be Gods Ordinance. Expressed in a letter to Sir Francis Knowls, concerning Doctor Bancrofts Sermon at Pauls-crosse, the ninth of February 1588. In the Parliament time.* Both these editions contain numerous inaccuracies. In addition, it appears to have circulated in MS. in Raynolds's lifetime and at least two late sixteenth- or early seventeenth-century MS. copies of it survive, B. L. Harleian MS. 3998, no. 2, and B. L. Sloane MS. 271, fols. 41v–43.

76 B. L. Lansdowne MS. 61, no. 27, fol. 78; *Informations, or a Protestation*, 73–4. The reference is to Bancroft, *Sermon*, 18–19, where Bancroft maintained that Aerius had been condemned as a heretic for holding that there was no distinction between a bishop and a presbyter.

77 B. L. Lansdowne MS. 61, no. 27, fols. 79v–80; *Informations, or a Protestation*, 84–7. The reference here is to Bancroft, *Sermon*, 14, 69.

78 For Hubbock, see *DNB*; Strype, *Whitgift*, ii, 32–4; Collinson, *Elizabethan Puritan Movement*, 405.

79 B. L. Lansdowne MS. 68, no. 77.

80 B. L. Lansdowne MS. 64, no. 32. Summarised in Strype, *Whitgift*, ii, 33–4.

81 The whole passage quoted by Knollys will be found in Whitgift, *Works*, ii, 378–9: 'It is a marvellous matter that you delight to run so fast upon a false string. . . . But such bold assertions without proof are meet principles for such a ruinous and tottering platform as you dream of'.

82 B.L. Additional MS. 48064 (Yelverton MS. 70), fols. 94–5.

83 B. L. Lansdowne MS. 64, no. 46. Strype printed it twice, in *Whitgift*, ii, 54–5, and *Annals*, iv, 9.

84 Strype, *Whitgift*, ii, 54.

85 For Marten's tract, see Cargill Thompson, 'Anthony Marten and the Elizabethan Debate on Episcopacy' in Bennett and Walsh, *Essays in Modern English Church History*, 44–75.

86 Knollys was quite justified in making this accusation in that Marten's arguments were very largely taken from Whitgift's writings against Cartwright. On the other hand, although Marten claimed that distinctions of authority had existed in the Church since apostolic times,

in the main part of the book (like Whitgift) he laid great weight on the argument that no set form of government was prescribed for the Church in Scripture and in places his conception of church government appears to be almost as Erastian as that of Knollys himself. It is only in the concluding pages of the book, written, as he admits in his preface, after he had read Saravia's *De Diversis Ministrorum Evangelii Gradibus*, that he suddenly shifted his ground and began to argue categorically that episcopacy was instituted by Christ and the Apostles and that it ought therefore 'to remain in most places perpetual'. (See *Essays in Modern English Church History*, 62–75.)

87 Knollys's reference appears to be to Anthony Marten, *A Reconciliation of all the Pastors and Cleargy of the Church of England*, London 1590, 31v, although the passage in question hardly justifies Knollys's attack: see *Essays in Modern English Church History*, 70.

88 B. L. Lansdowne MS. 64, no. 69. Summarised in Strype, *Whitgift*, ii, 53–4.

89 P.R.O. State Papers Domestic, Elizabeth, vol. 233, no. 62. Summarised briefly in *Cal. S.P. Dom., Elizabeth*, ii (1581–90), 687.

90 B. L. Lansdowne MS. 65, no. 60.

91 B. L. Lansdowne MS. 68, no. 84. Summarised in Strype, *Whitgift*, ii, 71–3.

92 Cf. his letter to Lord Burghley, 9 January 1591/2, B. L. Lansdowne MS. 66, no. 52, printed in *Queen Elizabeth and her Times*, ed. Thomas Wright, London 1838, ii, 417.

93 For an account of this debate and its aftermath, see Neale, *Elizabeth I and her Parliaments 1584–1601*, 267–79.

94 For Knollys's speech, see his letter to Lord Burghley, 29 April 1593, cited below.

95 B. L. Lansdowne MS. 73, no. 30. Printed in *Original Letters, Illustrative of English History*, Third Series, ed. Sir Henry Ellis, London 1846, iv, 111–12. See also Strype, *Whitgift*, ii, 123–4.

96 B. L. Lansdowne MS. 75, no. 37, Knollys to Lord Burghley, 29 April 1593. This letter was printed in 1604 as an appendix to [William Stoughton], *An Assertion for true and Christian Church-Policie* (Middleburgh), n.p., and again in 1608, along with Reynold's letter on Bancroft's Sermon, in *Informations, or a Protestation* (see above, 119 n.75), 88–93. It is also summarised very fully in Strype, *Whitgift*, ii, 124–7.

97 Read, *Lord Burghley and Queen Elizabeth*, 465.

THE PHILOSOPHER OF THE 'POLITIC SOCIETY'

1 J. W. Allen, *A History of Political Thought in the Sixteenth Century*, London 1928, 184.

2 *Hooker's Ecclesiastical Polity: Book VIII*, ed. R. A. Houk, New York 1931; C. J. Sisson, *The Judicious Marriage of Mr. Hooker and the*

Birth of The Laws of Ecclesiastical Polity, Cambridge 1940; David Novarr, *The Making of Walton's 'Lives'*, Ithaca 1958.

3 Chapter 10, 'The Last Years of Elizabeth', *Cambridge Modern History*, Cambridge 1904, iii, 348. In his *Constitutional History of England*, Hallam had written: 'Nothing perhaps is more striking to a reader of the Ecclesiastical Polity than the constant and even excessive predilection of Hooker for those liberal principles of civil government, which are sometimes so just and always so attractive. Upon these subjects, his theory absolutely coincides with that of Locke. The origin of government, both in right and in fact, he explicitly derives from a primary contract...', 7th ed., London 1854, i, 219.

4 Georg Jellinek, *Allgemeine Staatslehre*, 3rd ed., Berlin 1916; reprinted Berlin 1922, 205–6; Ernst Tröltsch, *The Social Teaching of the Christian Churches* (1911), trans. Olive Wyon, London 1931, 637. Tröltsch mentions Hooker merely as the source of Locke's ideas, and it is not altogether clear that he had read him. On the Continent, Hooker was also beginning to attract attention in the years before the 1914–18 War as a pioneering figure in the protestant revival of natural law at the end of the sixteenth century and as one of the precursors of Grotius; cf. August Lang's essay, 'The Reformation and Natural Law', *Princeton Theological Review* 7 (1909), reprinted in William Park Armstrong, ed., *Calvin and the Reformation: Four Studies by Emile Doumergue, August Lang, Herman Bavinck, Benjamin B. Warfield*, New York 1909, 76–81.

5 W. Pauck, *Das Reich Gottes auf Erden*, Berlin 1928, 159–71.

6 N. Sykes, in *The Social & Political Ideas of Some Great Thinkers of the Sixteenth & Seventeenth Centuries*, ed. F. J. C. Hearnshaw, London 1926, 63–89; R. H. Murray, *The Political Consequences of the Reformation*, Boston 1926, esp. 273–81; Allen, op. cit., 184–98.

7 The main arguments of d'Entrèves's *Riccardo Hooker* are summarised in his Oxford lectures, *The Medieval Contribution to Political Thought*, chs. 5 and 6, some passages being translated almost verbatim.

8 D'Entrèves had already advanced this view in an earlier article, 'Hooker e Locke', in *Studi filosofico-giuridici*, ii. 228–50; its arguments are summarised in *Riccardo Hooker*, Pt. II, ch. I, 81–102.

9 *Riccardo Hooker*, 46.

10 *Medieval Contribution*, 88–9.

11 Michaelis, *Richard Hooker als politischer Denker*, 58.

12 Previté-Orton, 'Marsilius of Padua', *Proceedings of the British Academy*, 21 (1935), 165–6. D'Entrèves had briefly noted the parallels between some of Hooker's ideas and those of Marsilius (*Riccardo Hooker*, 58, n.7), but he did not discuss them in such detail as Previté-Orton. See also Michaelis, 54, 70, 97.

13 H. F. Kearney, 'Richard Hooker a reconstruction', *The Cambridge Journal* 5 (1952), 300–11.

14 Munz, *The Place of Hooker in the History of Thought*. See esp. ch. 3, 'Hooker and Marsilius of Padua', 68–111.

15 *Journal of the History of Ideas* 24 (1963), 163–82.

16 *Political Thought in England*, ch. 9. Cf. his introduction to the Everyman's Library edition of *The Laws of Ecclesiastical Polity: Books I–V*.

17 Marshall, *Hooker and the Anglican Tradition*. See esp. ch. 8, 'Hooker as the Author of a Summa'.

18 Marshall, esp. 4 f. and 66 ff.

19 *Political Thought in England*, 176.

20 *The Works of . . . Mr. Richard Hooker*, ed. Keble, 7th ed., rev. 1888. All quotations are from this text, by book, chapter, and section; cited below as *Works*.

21 Cf. F. Paget, *An Introduction to the Fifth Book*, Oxford 1899, 115–25; F. J. Shirley, *Richard Hooker and Contemporary Political Ideas*, London 1949, 58–70; and E. T. Davies, *The Political Ideas of Richard Hooker*, London 1946, 36–43.

22 This was recognised at the time by the authors of *A Christian Letter* (1599), who complained that 'we, happily remembering your *Preface*, that there might be some *other cause*, opened at length our heavy eyes, and casting some more earnest and intentive sight into your manner of fight, it seemed unto us that covertly and underhand you did bend all your skill and force against the present state of our English Church': *The Fifth Book*, ed. Bayne, 1902, 592. Cf. also 621ff., where they attacked Hooker's account of Calvin and asked, 'what moved you to make choice of that worthy pillar of the Church above all other, to traduce him and make him a spectacle before all Christians!'.

23 *Laws* Pref.iv.3. Cf. Richard Bancroft, *A Sermon Preached at Paules Crosse the 9. of Februarie . . . Anno 1588[9]*, 24–5: 'For saie they . . . our preachers ought to conforme themselves to the example of Christ and his apostles. Their Master had not a house to put his head in. The apostles their predecessors had neither gold nor silver, possessions, riches, goods, nor revenues: and why then should they being in gifts and paines inferior unto them, have greater preferments in the world than they had? . . . Surelie these advancements which they have do greatlie hinder and hurt them'. Although his language is more moderate, Hooker's argument in Pref.iv.3 and 4 is clearly modelled on Bancroft's distinction between 'the clergie factious, and the laie factious' (*Sermon*, 24). There is another obvious echo of Bancroft's Sermon in Pref.iv.1, where Hooker writes: 'A very strange thing sure it were, that such a discipline as ye speak of should be taught by Christ and his apostles in the word of God, and no church ever have found it out, nor received it till this present time'. Cf. Bancroft, 10–11: 'A verie strange matter if it were true, that Christ should erect a forme of government for the ruling of his Church to continue from

his departure out of the world untill his comming againe: and that the same should never be once thought of or put in practise for the space of 1500. yeers ...'.

24 *Laws*, Pref.viii.6–12. Bancroft also draws an analogy between the Puritans and the Anabaptists in his *Sermon*, 25–6.

25 Cf. esp., *Laws* v.vi–x. In II.vi.4, where he defends Jewel's views on the negative authority of Scripture, Hooker describes Jewel as 'the worthiest divine that Christendom hath bred for the space of some hundreds of years'.

26 Cf. Hooker's claim that the Apostles were the first bishops (VII.iv, and passim) and his admission (VII.xi.8) that he had earlier held the view that bishops were first instituted only after the death of the Apostles. Hooker's conversion to the belief that episcopacy was a dominical institution is almost certainly attributable to the influence of Saravia's *De Diversis Ministorum Evangelii Gradibus* (1590), which had a profound influence on Anglican attitudes towards episcopacy in the 1590s. Contrary to what Shirley has argued (*Richard Hooker and Contemporary Political Ideas*, 45–57), there is nothing in the views on episcopacy which are expressed in Book VII which would lead one to suspect the authenticity of the book: Hooker's arguments are essentially in accordance with the new theory of the dominical origin of bishops, which was being advanced by a number of Anglican divines, such as Saravia, Bilson, and Bancroft, in the 1590s. For the development of this theory, see W. D. J. Cargill Thompson, 'Anthony Marten and the Elizabethan Debate on Episcopacy', in *Essays in Modern English Church History in Memory of Norman Sykes*, ed. G. V. Bennett and J. D. Walsh, London 1966, 44–75.

27 *The Works of John Whitgift*, ed. John Ayre, Parker Society, Cambridge 1851–3; reprinted New York and London, Johnson Reprint Corp., 1968, i. 363, 6. Cf. also Tract. II, 'Of the Authority of the Church in things indifferent', i. 175–295. For a fuller discussion of Whitgift's views, see my article in *Essays in Modern English Church History*, 50–4.

28 Thomas Fuller, *The Church-History of Great Britain* (IX.vii, sub A.D. 1591) quoted by Keble, *Works* i. 79, n. 2.

29 *Laws* Pref.vii, and *Works* i.196. Houk has argued that the whole work was already complete in some form when the first four books were published in 1593 (*Hooker's Ecclesiastical Polity: Book VIII*, 91–6). While some of Houk's arguments have been criticised by Sisson (*The Judicious Marriage of Mr. Hooker*, 60–4, 88–91), the fact that Hooker twice speaks of Book VIII in the Preface as if it were already in existence (vii.6; viii.2) would appear to lend strong support to Houk's view; cf. W. Speed Hill, 'Hooker's *Polity*: The Problem of the "Three Last Books"', *Huntington Library Quarterly*, 34 (1971), 317–36. Whether or not Books VI and VII existed in draft as early as 1593, I am inclined to take the view that Book VIII, in the imperfect

form in which it has come down to us, may well have been written by that date.

30 McGrade, *Journal of the History of Ideas*, 24 (1963), 165. For a more detailed discussion of this point, see Houk, 72, 79, 87–90.

31 D'Entrèves, *Riccardo Hooker*, 74. D'Entrèves has also drawn attention to the significance of the letter from Dr. John Rainolds to George Cranmer, printed by Keble in *Works*, i. 106–8 (*Riccardo Hooker*, 76). In this letter Rainolds writes: 'tamen in Scoto et Aquinate non esse nihil quod inservire possit tuo studio promovendo, libens agnosco. Illud inter meum et tuum judicium discriminis intercedit, quod tu de iis videris honorificentius sentire, quam ego. Nam ego minus tribuo Scoto quam Aquinati, Aquinati quam Scaligero, immo vero pluris unum Scaligerum quam sexcentos Scotos et Aquinates facio'. The letter is undated, but presumably belongs to the period when Cranmer was either an undergraduate or a fellow of Corpus Christi.

32 Cf. William T. Costello, *The Scholastic Curriculum at Early Seventeenth-Century Cambridge*, Cambridge, Mass. 1958; Hugh Kearney, *Scholars and Gentlemen: Universities and Society in Pre-Industrial Britain, 1500–1700*, London 1970, esp. ch. 5. That the scholastics were being read even by Puritans at the beginning of the seventeenth century is illustrated by the well-known story of John Preston, whose enthusiasm for Aquinas was so great that he took his copy along to the barber's and refused to put it down, even while his hair was being cut, but simply blew away the hair as it fell on the pages: Irvonwy Morgan, *Prince Charles's Puritan Chaplain*, London 1957, 19–20.

33 Paget, *Introduction to the Fifth Book*, 141–5. Cf. *Book I. Of the Laws of Ecclesiastical Polity*, ed. R. W. Church (1868), xvii.

34 Thomas Cartwright, *A Replye to an Answere made of M. Doctor Whitegift* (n.p., 1574?), cited in Whitgift, *Works*, i. 191 (italics in text mine). Interestingly, Hooker judiciously abridges an earlier section from the same passage in order to underline his own thesis. In his marginal reference to II.i.4, Hooker cites Cartwright as saying, 'I say, that the word of God containeth whatsoever things can fall into any part of man's life'. In fact, as Keble noted, what Cartwright actually wrote was 'I say that the word of God containeth the direction of all things pertaining to the Church, yea, of whatsoever things can fall into any part of man's life' (*Works*, i. 289, n. 1; for the full text of this passage from Cartwright, see Whitgift, *Works*, i. 190–1). For an illustration of Cartwright's views on the differences between the temporal and the spiritual sphere, see Whitgift, *Works*, ii. 356: 'For God hath left a greater liberty in instituting things in the commonwealth than in the Church', etc. For Cartwright's readiness to allow a certain degree of authority to philosophy and reason, see Whitgift, *Works*, ii. 442–3.

35 Whitgift, *Works*, i. 195.

36 *Laws* I. xvi. 5: 'There are in men operations, some natural, some

rational, some supernatural, some politic, some finally ecclesiastical: which if we measure not each by his own proper law, whereas the things themselves are so different, there will be in our understanding and judgment of them confusion'.

37 For a full discussion of Hooker's debt to Aquinas, see d'Entrèves, *Riccardo Hooker*, Pt. I, chs. 2–4, and, more briefly, *Medieval Contribution*, 117–24. Cf. Michaelis, *Richard Hooker als politischer Denker*, 47–9, and Munz, *The Place of Hooker*, ch. 2 and Appendix A, which contains a table of correspondences between Hooker's philosophy and that of Aquinas.

38 *Laws* I.viii.5–8. Cf. Aquinas, *Summa Theologica* II. I. Qu. 94, Art. 2.

39 *Laws* I.viii.10–11. Cf. Aquinas, Qu. 94, Arts. 4, 6.

40 Cf. d'Entrèves, *Riccardo Hooker*, 44 ff., and *Medieval Contribution*, 117 ff.

41 Hugo Grotius, *Prolegomena to the Law of War and Peace*, trans. Francis W. Kelsey, Library of Liberal Arts, Indianapolis 1957, sections 40 ff.

42 Cf. Lang, 'The Reformation and Natural Law', in *Calvin and the Reformation*, ed. Armstrong, 76–81, 93; Georges de Lagarde, *Recherches sur l'esprit politique de la Réforme*, Paris 1926, 191; Shirley, *Richard Hooker and Contemporary Political Ideas*, 74 ff.; and Morris, Everyman Hooker (1954), ix.

43 For a summary of the debate over whether or not Luther held a theory of natural law, see John T. McNeill, 'Natural Law in the Thought of Luther', *Church History*, 10 (1941), 215 ff.

44 Cf. Martin Luther, *Werke*, WA, 30 (2), 562: 'Aber ynn weltlichem reich, müs man aus der vernunfft (daher die rechte auch komen sind) handeln. Denn Gott hat der vernunfft unterworffen solch zeitlich regiment und leiblich wesen Gen 2'.

45 *Laws* I.viii.3. Cf. Luther, WA 46, 606; Calvin, *Institutes of the Christian Religion* II..ii.22.

46 *Laws* I.xii.1–2. For Luther's views on the relationship between natural law and the Decalogue, see *Wider die himmlischen Propheten*, WA 18, 80–2. Cf. Calvin, *Institutes* II.viii.1.

47 For Hooker's views on human law, see *Laws* I.x, esp. 6–11.

48 *Laws* I.x.8: 'That which we spake before concerning the power of government must here be applied unto the power of making laws whereby to govern; which power God hath over all: and by the natural law, whereunto he hath made all subject, the lawful power of making laws to command whole politic societies of men belongeth so properly unto the same entire societies, that for any prince or potentate of what kind soever upon earth to exercise the same of himself, and not either by express commission immediately and personally received from God, or else by authority derived at the first from their consent upon whose persons they impose laws, it is no better than mere tyranny'.

49 Cf. *Laws* Pref. v.2: 'A law is the deed of the whole body politic, whereof if ye judge yourself to be any part, then is the law even your deed also'.

50 Since the order of the text of Book viii in Keble's edition is not always identical with that of the Dublin MS. Houk used, in references to Book viii in this and the following sections I have included page references to Houk in addition to Keble's chapter and section numbers.

51 For the development of these ideas in the late Middle Ages and the sixteenth century, see Gough, *The Social Contract*, 2nd ed., chs. 4–6.

52 Cf. *Laws* viii.ii.5 (Houk, 170): 'First, unto me it seemeth almost out of doubt and controversy, that every independent multitude, before any certain form of regiment established, hath, under God's supreme authority, full dominion over itself, even as a man not tied with the bond of subjection as yet unto any other, hath over himself the like power. God creating mankind did endue it naturally with full power to guide itself, in what kind of societies soever it should choose to live. A man which is born lord of himself may be made another's servant: and that power which naturally whole societies have, may be derived into many, few, or one, under whom the rest shall then live in subjection'.

53 *Laws* viii.ii.10 (Houk, 175–6): 'May then a body politic at all times withdraw in whole or in part that influence of dominion which passeth from it, if inconvenience doth grow thereby? It must be presumed, that supreme governors will not in such case oppose themselves, and be stiff in detaining that, the use whereof is with public detriment: but surely without their consent I see not how the body should be able by any just means to help itself, saving when dominion doth escheat'.

54 *Laws* i.x.5: 'The case of man's nature standing therefore as it doth, some kind of regiment the Law of Nature doth require; yet the kinds thereof being many, Nature tieth not to any one, but leaveth the choice as a thing arbitrary'.

55 In *Laws* i.x.5, Hooker suggests that in all probability men's first rulers were absolute. 'At the first when some certain kind of regiment was once approved, it may be that nothing was then further thought upon for the manner of governing, but all permitted unto their wisdom and discretion which were to rule, till by experience they found this for all parts very inconvenient, so as the thing which they had devised for a remedy did indeed but increase the sore which it should have cured. They saw that to live by one man's will became the cause of all men's misery. This constrained them to come unto laws, wherein all men might see their duties beforehand, and know the penalties of transgressing them'. For a comparison between this passage and the arguments of George Buchanan's *De Jure Regni apud Scotos*, see below, 169.

56 Cf. Michaelis, *Richard Hooker als politischer Denker*, 58.

57 For an account of the way in which Hooker was used for purposes of Whig propaganda in the late seventeenth and early eighteenth centuries, see d'Entrèves, *Riccardo Hooker*, 9–12.

58 D'Entrèves, *Medieval Contribution*, 127–32; cf. *Riccardo Hooker*, Pt. II, ch. I, 81–102.

59 *Laws* VIII.ii.10 (Houk, 176), cited above, n. 53. In this passage Hooker does appear to allow that in the event of a dynasty of hereditary rulers dying out dominion might revert to the people by 'escheat'.

60 *Laws* VIII.ii.6 (Houk, 172): 'And therefore of what kind soever the means be whereby governors are lawfully advanced unto their seats, as we by the law of God stand bound meekly to acknowledge them for God's lieutenants, and to confess their power his, so they by the same law are both authorized and required to use that power as far as it may be in any sort available to his honour'. Cf. II.i.1, cited below, 174.

61 D'Entrèves, *Riccardo Hooker*, 95–7, *Medieval Contribution*, 130–1.

62 *Laws* VIII.ii.11 (Houk, 176). The whole passage is as follows: 'Touching kings which were first instituted by agreement and composition made with them over whom they reign, how far their power may lawfully extend, the articles of compact between them must shew: not the articles only of compact at the first beginning, which for the most part are either clean worn out of knowledge, or else known unto very few, but whatsoever hath been after in free and voluntary manner condescended unto, whether by express consent, whereof positive laws are witnesses, or else by silent allowance famously notified through custom reaching beyond the memory of man'.

63 George Buchanan, *De Jure Regni apud Scotos. or, A Dialogue, Concerning the due Priviledge of Government In the Kingdom of Scotland*, Eng. trans., London: Richard Baldwin, 1689, 6–7.

64 See above, n. 55.

65 *Laws* VIII.ii.5–6 (Houk, 171): 'By which of these means soever it happen that kings or governors be advanced unto their states, we must acknowledge both their lawful choice to be approved of God, and themselves to be God's lieutenants, and confess their power his. . . .

'Again, on whom the same is bestowed even at men's discretion, they likewise do hold it by divine right. If God in his own revealed word have appointed such power to be, although himself extraordinarily bestow it not, but leave the appointment of the person unto men. . .'.

66 Cf. Houk, 50–1.

67 Cf. Charles Howard McIlwain, *Constitutionalism: Ancient and Modern*, rev. ed., Ithaca 1947, chs. 4–5.

68 Cf. also *Laws* VIII.vi.1, 11 (Houk, 224, 241–2).

69 He cites Bodin's *De Republica* in the fragment which Keble prints as an appendix to Book VIII, 'Supposed Fragment of a Sermon on Civil

Obedience, hitherto printed as part of the Eighth Book', *Works,* iii. 457-8. Houk, 237, n. 28.

70 Cf. *Laws,* ii, 2-3; Houk, 168-9.

71 Cf. the 'Supposed Fragment of a Sermon on Civil Obedience' (*Works,* iii. 456-60), which contains a clear affirmation of the traditional protestant doctrine of nonresistance. Keble pointed out that this passage did not appear in the first edition (1648) of Book VIII and that the opening paragraph down to 'evangelists' is taken verbatim from III.ix.3. He therefore argued that it should be treated 'as a separate fragment, probably of a Sermon on Obedience to Governors, annexed by mistake to the eighth book in all the MSS.' (*Works,* iii. 456, n. 1). Houk, on the other hand, following the text of the Dublin MS., prints it as part of chapter 6 (235-41). In view of the fact that there are other instances of repetition in Book VIII, which can be accounted for on the assumption that the present text of Book VIII was compiled from Hooker's unpolished first draft, there would appear to be no strong reason why this passage should not be treated, in accordance with the MS. tradition, as forming an authentic part of Book VIII.

72 Munz, *The Place of Hooker,* chs. 1-3, esp. 96-111.

73 See Munz, esp. 89-96 and Appendix C, 'Marsilius in the Sixteenth Century', 199-204, which includes a useful list of references to earlier discussions of Marsilius's influence on Tudor thought (109, nn. 1, 2).

74 *Laws* VII.xi.8. For the manner in which Henrician writers used Marsilius as a source of historical arguments against the papacy, see Franklin Le Van Baumer, *The Early Tudor Theory of Kingship,* Yale Historical Publications, 35, New Haven 1940; reprinted New York 1966, 43. In the 1560s bishop Jewel cited Marsilius by name on a number of occasions in his *Apology* and other writings as an exponent of the view that the pope was Anti-Christ, and also as a historical source for the dealings between the Franks and pope Stephen in the eighth century; see John Jewel, *Works,* ed. John Ayre, the Parker Society, Cambridge 1845-50, iii. 81; iv. 680, 740-2, 1115). It is clear that in the sixteenth century Marsilius was regarded by English Protestants not as a dangerous secularist but as a proto-Reformer along with men like Valla, Hus, and Jerome of Prague. Jewel in his *Defence of the Apology* defends him against the charge of heresy (*Works,* iv. 742), while John Philpot in his translation of Curio's *Defence of Christ's Church* (c. 1550) describes him as one of the 'trumpets of the Gospel': *The Examinations and Writings of John Philpot,* ed. Robert Eden, Parker Society, Cambridge 1842, 393. Cf. John Foxe, preface 'To the True and Faithful Congregation of Christ's Universal Church', in *Acts and Monuments,* intro. George Townsend, ed. Stephen Reed Cattley, London 1841-3, i. 517.

75 Cf. Baumer, op. cit., 41-56 passim, 67-8; Shirley, *Richard Hooker and Contemporary Political Ideas,* 1-5, 130; Morris, *Political Thought*

in England, 54. On the other hand, the importance of these parallels should not be exaggerated. While Baumer and others have shown that the *Defensor Pacis* was one of the major sources used by Henrician propagandists in the 1530s, it was not the only one, and many of Marsilius's leading ideas were commonplaces not only of late medieval anti-papal and conciliarist thought but also of sixteenth-century protestant political thought as well (see Morris, 35). The evidence suggests that the Henrician pamphleteers of the 1530s used Marsilius as a convenient source of anti-papal propaganda, but that they ignored, and may not even have understood, the philosophical assumptions underlying his political thought.

76 For a classic statement of this doctrine, see Cranmer's Speech at the Coronation of Edward vi, printed in Thomas Cranmer, *Miscellaneous Writings and Letters*, ed. John Edmund Cox, Parker Society, Cambridge 1846, 126–7. The same theocratic conception of kingship is to be found in all the leading tracts produced in defence of the Royal Supremacy in the 1530s, such as Stephen Gardiner's *De Vera Obedientia*, Richard Sampson's *Oratio*, and Edward Foxe's *De Vera Differentia*.

77 Cf. the articles on the Church in the *Bishops' Book* (1537) and the *King's Book* (1543) in *Formularies of Faith put forth by authority during the Reign of Henry VIII*, ed. Charles Lloyd, Oxford 1825, 52–7 and 243–9.

78 *Laws* i.xv.2. Cf. iii.xi.14: 'First, so far forth as the Church is the mystical body of Christ and his invisible spouse, it needeth no external polity. That very part of the law divine which teacheth faith and works of righteousness is itself alone sufficient for the Church of God in that respect. But as the Church is a visible society and body politic, laws of polity it cannot want'.

79 Cf. *Laws* iii.xi.16, 20; v.lxxviii.4, 5, 12. These passages indicate that certainly by the time he wrote Book v, and probably by the time he wrote Book iii, Hooker had come to accept the doctrine, put forward by Saravia in his *De Diversis Ministrorum Evangelii Gradibus* (1590), that the origins of episcopacy were to be traced back to the distinction which Christ had made between the Twelve Apostles and the Seventy Disciples (see esp. v.lxxviii.5). In other words, Hooker's conversion from the Jeromian theory, held by most Elizabethan divines, that episcopacy was first introduced into the Church after the death of the Apostles (vii.xi.8) to the new theory of Saravia that episcopacy was a dominical institution almost certainly dates back to the period of the early 1590s, when this idea was beginning to be put forward by a number of other Anglican writers, such as Bilson and Bancroft.

80 *Obedience in Church & State: Three Political Tracts by Stephen Gardiner*, ed. Pierre Janelle, Cambridge 1930, 92–7. Whitgift, *Works* i. 21–2.

81 Cf. 'The Injunctions of Elizabeth, A.D. 1559', No. 78, in *Documents*

Illustrative of English Church History Compiled from Original Sources, ed. Henry Gee and William John Hardy, London 1896; reprinted 1910, 'An admonition to simple men deceived by malicious', 438–9.

82 *Laws* VIII.vi.11 (Houk, 241–2). The language of this passage bears a striking resemblance to that of Sir Thomas Smith's description of parliament in *De Republica Anglorum* II.i, and it is likely that Hooker was paraphrasing Smith at this point; see *De Republica Anglorum: A Discourse on the Commonwealth of England*, ed. L. Alston, Cambridge 1906, 48–9.

83 In addition to those already cited, see also Shirley, *Richard Hooker and Contemporary Political Ideas*, 96, 112; and Morris, *Political Thought in England*, 177, 184.

84 Cf. his remark in VIII.vi.11 (Houk, 242): 'The parliament is a court not so merely temporal as if it might meddle with nothing but only leather and wool'.

JOHN STRYPE AND ENGLISH CHURCH HISTORY

1 David C. Douglas, *English Scholars 1660–1730*, 2nd ed. London 1951.

2 For the details of Strype's life, see *DNB*; *Biographia Britannica*, London 1747–66, VI, i, 3847–50. The latter contains an interesting account of the circumstances of Strype's appointment as minister of Leyton (3847, n. A).

3 See the extract from the letter of Strype to Dr. Samuel Knight, 19 January 1729, printed in *Gentlemen's Magazine*, London 1791, i, 223.

4 John Strype, *Annals of the Reformation and Establishment of Religion, and other various occurrences in the Church of England, during Queen Elizabeth's Happy Reign*, Oxford 1824, I. i, vii.

5 Strype was granted permission to use the Harleian library on 26 May 1707; see *The Diary of Humphrey Wanley 1715–1726*, ed. C. E. and Ruth Wright, The Bibliographical Society, London 1966, i, Intr. xxi.

6 Strype's correspondence, which contains numerous letters from contemporaries relating to his historical collections, is preserved in the Baumgartner MSS. in the Cambridge University Library. See *A Catalogue of the Manuscripts preserved in the Library of the University of Cambridge*, Cambridge 1856–67, V, 1–159.

7 J. F. Mozley states that the Willys family 'lent' the Foxe papers to Strype: J. F. Mozley, *John Foxe and his Book*, London 1940, ix; and this appears to be confirmed by Strype's own remark in the preface to his *Cranmer* (1694) that 'I have been conversant in what remaineth of the papers of John Fox, communicated to me by the favour of my good friend William Willys, of Hackney, Esquire': John Strype, *Memorials of the Most Reverend Father in God Thomas Cranmer, Sometime Lord Archbishop of Canterbury*, Oxford 1840, i, xiii–xiv.

Later, however, in a statement made after all the parties concerned were dead, he claimed that they 'were given me long since by Mr Will. Willis of Hackney deceased, who was Executor to Sr Richard. Willis Kt. yt married ye Heir of Foxes Family'; see Cambridge University Library, Baumgartner MSS., Patrick Papers, vol. 40, no. 7, 'Mr Strypes Case' [August 1714], 4.

8   See *Wanley*, I, xxi–xxii, and C. E. Wright, *Fontes Harleiani*, British Museum Bicentenary Publications, London 1972, 321. The remainder of the Foxe papers, which Strype retained in his possession, were sold with the Burghley papers and are now in the Lansdowne collection.

9   The exact details of this transaction are obscure. For Strype's version of this episode, see 'Mr Strypes Case'.

10   *A Catalogue of the Lansdowne Manuscripts in the British Museum*, London 1819, preface, ix.

11   Historical Manuscripts Commission, *Calendar of the Manuscripts of the Most Hon. The Marquis of Salisbury, K.G., &c.*, preserved at *Hatfield House, Hertfordshire*, in progress, London 1883–, vols. 1–8.

12   In the preface to his *Cranmer*, Strype claims to be modelling himself on 'a good practice first begun by Mr. Sumner of Canterbury' in his *Antiquities of Canterbury* (i.e. William Somner, *The Antiquities of Canterbury. Or a Survey of that Ancient Citie, with the Suburbs, and Cathedrall*, London 1640) *Cranmer*, xv.

13   See John Strype, *Ecclesiastical Memorials, relating chiefly to Religion, and the Reformation of it, and the Emergencies of the Church of England, under King Henry VIII, King Edward VI, and Queen Mary I*, Oxford 1822, I, i, preface, xii–xiii.

14   S. R. Maitland, *Remarks on the First Volume of Strype's Life of Archbishop Cranmer, recently published by the Ecclesiastical History Society* reprinted from the *British Magazine*, London 1848, 4.

15   For examples from Strype's *Cranmer*, see Maitland, *Remarks*, 5 f.

16   Ibid., 10.

17   Strype, I, *Annals*, I, i, viii.

18   Ibid., I, ii, 372.

19   John Strype, *The Life and Acts of John Whitgift, D.D., the third and last Lord Archbishop of Canterbury in the Reign of Queen Elizabeth*, Oxford 1822, I, 227.

20   Ibid., 213.

21   Ibid., 530.

22   Strype, *Annals*, I, ii, 372.

23   Ibid.

24   Strype, *Whitgift*, I, 347.

25   Ibid., 38.

26   Ibid., 301.

27   Maitland, *Remarks*, 9–13.

28   Strype, *Annals*, I, ii, Appendix, 392–8 and 459–64.

29   Ibid., I, i, 74–6.

30 Gilbert Burnet, *The History of the Reformation of the Church of England*, Oxford 1829, II, i, 754–7, and II, ii, 459–64; William Camden, *The History of the Most Renowned and Victorious Princess Elizabeth, Late Queen of England*, 4th ed. London 1688, 16.
31 Strype, *Annals*, I, i, 119.
32 Ibid., 75.
33 Ibid., 120–1.
34 The most recent scholar to investigate the problem is W. P. Haugaard, who considers that Guest was the author of the letter but that it relates to an earlier scheme by Elizabeth for adopting the 1549 Prayer Book as the basis of the 1559 Settlement. See W. P. Haugaard, *Elizabeth and the English Reformation*, Cambridge 1968, 109 and 'The Proposed Liturgy of Edmund Guest', *Anglican Theological Review*, 46 (Evanston 1964), 177–89.
35 W. D. J. Cargill Thompson, 'A Reconsideration of Richard Bancroft's Paul's Cross Sermon of 9 February 1588/9', *JEH*, 20 (1969) esp. 253–6.
36 Ibid., 255–6.
37 S. R. Maitland, *Notes on Strype*, Gloucester 1858, which contains a draft prospectus which he had compiled some years earlier for a new edition of Strype's *Works* that was never published.

Index